CW00384971

FROM ABBOTSFORD
TO PARIS AND BACK

Sir Walter Scott by Andrew Geddes. (Scottish National Portrait Gallery)

FROM ABBOTSFORD TO PARIS AND BACK

SIR WALTER SCOTT'S JOURNEY OF 1815

DONALD SULTANA

ALAN SUTTON

First published in the United Kingdom in 1993 by
Alan Sutton Publishing Limited
Phoenix Mill · Far Thrupp · Stroud · Gloucestershire

First published in the United States of America in 1993 by
Alan Sutton Publishing Inc. · 83 Washington Street · Dover · NH 03820

British Library Cataloguing in Publication Data

Sultana, Donald
    From Abbotsford to Paris and back
    I. Title
    828.709

ISBN 0-7509-0324-4

Library of Congress Cataloging in Publication Data applied for

Typeset in 10/11 Palatino
Typeset by Bookman Ltd, Bristol
Printed in Great Britain by
The Bath Press, Bath

Contents

Preface

The purpose of this book is to fill a gap in Scott studies. There has hitherto been no full, comprehensive, and independent publication—even in monologue form—on Scott's memorable journey to Flanders and Paris in the summer of 1815, two months after the battle of Waterloo. His first biographer, Lockhart, has a chapter about it in his *Memoirs of the Life of Sir Walter Scott* (1837–8), but it is largely a loosely connected compilation of extracts from letters, journals, and reminiscences by Scott, his fellow-travellers, and other sources. The extracts alternate with passages of narrative and brief critical comment without proper sequence, and are not infrequently flawed by Lockhart's long-recognised tendency to inaccuracy and to substitute fiction for fact. His successors from Sir Herbert Grierson and John Buchan to Hesketh Pearson wrote only a few pages about Scott's journey, barely a few sentences in Grierson's *Sir Walter Scott, Bart.* (1938). Both he and Pearson were dismissive of the travel book called *Paul's Letters to his Kinsfolk* (1816), which was the principal literary product of Scott's journey, and which Lockhart had justly dubbed 'a true and faithful journal of this expedition'. Buchan echoed Lockhart's praise, hailing the book as 'a revealing piece of autobiography', and emphasising 'its moderation and good sense' as 'more remarkable than the vivid narrative of travel'. But he made no attempt to draw on it for anything like a bare outline of Scott's journey.

It was left to Professor Edgar Johnson and Carola Oman, in more recent times, to provide short, coherent sketches of the trip, the former in fifteen pages of narrative in somewhat high-figured language, but thoroughly documented; the latter in under that length and in much simpler style, but with ludicrously minimal references. Although Carola Oman endorsed Lockhart's and Buchan's view of *Paul's Letters to his Kinsfolk* as 'excellent reading', she drew on it only in the most perfunctory manner in her factual résumé of places, people, incidents, and anecdotes recorded by

Scott in his letters and travel book, which she supplemented by very brief information from the journals of two of his fellow-travellers.

This material, together with Lockhart's chapter and two or three other sources, served Professor Johnson to recapture to some extent the atmosphere of war and peace as well as the extraordinary international spectacles and brilliant festivities of high society, of which Scott became for a while both witness and participant. Drawing on Sir Arthur Bryant's *The Age of Elegance 1812–1822*, Professor Johnson focused a substantial part of his narrative on 'the *décor*' or physical background to Scott's movements and sight-seeing in Paris under Allied occupation. But he did not shed much light on the 'non-physical' or cultural aspects of Scott's journey, particularly as embodied in *Paul's Letters to his Kinsfolk*. Although he conceded in large measure, perhaps even echoed, John Buchan's remark that Scott's travel book was 'journalism at its best', his overall view of it was that of 'a hack job'.

A large part of my task, therefore, in this book is not only to write a much more extensive account of Scott's journey by incorporating into it fresh information, incidents, and insights from the sources already known to, but not fully tapped by, Scott's biographers, supplemented by other sources hitherto unknown, but, more importantly, to demonstrate in detail how Scott's journey drew out many of his central interests, ideas, and attitudes in history, politics, literature, religion, the theatre, art, aesthetics, and the supernatural in the context of its prominence as a feature of the Romantic Age. In other words, through a systematic and searching analysis of *Paul's Letters to his Kinsfolk*, I seek not only to confirm but to illustrate on an extensive scale Lockhart's dictum that 'the whole man, just as he [Scott] was, breathes in every line'. I attempt to achieve this purpose by relating Scott's journey, his travel book, and *The Field of Waterloo* (1815), which was the principal poetic product of his trip, to a very wide range of his novels and poems in respect of topography, themes, characters, *motifs*, imagery, and sources. Moreover, I relate Scott's journey and the more historical and political parts of his observations in his travel book to his *Life of Napoleon Buonaparte* (1827) in respect of genesis, characters, and sources as well as with a view to showing how he carried over certain ideas on several of his favourite themes from his earlier to his later work in an expanded or identical form.

Naturally I relate Scott's journey to his second visit to Paris in 1826, which he undertook specifically to collect material for the *Life of Napoleon Buonaparte*. And in the last chapter, which covers in detail his return journey from Paris to Abbotsford across the length of England by coach from London, I have fully exploited the topography of his route as recorded in the journal of one of his fellow-travellers in order to link it to many of his novels and poems, particularly the novels of his middle and later periods when he branched out from Scottish to English history. Moreover, I have taken full advantage of the same journal of his fellow-traveller, which contains a hitherto unnoticed hint of autobiography on Scott's part, in order to relate it not only to his novels and poems but to important incidents of his earlier life.

In tracing and illustrating a very large number of these links, arising out of hints and observations or associations with his journey, and in demonstrating how years later they came to be used or transmuted into the scenery, characters, or dialogue of his novels, I am making no claim for my book as a specific contribution to the working of Scott's wonderful memory or of his imagination as a creative artist. I am simply vindicating the truth of the remark first made by Lockhart and afterwards by Mrs James Skene, who, like her husband, knew Scott intimately for many years right up to his death. Lockhart underlined, in his chapter on Scott's journey, how 'every little peculiarity remain[ed] treasured in his [Scott's] memory, to be used in due time for giving the air of minute reality to some imaginary personage'. For her part, Mrs Skene explained that, having had 'the opportunity of meeting at his house with every person of rank or note that came to Scotland', she had been struck by 'the very happy use to which he turned every little circumstance that occurred to him', particularly in conversation. 'He not only never forgot anything he heard, but it was there to be made use of when he was writing his novels, and this probably gave many of his descriptions the air of truth that characterises them'.

Mrs Skene knew Scott in full maturity and as, intellectually, a beneficiary of what is known as the Scottish Enlightenment. It is precisely as a product of the Scottish Enlightenment that I present Scott throughout the book (indeed I even end it in that context) with particular reference to the good sense, moderation, and balanced judgement that he displayed in *Paul's Letters to his Kinsfolk* in his discussions of the political, religious, and constitutional issues that he found to be to the fore in Flanders and Paris in the wake of the restoration of the monarchy in France after the downfall of Napoleon, and the establishment by the victorious Allied Powers of the new Kingdom of the Netherlands through the union of Holland and Belgium.

It may be proper to explain, purely as a matter of nomenclature, that I use 'Belgium' and 'Flanders', and 'Belgians' and 'Flemish' interchangeably, as was common in the books of contemporary travellers. (Scott himself seems to have preferred to use 'Flemings' rather than 'Belgians'.) It may also be proper to explain that, in drawing extensively on *The Field of Waterloo*, particularly in the chapter about Scott in Flanders, my purpose has not been to elevate that poem to a high status, or make special claims for its quality. I seek simply to demonstrate how admirably it illuminates the Waterloo chapters in *Paul's Letters to his Kinsfolk*—the centre-piece of Scott's travel book and by general agreement the best section of that book—and how the two works complement each other in military history, drama, and personalities. Bearing in mind that Scott's celebrity at the time of his journey was that of a poet rather than of a novelist, I have sought to broaden the interest of *The Field of Waterloo* by linking

Scott with Byron and Robert Southey as contemporary visitors to the battlefield, complete with extracts from *Childe Harold's Pilgrimage* (1816) and *The Poet's Pilgrimage to Waterloo* (1816) respectively. Likewise I have attempted to place Scott firmly in the flood of visitors to Waterloo and Paris after Napoleon's second abdication not only by expanding on the personalities already noticed by Scott's biographers as hosts or friends or new acquaintances with whom he mingled at various places, but by drawing on the more literary of those visitors in order to illuminate Scott's own travel book.

In view of Lockhart's central position in Scott studies I have drawn attention to several inaccuracies or suspect anecdotes in his chapter on Scott's journey that have not yet been exposed by his biographers, and indeed that continue to be passed from biographer to biographer. I refer to them in the main body of the narrative as well as in the Notes and References. But, to avoid tedious reading and distraction from the narrative in this remedial exercise, I have relegated the misreadings or errors of fact of Scott's biographers to the Notes and References. Several of Carola Oman's factual errors can be detected only with a thorough advance knowledge of the text of Scott's letters and *Paul's Letters to his Kinsfolk* because of her lack of references. A few corrections of Grierson's occasional misinformation as editor of Scott's letters, including two or three slips of his that passed unnoticed by James Corson in *Notes and Index to Sir Herbert Grierson's Edition of 'The Letters of Sir Walter Scott'*, are also to be found in my Notes and References.

Perhaps the most important of the factual corrections is the long note in chapter three (no. 221) explaining for the first time how Professor Johnson came to be misled by Hesketh Pearson over the Duke of Wellington's supposed communications to Scott about his opinion of Napoleon and the battle of Waterloo after Scott's introduction to Wellington at the latter's headquarters in Paris. I should have wished to have incorporated this correction into the narrative of Scott's meeting with Wellington, but I detected it at a stage in the printing of the book that rendered my wish impracticable.

Finally, I should like to record with gratitude the encouragement and advice I received from Dr Ian Alexander, of the University of Aberdeen, who read an early draft of my book.

D.E.S.
Edinburgh, April 1993

List of Illustrations and Maps

ILLUSTRATIONS

Principal Abbreviations and References
(Place of publication is London unless otherwise stated.)

Bruce	Robert Bruce, *Journal of a Tour to the Continent in Autumn 1815*, with Sir Walter Scott, John Scott of Gala, and Alexander Pringle of Whytbank, MS 991, National Library of Scotland, Edinburgh
Byron's Letters	*Byron's Letters and Journals*, ed L A Marchand, 12 vols (1973–81)
Frazer	*Letters of Colonel Sir Augustus Frazer*, ed General Sir Edward Sabine (1859)
Gala	John Scott of Gala, *Journal of a Tour to Waterloo and Paris in company with Sir Walter Scott in 1815* (1842)
Gordon	Pryse Lockhart Gordon, *Personal Memoirs, or Reminiscences of Men and Manners at Home and Abroad*, 2 vols (1830)
Johnson	Edgar Johnson, *Sir Walter Scott The Great Unknown* 2 vols (New York, 1970)
Journal	*The Journal of Sir Walter Scott*, ed W E K Anderson (Oxford, 1972)
Letters	*The Letters of Sir Walter Scott* (centenary edition), ed Sir Herbert Grierson, 12 vols (1932–7)
Life of Buonaparte	Sir Walter Scott, *The Life of Napoleon Buonaparte*, 9 vols (Edinburgh, 1827)
Lockhart	John Gibson Lockhart, *Memoirs of the Life of Sir Walter Scott*, 10 vols (Edinburgh, 1856–8)
Longford *Wellington* I	Elizabeth Longford, *Wellington: The Years of the Sword* (1969)
Longford *Wellington* II	Elizabeth Longford, *Wellington: Pillar of State* (1972)
Malcolm	*The Life and Correspondence of Major-General Sir John Malcolm* by J W Kaye, 2 vols (1856)

Mathews *Memoirs*	*Memoirs of Charles Mathews, Comedian* by Mrs Mathews, 4 vols (1838)
Misc. Pr. W.	*The Miscellaneous Prose Works of Sir Walter Scott*, 3 vols (Edinburgh, 1841)
Notes & Index	James C Corson, *Notes & Index to Sir Herbert Grierson's Edition of 'The Letters of Sir Walter Scott'* (Oxford, 1979)
Oman	Carola Oman, *The Wizard of the North The Life of Sir Walter Scott* (1973)
PL	Anonymous [Walter Scott], *Paul's Letters to his Kinsfolk* (Edinburgh, 1816)
P.W.	*The Poetical Works of Sir Walter Scott*, ed J Logie Robertson (Oxford, 1951)
QR	*The Quarterly Review*
Lady Shelley	*The Diary of Lady Shelley*, ed R Edgcumbe, 2 vols (1912–13)
Simpson	James Simpson, *Paris after Waterloo, including a revised edition of 'A Visit to Flanders and the Field of Waterloo'* (Edinburgh & London, 1853)
Smiles	S Smiles, *A Publisher and his Friends: Memoir and Correspondence of John Murray*, 2 vols (1891)

CHAPTER I

Introduction and Journey to Brussels and Waterloo

'I expect a great deal from this trip,' Walter Scott wrote to an Irish correspondent on 26 July 1815, as he was about to leave for Brussels and Paris from his country house at Abbotsford in Scotland.[1] In the event, he was not disappointed. 'I shall always number the weeks I have spent here [in Paris] among the happiest of my life,' he declared at the end of the travel book[2] that he wrote as the principal record of his trip of six weeks and of his first journey abroad. It was called *Paul's Letters to his Kinsfolk* (1816), and was written in the traditional epistolary form of travel literature. It also served Scott as a means of funding his trip, which he supplemented by 'a new Gaudeamus poem'[3] in celebration of the victory won, only the month before his trip, by the British army at Waterloo under the Duke of Wellington over the French army under Napoleon Bonaparte, who was then a prisoner in a British warship bound for exile in the remote island of St Helena.

The 'new Gaudeamus poem' was to be called *The Field of Waterloo* (1815),[4] and the profits of its first edition were to be made over to the public fund that had been launched for the dependants of the fallen and the disabled at the battle of Waterloo,[5] in which the principal ally of the British had been the Prussian army under Field Marshal Blücher. Scott's object, therefore, in making Brussels his first destination, was to visit the field of Waterloo,[6] following the opening up of the continent for travel and the restoration of peace to Europe after twenty-six years of upheavals and warfare, from the outbreak of the French Revolution in 1789 to the downfall of Napoleon as Emperor of the French in 1815. Thus Scott was one of the earliest in the unending stream of travellers from Britain to Waterloo,[7] followed closely by his friend, Robert Southey,[8] the poet laureate, and, a few months later, by Lord Byron.

In making Paris his second destination,[9] in which again he was following what tens of thousands of his fellow-countrymen were doing after their pilgrimage to Waterloo, Scott was anxious to see the French capital under Allied occupation in the form of an unparalleled garrison of nearly 1 million troops drawn from the armies not only of Britain, Prussia, and their western allies (Holland, Belgium, Brunswick, Spain) but also of their eastern allies, notably Russia and Austria. Besides Wellington, Blücher, and all the heroes of Waterloo, the Emperors of Russia and Austria, the King of Prussia, and all their leading generals, ministers, and diplomats were then all in Paris, together with the newly restored King Louis XVIII of France. Accordingly Scott wrote to the same Irish correspondent, on the eve of his departure for Brussels, that 'the sight that is now in Paris is such as only occurs once in five hundred years'.[10]

Scott was then aged forty-four, and was married to Charlotte, née Carpenter, which was the anglicised surname for Charpentier. Born at Lyons of French parents, Charlotte had been brought to England as a girl by her mother a few years before the French Revolution, together with her only brother, Charles. Both of them had been baptised in the Church of England on becoming wards of the 2nd Marquess of Downshire. There is no evidence that they had set foot again in France. Charlotte spoke English imperfectly, and with a French accent. Her full family history does not appear to have been known to Scott, particularly the relationship of her mother, Mme Charpentier, to Lord Downshire, which has remained a subject of mystery and controversy to this day.[11] Charlotte herself was only a few months older than Scott, and had borne him four children: two sons and two daughters. The elder daughter, Sophia, was the future wife of John Gibson Lockhart, the author of *Memoirs of the Life of Sir Walter Scott* (1837–8). Sophia had been named after her mother's earliest and best friend in England, another immigrant from France called Sophia Dumergue, who had been baptised in the Church of England by her father, Charles Dumergue, a naturalised surgeon-dentist with a large practice in London.[12] The Dumergues were apparently related to the Charpentiers. Both families had settled in England at much the same time. Thanks to these links, Scott and his wife had always been warmly received by the Dumergues on their visits from Scotland to London, where the Dumergues had played hosts to royalist refugees from France.[13]

Although Scott was already a literary celebrity throughout Britain, he was not yet well known in France and other countries of the continent. His celebrity was principally that of a poet. In that capacity only Byron, with whom he had had his celebrated meeting in London the previous spring,[14] eclipsed him in popularity. As Jane Austen was to acknowledge in *Persuasion* (1817),[15] Byron and Scott were the most popular Regency poets. Recognising that his poetic star had passed its zenith (for his latest poems had been received less enthusiastically than his earlier),[16] Scott had turned to novel-writing the year before his trip to Brussels and Paris, and had scored a resounding success with *Waverley* (1814), which he had rapidly followed up—equally successfully—with *Guy Mannering* (1815).

But both these novels had been published anonymously, whereas all his major poems, with which he had opened up Scotland, especially the Highlands, to English readers, had been published under his own name, because the writing of poetry, unlike that of the novel, which was a comparatively young genre, had long been considered respectable among the gentry and professional class, to which Scott belonged as an Edinburgh advocate.[17] For Scott was a legal civil servant as a Principal Clerk to the Court of Session in Edinburgh (the supreme civil court of law in Scotland). Although his name was a household word in Britain as a poet, his identity as a novelist was a closely guarded secret except among a small circle of intimate friends, who themselves kept up the mystification that he enjoyed, and was an adept at, practising. To the public at large the author of *Guy Mannering* was known simply as 'the author of *Waverley*', which was to remain the *soubriquet* for him on the title-page of most of the subsequent Waverley Novels until he finally acknowledged his identity in 1827.[18]

Even as a traveller to Brussels and Paris, Scott intended to publish *Paul's Letters to his Kinsfolk* anonymously, whereas *The Field of Waterloo* was to be published under his own name by Archibald Constable in Edinburgh and by John Murray and Longman in England. It was significant that, while Scott was making this and other arrangements with his publishers by letter before setting off for the continent, Murray was himself in Paris in the flood of British tourists to Waterloo and the French capital.[19] It was in Murray's famous drawing-room that Scott's first meeting with Byron had taken place, at much the same time that Scott had had his first audience with the Prince Regent at Carlton House.[20] The prince was a great admirer of Scott's poetry. He had offered Scott the poet laureateship, and, a few years later, he was to create Scott a baronet. Scott had politely declined the laureateship, and had recommended Southey instead.[21] He treasured a gold snuff box set in brilliants that he had received from the Prince Regent, who had also entertained him to a merry dinner, attended by several leading Scottish peers, including the Marquess of Huntly, the eldest son of the Duke of Gordon.[22] Scott, for his part, had endeared himself to his royal host, as he had already widely done in high and low society in Scotland and England, with his genial personality and great powers as a raconteur. To these and other qualities he added an extraordinary range of erudition, particularly in history and literature, the most recent evidence of which was his edition of *The Life and Works of Jonathan Swift* (1814), published almost at the same time as *Waverley*. This pioneering feat of scholarship complemented his earlier major edition of *The Works of John Dryden* (1808). Thanks to these two editions he was excellently equipped with knowledge of the Stuart Restoration in England for parallel observations in *Paul's Letters to his Kinsfolk* on the Bourbon Restoration in France in the person of King Louis XVIII.

Scott was in very high spirits on setting off by coach on 28 July 1815 with three fellow-travellers shortly after the publication of a powerful review article on Wellington by Southey. It had appeared in the *Quarterly Review*,[23] which Scott and others had founded in support of the ruling Tory government. Its publisher was Murray, to whom Scott had written that 'Southey's article on Lord Wellington does him the highest honor'. He had also confirmed a promise to him to contribute 'a highland article on my return' from Paris[24] in full awareness that Murray and other publishers were anxious to exploit the so-called 'Tartan fever'[25] that Scott had generated among English readers with *The Lady of The Lake* (1810), *Waverley*, and *The Lord of the Isles* (1815).

Scott's three fellow-travellers were all familiar from the newspapers with the speech that he had recently made in Edinburgh at the launching of 'the Waterloo Subscription', as the national fund in aid of the dependants of the fallen and disabled was officially called.[26] His fellow-travellers were all Scots from neighbouring homes of the gentry in Edinburgh or of country squires on the border between Scotland and England. One of them, in fact, called Alexander Pringle of Whytbank, was associated with Scott's former cottage at Ashestiel on the river Tweed, in which picturesque setting he had been sketched by Scott in *Marmion* (1808) as 'one of the companions of my mountain joys'.[27] Pringle was now an advocate, like Robert Bruce, the second fellow-traveller, whose father was a colleague of Scott's as Deputy Clerk to the Court of Session.[28] Both Pringle and Bruce were much younger than Scott. So was his third companion, John Scott of Gala, who was commonly called 'Gala' by his territorial designation. He was a relation of Scott's as well as the most interesting of his fellow-travellers. Intelligent, good-humoured, cultured (including greater fluency in French than Scott), widely travelled, musical, and fond of the theatre, Gala kept a journal of their trip, which admirably complements Scott's own record in *Paul's Letters to his Kinsfolk* and in the letters he sent home from Brussels and Paris, mainly to Mrs Scott, to the 4th Duke of Buccleuch (his patron and chief of the Scott clan), and to his old friend, Joanna Baillie, the Scottish playwright.

Robert Bruce also kept a journal,[29] but short and incomplete; although useful, it lacks the many personal touches and amusing anecdotes of Scott in Gala's journal. Scott himself had not yet started keeping his celebrated journal. The year before, however, he had kept a brilliant diary of a memorable sea voyage to the northern and western coast of Scotland,[30] on which he had drawn for the scenery of *The Lord of the Isles*.[31] Extracts from the diary had appeared in the *Edinburgh Annual Register*,[32] which Scott had also founded at the same time as the *Quarterly Review*, originally as 'subsidiary' to it.[33]

His party landed at Hellevoetsluis in Holland from Harwich on 5 August after a rough crossing in a cutter, which induced a bout of prostrating sea-sickness, but which he afterwards described with characteristic humour, flavoured with one of his favourite Shakespearean quotations.[34] Their route to Brussels via the frontier town of Bergen-op-

Zoom and Antwerp covered very fertile country, although everywhere the ravages of war were visible in the shape of dismantled houses and abandoned châteaux.[35] The landscape seemed to Scott to have been drawn with strict realism in the paintings of the Flemish artists, with which he was familiar in Scotland.[36] The Flemish people bore striking resemblances to his own fellow-countrymen in figure, features, style of dress, and architecture, and in national character. He was inclined to 'favour the idea held by most antiquaries', that the lowlanders of Scotland and the Flemish were 'kindred tribes'.[37] The similarities between them reinforced the long-standing historical and military appeal of Flanders to Scott as a poet and novelist who excelled in describing 'what was striking and picturesque in historical narrative'. For 'a thousand memorable actions' had made Flanders the 'classic land' in European military history.[38] Moreover, two of Scott's favourite authors had both been Flemish. The first was Jean Froissart, 'the most picturesque of historians',[39] on whose mediaeval chronicles, with their 'heart-stirring and eye-dazzling descriptions of war and tournaments',[40] Scott had already drawn heavily for *The Lay of the Last Minstrel* (1805), *Marmion*, and other romances. The second was Philippe de Comines, 'perhaps the most faithful [truthful]' of historians,[41] who was to serve Scott as principal source for *Quentin Durward* (1823) as well as to rally his drooping spirits with his *Mémoires* (1524) at a critical phase in the composition of *Anne of Geierstein* (1829).[42] Comines himself, moreover, was to figure as one of the characters in *Quentin Durward*.

Scott had long known of Bergen-op-Zoom as not only 'the strongest fortress in the Netherlands' but as 'the masterpiece of Coeho[o]rn, that prince of engineers',[43] whom he had compared in *Guy Mannering*[44] to the great military architects who had put up Hadrian's Wall on the border between England and Scotland. Initially, however, Bergen-op-Zoom's appearance in a flat country setting disappointed Scott as a traveller with an eye for 'the picturesque'.[45] Its modern fortifications fell short of his ideal of a castle in romantic scenery, examples of which already abounded in his poetry as well as in his two novels, such as the castles of Doune, Stirling, and Edinburgh in *Waverley*,[46] and that of Ellangowan in *Guy Mannering*.[47] They all had an 'antique' air, were mediaeval in origin, and were placed on 'steepy ascents' or in precipitous settings commanding panoramic views of land or sea for maximum effect of beauty or sublimity. Accordingly Scott, after his great success with *Marmion*, had been painted, in a celebrated portrait by Henry (later Sir Henry) Raeburn, against a background of his favourite mediaeval castle called Hermitage in a luminous, hilly setting.[48]

Despite his initial disappointment with Bergen-op-Zoom, it did manage eventually to draw out the romantic poet in him in a typical blend of landscape and sensibility towards the end of his party's close inner survey of its formidable fortifications. For, the year before his visit, Bergen-op-Zoom had been the scene of a bold, but ill-fated, martial

Great Britain, showing places connected mainly with Scott's return journey from Paris to Abbotsfor

Key

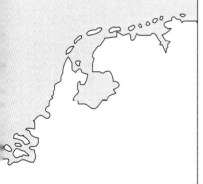

exploit by one of the Scottish heroes in the campaign against Napoleon, namely, General Sir Thomas Graham, whose bravery in the Peninsular War Scott had already celebrated in *The Vision of Don Roderick* (1811).[49] Therefore, after listening to his guide's details of Graham's desperate attempt to carry Bergen-op-Zoom by storm, and after walking from one bastion to another, 'admiring the strength of the defences, which British valour had so nearly surmounted, and mourning over the evil fate which rendered that valour fruitless', Scott fell into 'solemn reflections'. His state of mind was touched with that 'melancholy' dear to the Romantics, as the evening matched Scott's mood with flashes of lightning before turning from twilight into darkness, while 'the hollow roll of the drum announced the setting of the watch'.[50] This nocturnal scene provided a striking parallel to that in *Waverley*[51] on the eve of the battle of Prestonpans.

Scott had a personal link with Graham, in that both of them had been given the freedom of the city of Edinburgh at the same ceremony[52] only the month before Graham's assault on Bergen-op-Zoom. The assault had been combined with a bombardment of Antwerp's harbour, of which Scott now saw evidence in the form of shattered houses and sunken vessels. At the same time he expressed surprise at hearing the people of Antwerp speak without much respect for the talents of the celebrated military engineer, General Carnot, who had defended the city at the time of Graham's assault. On the other hand, their fears over Carnot's appointment by Napoleon as governor of their city had happily proved unfounded, for his tactful and moderate measures had belied his earlier record as a collaborator with the notoriously ruthless Robespierre.[53]

Although Scott coupled Antwerp with Bergen-op-Zoom as both 'very strongly fortified', the latter had nothing to match the former's 'magnificent' cathedral and other splendid churches,[54] or indeed the extraordinary dockyard that Napoleon had created at Antwerp, following the annexation of Belgium to France. One of his most ambitious projects was to create a navy at Antwerp, for which reason the trees fit for ship timber had been cut down by his orders, which explains why Scott stated that 'the forests of Flanders were formerly of a more valuable description than at present'.[55]

Antwerp's cathedral of Nôtre Dame and the other churches, which Scott found to be full of worshippers,[56] drew out his feeling for Gothic architecture at a time when, although the dominant national taste in England was for Regency neo-classical architecture, the cult of mediaeval art and literature, and the Gothic Revival, were gaining ground in the wake of Horace Walpole, Thomas Chatterton, Ann Radcliffe, and their followers. Scott, with his extraordinary fund of antiquarian lore embodied in popular poems and tales of chivalry and romance set in the period of Gothic architectural ascendency, was an outstanding contributor to the mediaeval cult and Gothic Revival. Moreover, it was his ambition to enlarge and convert his small estate at Abbotsford into a Scottish baronial

Lieut-General Sir Thomas Graham (Lord Lynedoch) by Sir Thomas Lawrence. (Wellington Museum, Apsley House. By permission of Victoria and Albert Museum, London)

manor[57] befitting a *laird* (Scottish country gentleman) as his own distinct architectural contribution to the Gothic Revival.

Aware that Antwerp was the city of Rubens, Scott made a point of visiting his tomb in the church of St James's,[58] but was dismayed to find that all Antwerp's art treasures (including Rubens's masterpiece, *The Descent from the Cross*) had been carried to Paris on Napoleon's orders for display in the Louvre. He therefore complained that 'we hardly saw a single good picture'[59] not only by Rubens but by other Flemish artists, who, with the Dutch, were renowned for genre paintings,[60] the literary counterparts of which were the low Scottish characters that Scott was creating as one of his outstanding achievements in the Waverley Novels. Perhaps the Flemish painter best known in Britain for genre was David Teniers the younger, so that Scott was to allude to him in *The Field of Waterloo*, in a stanza[61] contrasting the normal, happy, simple life of the rural inhabitants of Waterloo village with the destruction, carnage, and scorched landscape resulting from the battle. Teniers' counterpart in Scotland was Scott's future friend, David Wilkie, so much so that Scott was to refer to him in *The Bride of Lammermoor* (1819) as 'the Scottish Teniers'.[62]

As for Rubens, 'the cumbrous solidity' of his female figures seemed to Scott to bear a curious resemblance to the instruments of labour of the Flemish peasants, which were 'strong and solid, but clumsy and inelegant'.[63] Personally, Scott was drawn to Rubens for his horses, boar hunts, and groups of Flemish peasants.[64] For Scott himself loved horses, and excelled in describing hunting scenes on high ground as part of his comprehensive portrayal of Scottish 'manners', in which accomplishment Byron, on arriving at Brussels a few months after Scott, was to declare to his British host that Scott was without a rival.[65] On the other hand, as a poet and novelist with an encyclopaedic knowledge of history, Scott certainly responded, on going to Paris from Brussels, to 'that splendid series of historical pictures' by Rubens in the Luxembourg Gallery 'commemorating the principal actions in the life of Mary de Medici'.[66] The series, moreover, provided an excellent example of Rubens's 'profusion of imagination', which Scott was to compare, in *Lives of the Novelists* (1821–4),[67] to the literary inventiveness of his fellow-countryman, Tobias Smollett.

Scott was keenly interested in the 'new political existence'[68] that Brussels and the whole of Flanders had just acquired, following Bonaparte's defeat and abdication. For the victorious Allied Powers, on the insistence of Britain, led by her Foreign Secretary, Lord Castlereagh, had formed the new Kingdom of the Netherlands by uniting Belgium or Flanders to Holland under King William I of the House of Orange. Although Scott, who had so vigorously supported the war against Bonaparte by Britain and her allies, approved, in general, of the new United Kingdom of the Netherlands, he did so not without grave reservations. Indeed his fears over the ultimate success of the new arrangement were to prove prophetic, for he was to live to see the Belgians rise up in 1831 against the new union and break it up,[69] so as to form a separate Kingdom of Belgium under Leopold I. Scott's deep-rooted Tory instincts and faith compelled him to protest eloquently against 'the modern political legerdemain' of wholesale and forced transfers of cities, districts, and even kingdoms from one state to another on the pretext of 'natural boundaries' of rivers and mountains (*arrondisements* was then the coined word for them), in disregard of ancient ties of morals, manners, habits, language, and religion.[70] This iniquitous pretext had prevailed in Scott's own lifetime for the partition of Poland and the separation of the Tyrol from Austria—with disastrous consequences. Accordingly, he held it to be 'in general, sound and good doctrine, to beware of removing ancient landmarks', for which reason the new union between Belgium and Holland 'must be admitted to form a grand exception to the general rule'. Indeed, Scott argued that it was 'rather a restoration of the natural union which subsisted before the time of Philip the Second' of Spain.[71]

After his party's arrival at Brussels on 7 August 1815[72] Scott was quick to perceive that the principal threat to the new Kingdom of the Netherlands sprang from the religious differences between Flanders, which was a Catholic country, and Holland, which was Protestant. King William had proclaimed religious toleration in his new Catholic dominions, to which the Flemish clergy, led by the Bishop of Ghent,[73] were opposed. The King, to conciliate his new subjects, had promised to procure the restoration of the treasures that had been removed by the French from the Flemish churches to Paris.[74] Scott represented the Flemish Catholics as 'sincere' but 'unenlightened' and 'very zealous'.[75] He criticised the alleged 'idolatry of the Romish church' on observing worshippers in Antwerp's cathedral at their devotions before 'a wax figure of the Virgin'. For this and other reasons he admitted that 'the rites and solemnities of the Catholic Church', the pageantry of which he had fully exploited in those poems of his set in the Middle Ages, 'made less impression on me than I expected'.[76] On the other hand, he continued, in novel after novel as well as in his private correspondence, to refer to 'those beautiful old Latin hymns which belong to the Catholic service.'[77]

As a Protestant himself Scott had moved from the gloomy Calvinistic doctrines and rigid practices of the Church of Scotland, in which he had been born and brought up, to the more moderate Anglican Church, whose ritual was more to his liking.[78] The implication of his criticism of the Flemish Catholics as 'unenlightened' was that Scott, for all his antiquarianism and preoccupation with mediaeval chivalry and romance, regarded himself with pride as being a product of the eighteenth-century Scottish Enlightenment with its pursuit of 'good sense', reason, moderation, and distrust of 'enthusiasm' or religious fanaticism. He had lately paid a hearty tribute in *Guy Mannering*[79] to the Scottish Enlightenment—the age of David Hume, Adam Smith, William Robertson, and Adam Ferguson—as perhaps unrivalled for 'the depth and variety of talent which it embraced and concentrated', largely in his own home town of Edinburgh. Before *Guy Mannering* he had brilliantly caricatured Presbyterian bigotry in *Waverley*[80] in the person of Gifted Gilfillan, which he was to follow up in *Old Mortality* (1816), and even to extend to the more extreme representatives of the English Puritan sects in *Peveril of the Peak* (1823) and *Woodstock* (1826).

Except for his criticism of the Flemish Catholics and of some of the Belgian troops who had formed part of the army of the Duke of Wellington, and who had not acquitted themselves well in the battle of Waterloo,[81] Scott had only praise for Brussels, whose celebrated Hôtel de Ville and the buildings surrounding the Grande Place served to confirm him in his admiration of Gothic architecture.[82] The great tower of the Hôtel de Ville impressed him so much that he afterwards incorporated it into the opening stanza of *The Field of Waterloo*.[83] The Hôtel de Flandres, where his party was accommodated, lay in the Grande Place,[84] which conveyed the impression of a square of palaces, with streets running out from it, and enclosing the celebrated *parc* or public walk. Tastefully planted and adorned with elegant houses and statuary, the *parc* was the fashionable quarter of Brussels. Its buildings included the hotel where Wellington had stayed on arriving to take command of the Anglo-Belgian army.[85]

The shops in the vicinity of Scott's hotel displayed specimens of the famous Brussels lace, which he had apparently gathered from his literary reading had been much in fashion in Restoration England, especially among the dandies in the court of King Charles II: hence its prominence in the dress of his sketches of the fops of that period in his later novels.[86]

He observed that the old châteaux outside Brussels as well as the grounds around them seemed to have been maintained in their original style of construction. Many of the houses in Brussels and other parts of Flanders had dates inscribed on their fronts which went back nearly as far as the time of Froissart. 'An appearance of antiquity' seemed to Scott to be 'one of the most distinguishing features which strikes [*sic*] the traveller in the Low Countries'.[87]

The finest château was undoubtedly the royal palace of Lacken, whose classical façade was commonly likened by visitors from Scotland to the famous Register House in Edinburgh by Robert Adam.[88] Prettily situated on rising ground, the château had been furnished by Napoleon from Paris. It was now earmarked for King William's official residence after his forthcoming coronation. For the principal seat of government of the new Kingdom of the Netherlands was to be Brussels, not the Hague, which Scott foresaw as a potential source of jealousy on the part of the Dutch, who might also not like the new stipulation of opening up the river Scheldt to Flemish commerce, particularly the trade of Antwerp. On the other hand, Scott argued that the Dutch, bearing in mind Flanders' historic rôle as 'the common stage upon which all the prize-fighters of Europe [had] decided their quarrels', now had 'the inestimable advantage of having the battle turned from their gates, and of enjoying the protection of a strong barrier placed at a distance from their own frontier'.[89]

Scott's impression of an air of antiquity in the Low Countries was reinforced by the dress of the Flemish women, for it was marked by a black mantle, which he was given to understand had been derived from the Spanish *mantilla*, when Flanders had formed part of the so-called 'Spanish Netherlands'. Scott represented the mantle as the counterpart of the 'screen' or tartan plaid, 'which was formerly peculiar to Scotland'.[90] On that account, therefore, he was to take pains to make his female characters wear it in nationalistic scenes or contexts.[91] He was also to dress a number of his Scottish characters in the so-called 'Flemish fashion',[92] in keeping with 'the constant intercourse our ancestors maintained with Flanders, from which, according to contemporary accounts, they derived almost every article which required the least skill in manufacture'.[93]

Foremost among these articles were fine tapestries of the kind that Scott and his companions saw with admiration in the royal palace of Lacken,[94] and of which the cathedral of Brussels had a collection comparable to the celebrated Gobelin tapestries outside Paris.[95] Bearing in mind that tapestry hangings were the invention of the Low Countries, Scott afterwards exploited them in several ways in his novels, usually for effects of opulence, as in the description of the Earl of Leicester's private apartments in *Kenilworth* (1821), and of the pavilion of the Constable of Chester in *The Betrothed* (1825). The latter, moreover, included a Flemish weaver, Wilkin Flammock, as one of the principal characters, complete with a 'bulky figure'[96] matching the 'cumbrous solidity' of Rubens's women.

In every corner of Brussels Scott observed 'ballad-singers bellowing out songs' in praise of the Prince of Orange, the heir to the throne of the new Kingdom of the Netherlands, whose gallantry had made up for the poor performance of some of the Belgian troops.[97] Scott, who was a renowned 'collector of popular effusions, did not fail to purchase specimens of the Flemish minstrelsy'.[98] His own poetic career had opened with *Minstrelsy of the Scottish Border* (1802–3), followed by an impressive output of ballads and songs incorporated into his verse romances and, more recently, into *Waverley* and *Guy Mannering* as his own contribution to the wealth of balladry marking English Romantic poetry.

All the English society of Brussels, to whom Scott was introduced, and whom he afterwards reported to be 'so far as I saw it, of the very first order',[99] related to him how the citizens had vied with each other in acts of kindness and hospitality to the thousands of wounded British troops who had struggled back to Brussels from the battlefield, or had been carried to the city in waggons.[100] Many of the wounded, of whom Scott and his party found the hospitals of Brussels and Antwerp to be full, told him that they would have perished but for the attention they had received from the Flemish people.[101] Scott, for his part, fully entered, in imagination as well as in sympathy, into 'the agony of suspense' that the citizens of Brussels had suffered as they had awaited the outcome of the battle in the knowledge that Napoleon, confident of victory, had vowed revenge on their city. Their sensations were afterwards recreated by Scott in *The Field of Waterloo*[102] as well as in the longer prose account of the battle in *Paul's Letters to his Kinsfolk*.[103] Drawing on the conventional rhetorical devices of eighteenth-century poetry in *The Field of Waterloo*, he wrote:

> Pale Brussels! then what thoughts were thine,
> When ceaseless from the distant line
> > Continued thunders came!
> Each burgher held his breath to hear
> These forerunners of havoc near,
> > Of rapine and of flame.
> What ghastly sights were thine to meet,
> When rolling through thy stately street,
> The wounded show'd their mangled plight
> In token of th'unfinished fight,
> And from each anguish-laden wain
> The blood-drops laid thy dust like rain!

In *Paul's Letters to his Kinsfolk* Scott explained that 'the horrors of this agonizing period' for the citizens of Brussels had been aggravated by rumours of treachery inside the city on the part of friends of Napoleon. One of them—a man of rank and wealth—had gone over to Napoleon during the battle, when its outcome was still undecided, and after an immense mass of defiant French prisoners had spread terror and dismay in the city. Scott saw the Belgian defector's mansion, which had been converted into a military hospital, covering a considerable part of one side of the Grande Place.[104] At the hospital were many young surgeons who had volunteered from Britain. They included Charles (later Sir Charles) Bell, the future discoverer of the nervous system of the human body. His brother George was a fellow-advocate of Scott's in Edinburgh. George had passed to Scott a vivid letter that Charles had written to him from Brussels. It had quickened Scott's determination to travel to Brussels as soon after the battle of Waterloo as possible.[105] Moreover, one or two passages in it were echoed by Scott in *Paul's Letters to his Kinsfolk*[106] in his own remarks on the similarities between the Flemish and the Scots.

In *Paul's Letters to his Kinsfolk* Scott preceded his account of the anxieties suffered by the citizens of Brussels with an evocation of the drama that had followed the celebrated scene at the Duchess of Richmond's ball in Brussels, when the news had first reached Wellington that Napoleon was advancing on the city.[107] Although he presented much of the drama from a Scottish focus by dwelling, understandably, on the two distinguished Highland corps in Wellington's army, he again brought in the feelings of the citizens of Brussels as they had seen 'so many brave men take their departure ... for the slaughter which awaited them'.

Scott eulogised the Highlanders' bravery in an emotionally charged stanza in *The Field of Waterloo*,[108] which was designed as a roll of honour as well as of blood, for it contained the names of several of the outstanding heroes who had fallen in the battle. It was headed by that of the commander of the division of which the Highland corps had formed part: Lt-General Sir Thomas Picton,[109] perhaps the greatest soldier that Wales had produced. The stanza itself followed the metrical pattern that Scott had already used in *Marmion*[110] for the description of the battle of Flodden. He called it 'the irregular Pindaric measure':[111]

> Period of honour as of woes,
> What bright careers 'twas thine to close!
> Mark'd on thy roll of blood what names
> To Briton's memory, and to Fame's,
> Laid there their last immortal claims!
> Thou saw'st in seas of gore expire
> Redoubted Picton's soul of fire ...

Picton had died leading a desperate charge of Highlanders against masses of French infantry. His name on Scott's list was followed by that of Wellington's favourite aide-de-camp, Lt-Colonel Sir Alexander Gordon, whom Scott had known and valued.[112] He had fallen, according to Scott, 'while he watched his leader's [Wellington's] life'. Indeed Wellington had suffered the mortification of seeing the greater part of his staff, 'who had shared so many glories and dangers by his side, fall man by man around him';[113] hence Scott's memorable lament in *The Field of Waterloo*:[114]

> Ah! though her guardian angel's shield
> Fenced Britain's hero through the field,
> Fate not the less her power made known,
> Through his friends' hearts to pierce his own.

Colonel Gordon's clan was the same as that to which Byron belonged on his mother's side. Scott's tribute to Gordon and to the other Scottish heroes was to earn him a generous compliment from Byron in his own Waterloo stanzas[115] in canto three of *Childe Harold's Pilgrimage* (1816). 'Their praise is hymn'd by loftier harps than mine,' Byron was to write towards the end of those stanzas,[116] in which he was to upstage Scott with his own description of the drama that had followed the summons to arms at the Duchess of Richmond's ball. Scott, for his part, anticipated Byron's compliment to him with his own tribute in *The Field of Waterloo*[117] to 'the gifted bard', who, following Napoleon's first abdication in 1814, had vehemently denounced him in *Ode to Napoleon Bonaparte* for having allegedly betrayed the republican and democratic ideals of the French Revolution by crowning himself emperor in France and setting up a family dynasty of kings all over conquered Europe.

On the other hand, Scott, for all his high regard for Byron as a poet, and for all their eminently happy meeting in London a few months before Scott's trip to Brussels, could not have been more opposed to Byron in politics in view of the latter's Whig and republican principles. These were to culminate in Byron's denunciation in *Childe Harold's Pilgrimage*[118] of 'the king-making victory' of 'deadly Waterloo', which had brought about the restoration of the Bourbons in France in the person of King Louis XVIII. Therefore, when Scott, shortly after his return to Britain from Paris, reviewed *Childe Harold's Pilgrimage* in the *Quarterly Review*,[119] he did not hesitate to expose the inconsistency of Byron's politics in general, and the hollowness of his attitude to Waterloo in particular, in the light of Byron's past stance and writings. At the same time Scott extolled Byron's poetry, citing precisely the Waterloo stanzas as perhaps unsurpassed by 'any verses in our language ... in vigour and feeling'.

Whereas Byron was to compound his political sins, in Scott's eyes, by deliberately cutting out all mention of Wellington from the Waterloo stanzas, Scott drew Wellington as a heroic figure in his brilliantly gripping narrative of the two battles of Quatre Bras and Waterloo fought by the British at the same time as the battle of Ligny fought by their Prussian allies under their redoubtable veteran, Field Marshal Blücher.[120] Scott's narrative, comprehending all three battles, provided the longest and fullest display yet of his mastery of battle scenes, which he had first begun to develop in verse in *Marmion*, and which he had recently refined in prose in *Waverley*,[121] and again in verse in *The Lord of the Isles* with his description of the battle of Bannockburn. He was to exploit the same technique again and again in *Old Mortality*, *A Legend of Montrose* (1819), and other Waverley Novels. It consisted essentially of close topographical detail combined with analysis of tactics, and highlighted by dramatic action scenes, complete with dialogue and anecdotes, often of 'feats of personal strength and valour',[122] in swift-moving narrative. Scott's dramatic method was not unrelated to his love of, and regular attendance at, the theatre, which was in evidence even in Brussels, where he went with his fellow-travellers to see a play in French on the evening of their arrival.[123]

Scott was particularly effective with his dramatic method in bringing out Wellington's inspiring leadership and fearless self-exposure, which ensured him the devoted attachment of his army, especially in moments of crisis.[124] These two qualities of leadership and fearlessness were also distilled into Scott's presentation of Wellington in *The Field of Waterloo*, first, in the stanza[125] describing how

> HE, his country's sword and shield,
> Still in the battle-front reveal'd
> Where danger fiercest swept the field,
>   Came like a beam of light;
> In action prompt, in sentence brief,
> 'Soldiers, stand firm,' exclaimed the Chief,
>   'England shall tell the fight!'

and then in the passage[126] marking the turning-point of the battle, when Wellington, at the head of a brigade of guards, gave the order for his men to go on the offensive:

> Then, Wellington, thy piercing eye
> This crisis caught of destiny;
> The British host had stood
> That morn 'gainst charge of sword and lance
> As their own ocean-rocks hold stance,
> But when thy voice had said, 'Advance!'
> They were their ocean's flood.

Wellington's determination to die with his men on the field of battle, if necessary,[127] was sharply contrasted by Scott with Napoleon's alleged poorness of spirit in adversity,[128] in that, at seeing the final desperate charge of his imperial guards broken and turned into a rout by the celebrated 'squares' of British infantry, he had fled towards Paris to avoid capture by the advancing Prussian divisions of Blücher, who had joined up from Ligny with Wellington's army.[129] In this context, Scott, bearing Napoleon's fondness for Roman history in mind, also contrasted his flight to Paris with the gallant end of Catiline:[130]

> That Chieftain, who, of yore,
> Ambition's dizzy paths essay'd,
> And with the gladiators' aid
> For empire enterprised:
> He stood the cast his rashness play'd,
> Left not the victims he had made,
> Dug his red grave with his own blade
> And on the field he lost was laid,
> Abhorr'd—but not despised.

One great advantage of Scott's in making his dramatic presentation of character vivid with anecdotes in dialogue was that he drew them from several eye-witnesses, as he himself explained in *Paul's Letters to his Kinsfolk*:[131] 'the details which I have ventured to put into writing, are most of them from the authority of officers high in command upon that memorable day'. One of these senior officers was Major-General (later Sir) Frederick Adam, who had commanded a brigade of infantry, which, as Scott related,[132] had played a crucial part in the battle by engaging in the final manoeuvre that had brought about the destruction of Napoleon's imperial guards. He was Scott's principal host at Brussels,[133] thanks to a recommendation that Scott had brought with him from General Adam's father, William Adam, who had presented Scott to the Prince Regent the previous spring in London.[134] Having been wounded in the fighting, General Adam had been left in command of the small British garrison at Brussels, who were paraded under the windows of Scott's apartment in the Hôtel de Flandres.[135] All their able-bodied comrades in arms had crossed into France with the Prussian troops in pursuit of the retreating enemy or were encamped at Paris in the Allied army of occupation.

Scott referred to General Adam as 'one of our best and bravest officers'.[136] A veteran of the Peninsular War, he was barely thirty-five years old when Scott met him and heard graphic details from him of how the British 'squares' had operated against the furious onsets of the French cavalry led by the celebrated cuirassiers and lancers. Scott afterwards dubbed the cuirassiers 'those men of iron and steel whose hearts were as much proof as their armour ... They rode at the British squares round and round them attempting to penetrate on every side with the most determined perseverance, although the fire was the best supported and most tremendously destructive that was ever known'.[137] Eventually the heavy British dragoons had fallen upon them, and, together with the fire from the squares and the artillery, had despatched nearly twelve entire regiments of them.[138] The meeting of the two bodies of cuirassiers and heavy dragoons was represented to Scott as having 'occasioned a noise not unaptly compared to the tinkering and hammering of a smith's shop'.[139] Scott's imagination was fired by the charges and final annihilation of the cuirassiers and lancers, which he evoked forcefully in *The Field of Waterloo*,[140] complete with the image of the 'smith's shop':

> Then down went helm and lance!
> Down were the eagle banners sent,
> Down reeling steeds and riders went,
> Corslets were pierced, and pennons rent,
>   And, to augment the fray,
> Wheel'd full against their staggering flanks,
> The English horsemen's foaming ranks
>   Forced their resistless way.
> Then to the musket-knell succeeds
> The clash of swords, the neigh of steeds;
> As plies the smith his clanging trade,
> Against the cuirass rang the blade;
> And while amid their close array
> The well-served cannon rent their way,
> And while amid their scatter'd band
> Raged the fierce rider's bloody brand,
> Recoil'd in common rout and fear
> Lancer and guard and cuirassier,
> Horsemen and foot, a mingled host,
> Their leaders fall'n, their standards lost.

Scott was also introduced by General Adam to an unnamed 'officer of engineers', who had been entrusted by Wellington with the task of keeping up the vital communications with the Prussians at Ligny, where they had originally been defeated by Napoleon, but whence they had been able to retreat and regroup in good order with a view to hastening to Wellington's assistance. Scott heard from this 'officer of engineers' of 'the eager and enthusiastic desire' of the Prussians to press forward 'to obtain their share of the glories and dangers' at Waterloo, and to avenge their defeat at Ligny.[141] It was only after many hours had passed, however, that they had been able to appear towards sunset at Waterloo. By that time Wellington's troops, having stood their ground, had deployed into line for a general charge on Napoleon's 'routed bands',[142] as Scott put it in the stanza[143] referring to this decisive phase of the battle. In the same stanza Scott hinted at the fatal prospect that had opened up for Napoleon at the appearance of the Prussians on his flank at the woody edge of Waterloo:

> Where coming squadrons gleam afar,
> And fresher thunders wake the war,
> And other standards fly ...

Scott was able to see where the junction between the British and Prussian troops had taken place when his party was escorted to the battlefield by General Adam's aide-de-camp, Captain Campbell, and a French royalist officer, formerly on Napoleon's staff, who had deserted to the British army on the morning of the battle.[144] Scott represented the French officer in *Paul's Letters to his Kinsfolk*[145] as having communicated valuable information to Wellington about Napoleon's plan for the opening attack. Scott also represented Captain Campbell as having had the honour of firing the last gun at the retreating French troops with their own armour. For they had abandoned all their guns, which Scott, on finding them on public display in Brussels, had observed to be engraved with 'the emphatic inscriptions, *Liberté, Egalité, Fraternité*', or with the names of the philosophers commonly regarded as forerunners of the French Revolution, such as Voltaire and Rousseau.[146]

A share of this booty had fallen to the Prussians, particularly in their pursuit of the broken French army after the battle at nightfall under moonlight. For, as Scott explained in *Paul's Letters to his Kinsfolk*,[147] 'the British cavalry were completely wearied with the exertions of the day, and utterly incapable of following the chase'. The arrival of the Prussians, therefore, 'with all their cavalry fit for instant and rapid operation', had been 'essential to gathering in the harvest, which was already dearly won and fairly reaped'.

Scott afterwards attempted to evoke the moonlight 'chase' of the French troops by the Prussian cavalry towards the end of the *The Field of Waterloo*[148] in a direct and dramatic address to Napoleon, complete with one of Scott's favourite similes, and rounded off with a picture of the plight of the French at the conclusion of the battle contrasted with their defiant enthusiasm at its start:

> Look, ere thou leav'st the fatal hill,
> Back on yon broken ranks
> Upon whose wild confusion gleams
> The moon, as on the troubled streams

> When rivers break their banks,
> And, to the ruin'd peasant's eye,
> Objects half seen roll swiftly by,
>   Down the dread current hurl'd:
> So mingle banner, wain, and gun,
> Where the tumultuous flight rolls on
> Of warriors, who, when morn begun,
>   Defied a banded world.

Scott gathered that the Prussians had also captured Napoleon's handsome carriage, the contents of which included a proclamation to the citizens of Brussels in expectation of their city's capitulation to him.[149] It was dated from the royal palace of Lacken. Among other papers was a list of spies and emissaries of France in all the countries of Europe, including 'the names of twenty citizens [of Brussels] who, as friends of France, were to be exempted from the general pillage'.[150] Among the swords and firearms captured in Napoleon's carriage was a pair of beautifully engraved, ornamented pistols, which were afterwards presented to Scott[151] for a splendid collection of weapons and armour that he was forming for his projected Scottish baronial manor at Abbotsford. His enthusiasm as a collector extended to curiosities of all sorts, which he was to exploit brilliantly in his next novel, *The Antiquary* (1816), in the person of its principal character, Jonathan Oldbuck.

Besides Captain Campbell and the royalist French officer, Scott's other guide to the field of Waterloo was a leading British resident of Brussels, Major Pryse Lockhart Gordon. Scott had met him at General Adam's house.[152] Gordon was widely travelled, well connected, and had a flair for reminiscences and anecdotes, on the evidence of the memoirs that he published many years after his meeting with Scott, and in which he left a record of Scott's visit as well as of Byron's later one.[153] As another member of the Gordon clan, he enjoyed the friendship of the Marquess of Huntly, who had attended the Prince Regent's dinner in Scott's honour in London,[154] and who had raised the celebrated Gordon Highland Regiment,[155] to whose gallant stand in the battle of Quatre Bras Scott paid tribute in *Paul's Letters to his Kinsfolk*.[156] The regiment's commanding officer, Colonel John Cameron, had perished in that battle, so that he also figured in Scott's roll of honour and of blood in *The Field of Waterloo*.[157] His body had been hastily buried in a green valley by his foster-brother and his faithful soldier-servant, but at the time of Scott's visit to Brussels Cameron's family were arranging for his remains to be disinterred and taken to Scotland by the Royal Navy for proper burial in his Highland home. Scott was to compose the inscription on the tall obelisk over Cameron's grave.[158]

Needless to say, Scott knew that the Marquess of Huntly's sister was the Duchess of Richmond, and that their father was the chief of the Gordon clan. Availing himself of his acquaintance with several members of the Duchess's family, Scott called on her, and afterwards gave Southey

Major Pryse Lockhart Gordon. From an engraving by H Meyer. (Private Collection)

a letter of introduction to her for his own visit to Brussels.[159] He told Southey that she had given him 'an interesting account of her ball which was broken up in so particular a manner', and which had been followed by a general, albeit temporary, exodus of the British residents to Ghent, although not by Major and Mrs Gordon, who thus served Scott as his principal source for his description of 'the varied emotions' that had gripped the people of Brussels, pending the outcome of the battle.[160]

The break-up of the Duchess of Richmond's ball and the general exodus of the British residents were afterwards to be immortalised by William Thackeray in *Vanity Fair*.[161] The ball itself had already become a subject of dispute by the time of Scott's visit, particularly among military and lay commentators on the battle of Waterloo. For its break-up was being adduced as proof that Wellington, despite the formidable reputation that he had built up in the Peninsular War for gathering advance intelligence of his enemy's movements, had allowed himself to be taken by surprise in Flanders by Napoleon's bold and rapid advance on Brussels from the French frontier.[162] Accordingly, in *Paul's Letters to his Kinsfolk*,[163] Scott opened his account of the battle of Quatre Bras, which took place two days before the battle of Waterloo, with an admission that 'his [Napoleon's] first movements seem to have partaken of a surprise', but he was quick to dismiss any imputation that Wellington had neglected 'the necessary means to procure intelligence ... for skill in obtaining which, as well as for talent in availing himself of the information when gained, he was pre-eminently distinguished on the peninsula'. On the contrary, Scott's information 'from good authority', by which presumably he meant either General Adam or Captain Campbell, was that 'a detailed and authentic account of Buonaparte's plan for the campaign, was actually dispatched from Paris in time to have reached Brussels before the commencement of hostilities', but, owing to a combination of unforeseen circumstances on the frontier of France with Belgium, the intelligence had not arrived till after the battle of Quatre Bras.[164] Wellington himself had admitted, at the break-up of the Duchess of Richmond's ball, that 'Napoleon has *humbugged* me, by God! he has gained twenty-four hours' march on me'. For that reason Wellington had first ordered his army to concentrate at Quatre Bras, a few miles south of Waterloo; 'but we shall not stop him [Napoleon] there,' Wellington had declared, 'and if so, I must fight him here [at Waterloo]'.[165]

Scott, for his part, does not seem to have gone with his fellow-travellers to the village of Quatre Bras. They went straight to Waterloo with Major Gordon in a *voiture* on a beautiful day, Captain Campbell following them in a gig. They reached the battlefield after a delightful drive through a beech forest,[166] which Scott afterwards described in the opening stanza of *The Field of Waterloo*. It bore the name of Soignes,[167] and was supposed to be 'a remnant of the forest of Ardennes, famous in Boiardo's *Orlando*, and immortal in Shakespeare's *As You Like It*'.[168] Although Scott's party had set off shortly after daybreak, they found half a dozen other parties of English tourists already on their pilgrimage to Waterloo.[169]

An inn adjoined the forest of Soignes. Wellington had used it as his headquarters before the battle. Scott's party breakfasted in the very room where Wellington had slept during the stormy night before the battle.[170] There he had made his final dispositions with his quartermaster-general, Colonel Sir William De Lancey, whose subsequent fate had saddened all the citizens of Edinburgh, including Scott. For De Lancey had married the daughter of a leading Edinburgh baronet only a few weeks before he had sailed from Scotland for Wellington's headquarters at Brussels,[171] where his young wife had rejoined him. Mortally wounded by a cannon-ball while speaking to Wellington, he had fallen off his horse on his face. All the staff had dismounted and run to him, but he had said to Wellington, 'Pray tell them to leave me and let me die in peace.' Having been moved to a peasant's cottage in the village of Waterloo, he had died after a few days, tenderly nursed by his bride.[172]

According to Scott's information, apparently from Captain Campbell, the plan that Wellington had drawn up with De Lancey had been found in the breast of the latter's coat, 'when he fell, and stained with the blood of that gallant officer'.[173] Scott represented De Lancey, in the role of honour and of blood in *The Field of Waterloo*,[174] as having changed 'Love's bridal wreath/For laurels from the hand of Death'. On the other hand, Scott was then not aware that De Lancey's widow, on returning to Scotland, had written a journal of her extraordinary ordeal for her brother's private reading. It was only some ten years later, by which time she had died, and Scott had become very friendly with her brother, Captain Basil Hall, that he was shown a manuscript of her journal. He pronounced it 'most interesting and affecting', so much so that, in agreement with Constable, his publisher, he proposed to Hall that it be published anonymously as 'an addition' to a fresh edition of *Paul's Letters to his Kinsfolk*. He considered it 'one of the most valuable and important documents which could be published as illustrative of the woes of war'. Its appearance in print, however, would be subject to the overriding condition that 'it should not awaken the distress which time may in some degree have abated'.[175] Although Hall seemed to be in favour of publication, and although Scott's letter to him for submission to the other members of De Lancey's family was couched in language that might have served as a model of tact and delicacy, permission for the journal's publication was withheld.[176] Eventually, however, after another lapse of some eighty years, it *was* published under the title of *A Week at Waterloo in June 1815*. It was instantly recognised as one of the most moving pieces of narrative ever written.[177]

As for Scott's impression of the field of Waterloo, he found the ground still torn with the shot and shells, and broken up and rutted with the wheels of the artillery.[178] Fortunately, however, Major Gordon had sent out in advance a couple of saddle horses as a precaution against fatigue

Colonel Sir William De Lancey by an unknown artist. (Private Collection)

in going over the rough ground, so that Scott afterwards reported to his wife that 'I saw the field of battle in great stile [*sic*]', mounted on a most docile animal.[179] The tree where Wellington had stationed himself during the battle provided Scott with the most telling evidence of his fearless self-exposure, for it 'is barked in several places by the can[n]on balls levelled at him'.[180] In contrast, Scott represented Napoleon as having been 'well sheltered', first, 'in a high wooden observatory', recently constructed by the King of the Netherlands for a survey of the country, and then in a farm-house on high ground near a ridge, where he had stationed his army. The ridge was called La Belle Alliance, and had already become celebrated by the time that Scott saw it, because near it lay the spot where Wellington and Blücher had met to congratulate each other on their joint success at the victorious conclusion of the battle.[181]

At the beginning of the battle, however, shortly after Napoleon had defeated Blücher at Ligny, and had forced Wellington to retreat on Waterloo from Quatre Bras in order to maintain his vital communication with Blücher, it had seemed as if the victory would go to Napoleon on the score of a much larger number of veteran troops in his army than in that of Wellington. Scott, in fact, heard a stark attestation of this circumstance in an anecdote related to him by General Adam, whose brigade of infantry had formed part of the right wing of Wellington's army, against which Napoleon had ordered the first French attack to be made from La Belle Alliance with a combined force of cavalry, infantry, and artillery.[182] Adam told Scott that, just before the attack, on the morning after the stormy night, he had seen, 'the clouds of cavalry, which had mustered thicker and thicker upon the skirts of the horizon in the line of La Belle Alliance'. As they had begun to move forward, he had looked around him at Wellington's army, stationed on another ridge called Mont St Jean, facing La Belle Alliance. Adam, in Scott's words, 'confessed to me a momentary sinking of the heart when ... he considered how small was the part of our force properly belonging to Britain'. For the British troops had numbered 'not above 35,000', the rest of Wellington's army having been composed—besides the Belgians—of Brunswickers, raw Hanoverian recruits, and other foreigners. A slight incident, however, had reassured Adam. 'An aide-de-camp'—again to quote Scott—'galloped up, and after delivering his instructions, cautioned the battalion of the Guards, along whom he rode, to reserve their fire till the enemy were within a short distance. "Never mind us, sir," answered a veteran guardsman from the ranks, "*we know our duty.*" From that moment my gallant friend said, that he knew the hearts of the men were in the right trim, and that though they might leave their bodies on the spot, they would never forfeit their honour.'[183]

It was estimated that the number of the slain had exceeded 30,000, and that some 12,000 horses had piled up on 'a field scarcely two miles long, and not above half a mile in breadth'.[184] Scott was shown 'a sort of precipitous gravel pit' by Captain Campbell, into which the heavy

British dragoons had forced a great number of Napoleon's cuirassiers, 'who lay there, a living and struggling mass of men and horses, piled together in common destruction'.[185] Mercifully, however, 'these more ghastly tokens of the carnage' had been removed by the time of Scott's visit, 'the bodies both of men and of horses having been either burned or buried'.[186] Instead, the ground was strewn with 'old hats, old shoes, a vast number of letters and memorandum books and other trumpery', which the Flemish peasants had not thought worth recovering after they had plundered the French and British baggage of the dead or retreating soldiers and cavalry. Even the casques or head-pieces of the soldiers, which had littered the battlefield, had disappeared well before Scott's visit, 'for the peasants immediately sold them to be beat [sic] out for old copper, and the purchasers, needlessly afraid of their being reclaimed, destroyed them as fast as possible'.[187]

All the neighbouring houses exhibited to Scott 'a most striking picture of desolation', as they had been broken down by cannon-shot and shells.[188] Drawing on his extraordinary memory for poetic quotations, Scott cited a graphic passage from one of the plays of his friend, Joanna Baillie, to visualise the sensations of 'the inhabitants of these peaceful cottages' as 'the loud battle' had clanged around them, and as their 'warm and cheerful hearths', where their children had played, had become 'the bloody lair of dying men'.[189] At the same time Scott also cited, with a touch of dry humour, another anecdote, that he picked up from his guides, to intimate that the Flemish were not being overscrupulous in the claims on 'British generosity' that they were putting in as compensation for damage to their property. They had got wind of the liberal payments that the Spanish peasants had received for similar damage in the Peninsular War.[190]

Notwithstanding the care that had been taken in burning or burying the dead, the stench in several places of the battlefield, particularly in a small château called Hougoumont, which had been the scene of some of the fiercest fighting, was such as to indicate that the burials 'had been but hastily and imperfectly performed':[191]

> And feel'st thou not the tainted steam,
> That reeks against the sultry beam,
>> From yonder trenchéd mound?
> The pestilential fumes declare
> That Carnage has replenished there
>> Her garner-house profound.[192]

On the other hand, Scott found that parts of the ground were already being ploughed up by the Flemish farmers, so that the prediction in *Paul's Letters to his Kinsfolk*,[193] that 'the corn, which must soon wave there ... will speedily remove from the face of nature the melancholy traces of the strife of man', was to be fulfilled by the time of Southey's and Byron's visits. Accordingly Southey was to record that

> Nature everywhere resumed her course;
> Low pansies to the sun their purple gave,
> And the soft poppy blossom'd on the grave;[194]

while Byron, who was to be genuinely touched at identifying the grave of a gallant relation of his, was to make effective elegiac use of the contrast between reviving nature and the unreturning dead buried under the tall crops of maize and rye:

> There have been tears and breaking hearts for thee,
> And mine were nothing had I such to give:
> But when I stood beneath the fresh green tree,
> Which living waves where thou didst cease to live,
> And saw around me the wide field revive
> With fruits and fertile promise, and the Spring
> Come forth her work of gladness to contrive,
> With all her reckless birds upon the wing,
> I turned from all she brought to those she could not bring.[195]

Scott absorbed the topography of the battlefield so thoroughly, complete with the various positions and manoeuvres of the two armies, that he was afterwards congratulated by Southey for having 'featured it with your characteristic force and animation' in *The Field of Waterloo*.[196] He lingered for two whole hours, according to Major Gordon, in the farm and little wood of the château of Hougoumont, which had been heroically defended by the Scots and Coldstream Guards under the command of one of Wellington's most trusted officers, Colonel James Macdonell, a brother of the chief of the Highland clan of Glengarry.[197] Scott found Hougoumont almost entirely destroyed, only its fruit trees in the wrecked garden giving 'some idea of the Dutch neatness with which it had been kept ere the storm of war approached it'. In fact, its owner, whom Scott afterwards described as 'a quiet-looking gentleman', was being fully compensated by the new government of the Netherlands.[198]

As Hougoumont had already become prominent in the iconography of Waterloo, together with 'Wellington's tree' on Mont St Jean, and the farm-house of La Belle Alliance, Scott found most of the English visitors buying peaches and gathering hazel-nuts and filberds in the garden of Hougoumont 'with the pious purpose of planting, when they returned to England, trees which might remind them and their posterity of this remarkable spot'.[199] Scott himself, who had already begun to develop a passion for planting tress at Abbotsford, was to plant two knolls at a cottage on his estate and call them 'Mount Saint John and Hugomont [*sic*]'.[200]

At the farm-house of La Belle Alliance the enthusiasm of one of the visitors who preceded Scott's party was such that 'he actually purchased the door of the said mansion for two gold Napoleons'.[201] Even 'Wellington's tree' was to be stripped of its bark by visitors after

Scott's departure, so that eventually another visitor, seeing that it was about to be cut down, bought it from the owner of the land, sent it back to England, and commissioned Thomas Chippendale the younger to make three chairs from it, one for presenting to the Prince Regent, the other to the Duke of Wellington, and the third to the Duke of Rutland, of Belvoir Castle, the patron of the poet Crabbe, of whose verse tales Scott was a great admirer.[202]

All the visitors to Waterloo, including Scott and his party, had first heard of Wellington's victory over Napoleon through the 'London Gazette Extraordinary', which had been printed all over Britain, following the receipt of Wellington's celebrated 'Waterloo Despatch' in London from Brussels.[203] The gazette had carried his own account of the battle, in which Hougoumont, as Scott himself afterwards explained in *Paul's Letters to his Kinsfolk*,[204] had been the key to his position, so that, in view of the repeated assaults on it, Wellington had reinforced its garrison under Colonel Macdonell with a detachment of Scots Guards under Colonel Francis Hepburn. But, owing to an official blunder, which had appeared even in Wellington's despatch as published in the gazette, the credit for the important service rendered by Hepburn had been given to Colonel Home, a junior officer.[205] Although the mistake was officially explained, it was never notified publicly, with the result that Scott and all the visitors to Waterloo, many of whom took copies of the gazette with them to the battlefield, were under the impression that the hero of Hougoumont, next to Macdonell, was not Hepburn, but Home. Accordingly, when Scott learned of the blunder from his military friends, who also told him that Hepburn had taken over the command of the orchard at Hougoumont when it was being attacked by the whole French division of Joseph Bonaparte, Napoleon's brother, he made a point of giving as much publicity as possible to Hepburn's gallantry as was in his power through *Paul's Letters to his Kinsfolk*,[206] particularly as he was proud to hold Hepburn's family 'in old and sincere friendship'.

Scott was not aware at this stage that among the visitors who took copies of the 'London Gazette Extraordinary' with them to Waterloo was a young advocate from Edinburgh called James Simpson, who, on walking up to the ridge of La Belle Alliance, not only reread Wellington's account of the battle but also the speech that Scott had lately made in Edinburgh at the launching of 'the Waterloo Subscription'. Moreover, on observing that many names were written on the white-washed walls of the farm-house, Simpson, 'possessed by the spirit of the moment', took the liberty of quoting, 'on the very spot of Napoleon's final defeat and ruin, and on his *first* trial of strength with Wellington', the concluding lines of Scott's *The Vision of Don Roderick*.[207] Scott had predicted in those lines that Wellington, fresh from his victories over Napoleon's marshals in Spain, would defeat Napoleon himself if and when they would encounter each other.

At La Belle Alliance as well as at every hamlet in the vicinity of the battlefield Scott found that the local people had established a market of souvenirs for English tourists.[208] His own purchases included a cross of the Legion of Honour and two large French cuirasses, one of which was for his own collection of weapons and armour at Abbotsford. The other was for his patron, the Duke of Buccleuch, who, as Earl of Dalkeith before he succeeded to the dukedom, had served as a fellow-volunteer in the regiment of Edinburgh Light Dragoons that Scott had been instrumental in raising at the time of Napoleon's threatened invasion of England.[209]

Scott afterwards informed the Duke of Buccleuch from Cambrai on the road to Paris that Major Gordon had promised to get the two cuirasses safely over to England. Scott also sent the duke a shortened version of his account of the battle of Waterloo with particular reference to 'feats of personal strength and valour' in the desperate hand-to-hand fighting between the cuirassiers and the dragoons. He singled out a corporal of the Life Guards named John Shaw, who was well known to many, including the Duke of Buccleuch, as 'a pugilistic champion and equally formidable as a swordsman'.[210] Shaw was supposed to have 'slain or disabled ten Frenchmen with his own hand before he was killed by a musket or pistol shot'. Being a remarkably well-made man, Shaw had served as model to the artist Benjamin Haydon, who, although only casually acquainted with Scott at the time of his visit to Brussels, afterwards became both a friend and warm admirer of him. When, therefore, Haydon offered to supply him with anecdotes of Waterloo, Scott declared himself 'particularly desirous to know Shaw's fate', especially as Scott claimed to be 'in possession of his skull, poor fellow'.[211] There seems to be no evidence, however, that Scott could ever have come into possession of Shaw's skull,[212] although it is conceivable that Scott might have meant that he had a *cast* of Shaw's skull like that which is still preserved in the Household Cavalry Museum at Windsor Castle. Nor is there any evidence to support the statement of Elizabeth Longford in her biography of Wellington,[213] that Scott, 'having once met and admired Shaw in Haydon's studio, had his body brought home to his native Nottinghamshire'.

Scott sent the Duke of Buccleuch the shortened version of his account of the battle of Waterloo shortly after he had himself received at Brussels, on the eve of his departure for Paris, a letter of introduction from the Duchess of Buccleuch to the Duke of Wellington,[214] who was powerfully instrumental in releasing Scott's historical imagination and sensibility on the battlefield. For, after completing his examination of every point of defence and attack, Scott detached himself from his party, and, as he had done at Bergen-op-Zoom, fell into solitary reflections.[215] 'To recollect', he afterwards wrote in *Paul's Letters to his Kinsfolk*,[216] 'that within a short month, the man whose name had been the terror of Europe, stood on the very ground which I now occupied, that right opposite was placed the commander whom the event of the day hailed *Vainqueur de vainqueur de la terre*—that the landscape, now solitary and peaceful around me, presented

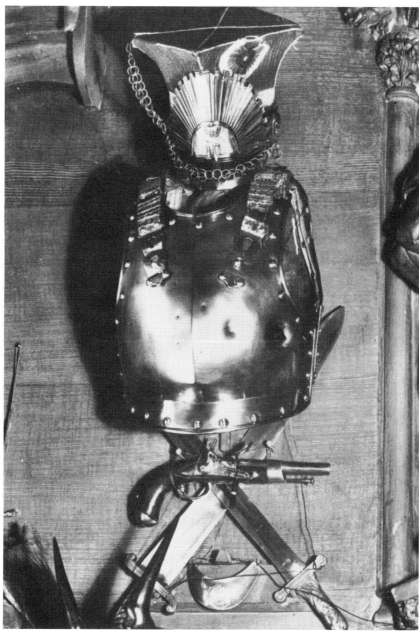

French cuirass worn at the battle of Waterloo and purchased by Scott on his visit to the battlefield; a bullet pierced it on the wearer's left side. The head-dress above it is a Polish chapka, originally belonging to one of the Polish squadron that formed part of Napoleon's bodyguard. (Abbotsford House. By permission of Mrs P Maxwell-Scott)

so lately a scene of such horrid magnificence—... to recollect all this, oppressed me with sensations which I find it impossible to describe.'

Scott's historical imagination and sensibility were often most intense when linked to moral reflection, for, as a product of the Scottish Enlightenment, he aspired to follow the so-called 'philosophical historians' of the eighteenth century by formulating 'a philosophy of history'.[217] In effect, this exercise usually took the form of close, trenchant arguments with deductions illustrated from history.[218] Alternatively, Scott indulged in moral generalisation on historical events or personalities, leading him repeatedly to point the moral of the revolutions of time and fate and the ironies of history. On this theme, the supreme poem, to his mind, was Dr Johnson's *The Vanity of Human Wishes*, which was his favourite piece in all literature.[219] When he himself handled the theme, he charged it, not infrequently, with imagery drawn from what he had called, in a climactic scene in *Guy Mannering*,[220] 'the emphatic language of Scripture'. (The scene was the recognition of Harry Bertram by Dominie Sampson.) Having lived through the whole of the French Revolution and Napoleonic Wars, Scott believed that no other age had witnessed so many vicissitudes as his own. The most explicit expression of this belief was in the moral envoy that he attached to *The Field of Waterloo*:

> Stern tide of Time! through what
> mysterious change
> Of hope and fear have our frail barks
> been driven!
> For ne'er before, vicissitude so
> strange
> Was to one race of Adam's offspring
> given.

The first example of Scott's preoccupation with the ironies of fate sprang from a manuscript collection of French songs that had been picked up from the field of Waterloo, and which was presented to him by Mrs Gordon on his accepting an invitation to dine with Major Gordon and herself after his survey of the battlefield.[221] The collection still bore stains of blood and clay, but as it contained specimens of his valued minstrelsy, he came to account it 'more precious than any of the other remains of Waterloo which had fallen into my possession'.[222] In fact, he afterwards translated the songs and incorporated them into *Paul's Letters to his Kinsfolk*,[223] with the comment that the collection had probably belonged to 'some young and gay French officer, who, little caring about the real merits of the quarrel in which he was engaged, considered the war by which the fate of Europe was to be decided only as a natural and animating exchange for the pleasures of Paris'. Accordingly Scott could not resist contrasting 'the hours of mirth or leisure' intended by the collection with 'the place in which the manuscript was found, trampled down in the blood of the writer, and flung away by the hands of the spoilers who had stripped him on the field of battle'.[224]

Scott incorporated the French songs and the translation immediately after the long narrative of the three battles of Quatre Bras, Ligny, and Waterloo, the last-named of which was intended to be the centre-piece of *Paul's Letters to his Kinsfolk*. It was also intended to appear in print as early as possible, in view of its topicality as well as the certainty of numerous impending similar publications.[225] Scott, moreover, preceded the military narrative with a political and psychological analysis of the reasons why, despite Napoleon's first abdication in 1814, followed by the restoration of the Bourbons on the part of the victorious Allies, he had succeeded in escaping from exile in the island of Elba, and in returning triumphantly to the imperial throne of France,[226] thereby precipitating a renewal of the war in Europe, which had led to a second restoration of Louis XVIII, following the Allies' victory at Waterloo.

It was in his political discussion relating to the two restorations of the Bourbons before and after the battle of Waterloo that Scott drew on the immense knowledge of the period of English history relating to the restoration of the Stuarts that he had acquired from his editorship of the works of Dryden and Swift. He stated, in fact, that 'we almost involuntarily resort [to the Stuart Restoration] as a parallel case'.[227] At the same time he supplemented his observations on the parallels and contrasts that he perceived in the Stuart and Bourbon Restorations by dicta[228] from Edmund Burke's *Reflections on the Revolution in France* (1790) in implied acknowledgement of that political thinker's unrivalled influence on Scott's generation. Burke, moreover, stood out, retrospectively, in Scott's view, as a political visionary, for his predictions about the progress and effects of the French Revolution had been fully vindicated.[229]

All this political and military material in *Paul's Letters to his Kinsfolk* was reworked by Scott after his return to Scotland, and incorporated in revised form, first, in the *Edinburgh Annual Register*,[230] and, several years later, into his longest and most ambitious historical work: *The Life of Napoleon Buonaparte* (1827).[231] Scott's journey to Flanders and Paris, therefore, served two purposes: one, short-term, the other long-term. First, it enabled him to collect material for a travel book displaying his varied political, military, historical, literary, and antiquarian interests. Second, it set him on the track of a major historical biography, which was to draw him back to Paris within eleven years.

CHAPTER II

Carriage Drive to Paris

As far as Scott's stay in Brussels was concerned, there was little temptation for him and his party to rest there after they had seen what there
was to be seen at Waterloo. Therefore, Scott hired a low carriage for his
party for the whole way to Paris, with the intention of changing horses at
the established post-houses, which, unlike their counterparts in England,
were 'entirely in the charge of the government.'[1] Scott also obtained a
letter of introduction to the governor of the frontier town of Mons from
a tourist named Richard Sass, who had recently been appointed landscape
painter to the Prince Regent.[2] Scott afterwards recommended Sass to his
publishers in Edinburgh and London,[3] but without indicating exactly if
Sass's 'proposals' were connected with a project to furnish illustrations
to a publication about the battle of Waterloo and the Allied occupation
of Paris.

Scott had apparently been introduced to Sass at Major and Mrs
Gordon's dinner party,[4] at which Scott had also promised his hostess
to write a stanza in her album (as was common practice) before his
departure from Brussels. Therefore he called again at her house in the
Parc, and was led to Major Gordon's library to avoid interruption, as
many persons had dogged Scott from his hotel, and were parading in
the park to get a peep of him. Inevitably his stanza was on Hougoumont,
whose name in the annals of British history he ventured to predict
would outlast that of Crecy, Agincourt, and Blenheim. His patriotic
sentiment was echoed by the more literary of the English travellers to
Waterloo, including Southey, who shared his sense of history. His stanza
afterwards drew praise from Byron on his own visit to Brussels, when he
too consented to contribute to Mrs Gordon's album.[5]

At Mrs Gordon's dinner party Scott's sympathy had been drawn to her
son, Huntly, who suffered from a severe hearing disability. Moreover,
Huntly's job at the British Commissariat, which he owed to General
Adam, and where he was arranging for the shipment of Scott's two

newly purchased cuirasses to Abbotsford,[6] was only temporary, in view of the move of the British army from Brussels to Paris. Accordingly, before his departure for Paris, Scott urged Huntly not to forget that he had a friend in Scotland if he were to return home and need assistance. In the event, Scott was to become Huntly's benefactor in several ways, including helping him to become a minister of the Church of Scotland, and welcoming him to Abbotsford as if he belonged to his own family circle. Huntly, for his part, was to serve Scott as amanuensis and transcribe several of the manuscripts of the Waverley Novels, running from twenty to thirty volumes. He was also to catalogue Scott's library.[7]

On 11 August 1815 Scott heard that the French garrison of the other frontier town of Valenciennes had surrendered, and that the road to Paris was open and safe. His party, therefore, drove again through the forest of Soignes, and entered French territory from Mons,[8] which was indelibly associated in Scott's mind with the celebrated cannon of large size and great antiquity in the castle of his own native city. The cannon, as Scott was himself to explain in a note to *Rob Roy*,[9] had been manufactured in Mons for the Scottish army on the orders of King James IV in the Middle Ages. It was popularly called 'Mons Meg', and had stood out in antiquarian records familiar to Scott as 'a great favourite with the Scottish common people', who had 'decked her carriage with ribands, and played on pipes before her when she was brought from the Castle to accompany the Scottish army on any distant expedition'.

From Mons Scott's party followed the route of the victorious British, Prussian, and Allied armies, as reinforcements from numerous countries of Europe were rushing on to Paris 'on foot, on horse-back, in waggons, and in every possible mode of conveyance'.[10] English regiments were newly arriving even from America, and several of their officers expressed their regret to Scott's party at having disembarked too late for the battle of Waterloo.[11] At the same time disbanded French garrisons, looking dirty and like banditti, were roaming the countryside.[12] Scott's immediate interest in their appearance and character served as a reminder of the confession he had made, on publishing *Waverley*, to 'an unfortunate propensity', as a creative artist, 'for the dubious characters of borderers, buccaneers, Highland robbers, and all others of a Robin-hood description'.[13] Indeed he had lately added to his list of 'dubious characters' a remarkable set of smugglers and gypsies in *Guy Mannering*. The gypsies included one of his greatest character creations: Meg Merrilies.

Every part of the French countryside traversed by Scott's carriage displayed marks of invasion and plunder. Although it was the harvest season, and a fine crop lay on the ground, he hardly saw any labourers. The few houses by the roadside that had survived the burning and pillage were shut and deserted.[14] 'All was indeed new to me,' Scott afterwards wrote about the ravages and military requisitions,[15] as if to imply that the scenes he had himself visualised in *Waverley*[16] for the advance of the Jacobite army from Scotland into England, followed by its retreat and crushing defeat at Culloden, paled into insignificance compared with the devastation and 'the ocean of humanity in a most glorious storm of confusion' that he saw on the spot in Picardy.[17] The Prussian invaders, in particular, were merciless in revenging the great wrongs that Napoleon's armies had perpetrated in their own homeland,[18] as Scott first hinted in *The Field of Waterloo*:[19]

> What notes of hate and vengeance thrill
> In Prussia's trumpet tone?

and then detailed in *Paul's Letters to his Kinsfolk*.[20] By contrast, the British troops maintained the strictest discipline, in obedience to the orders issued by Wellington and enforced by his officers. But even they had to be maintained at the expense of the country through which they passed, so that the heavy requisitions issued by the commissaries, and enforced by the French authorities themselves, were necessarily distressful.[21]

In consequence the scenes that Scott witnessed called forth not only his sharp powers of observation but pressed strongly on his feelings. They drew out 'deep emotions of compassion',[22] similar to the brilliantly poignant scene in *Waverley*,[23] describing the sacking of Tully-Veolon after the Jacobite defeat at Culloden. At one place, for instance, Scott saw an old Frenchman in full costume sitting on a bench with a snuff-box in hand, with a Dutch or German soldier on one side of him smoking a long pipe, and an English soldier with a glass of brandy and water on the other side. 'The poor Frenchman cast his eyes from time to time on his two extraordinary companions shrugging his shoulders and uttering deep groans.'[24] At another place one of Scott's military friends entered a garden of a pillaged cottage, and, on looking around him, perceived that he was being watched behind the bushes by two or three children. On their running away, he called after them. At the sound of his English accent, their mother, who understood English, felt emboldened to show herself from the neighbouring thicket, and to approach him. She told him that her family were just venturing back from their refuge in the woods, where they had been without shelter and almost without food for two days. On his assuring her that he was in a troop of English soldiers, she readily agreed to remain, 'under the confidence which the national character inspired'; and having accepted what assistance her visitor had to offer her, 'she sent one of the children to pull and present to her guest the only rose which her now ruined garden afforded'.[25]

This incident of 'sentimental delicacy', as Scott called it, was in the tradition of Sterne's *A Sentimental Journey* (1768), or, better still, of Sterne's Scottish counterpart, Henry Mackenzie, *alias* 'the man of feeling', to whom Scott had dedicated *Waverley*. The incident was typical of the anecdotal method of narrative that Scott again adopted in *Paul's Letters to his Kinsfolk* for his journey to Paris. 'It is only', he declared to his readers, 'by selecting such individual instances that I can make you comprehend the state of the country between Mons and Paris.'[26] Several of the instances he selected recurred in the journal of John Scott of Gala[27] with or without the extempore comment made by Scott in such places as roadside inns or market-places, or when changing horses at the post-houses, which Scott's party were relieved to find were unaffected by the general desolation of the country. For the regulations governing the horse-posting were, in general, supported and respected. A proclamation in French, English, and German was stuck up in every post-house, forbidding all officers and soldiers—whether French or Allied—to requisition horses or to interfere in any way with the usual communications of Paris with the provinces. Thus Scott's party experienced no interruption on the road to Paris.[28]

As for his response to the landscape and highways from Brussels to Paris, his extended commentary on these two subjects provided an illuminating revelation of some of his central aesthetic and Tory ideas combined with pointers to his remarkable erudition in French mediaeval and Renaissance history as a reader of Froissart, Comines, and later chroniclers, especially Pierre Brantôme. All of them had already been represented in *Waverley*[29] as favourite authors of its hero. Scott, for his part, had already represented himself as 'deeply bit with the madness of the picturesque',[30] as it related, not to 'historical narrative', but to the age's preoccupation with 'picturesque scenery' in landscape gardening, architecture, and travel. As an ardent reader of the classic *Essay on the Picturesque* (1794) by Uvedale Price as well as of other standard works on the subject,[31] Scott aspired to translate Price's ideas into reality in the Scottish baronial manor that he projected as laird of Abbotsford. It was in this context that he subjected the road and landscape from Mons to Paris to systematic scrutiny, and concluded that 'much of the picturesque delights of travelling are lost in France, owing to the very circumstances which have rendered the roads so excellent'. For 'the long and inflexible line of the French highways offered the least promising' of prospects to the traveller, 'who longs for gradual openings of landscape' afforded by variously modulated and winding roads.[32] The forward and 'rectilinear direction of the road on which he [the traveller] journeys', aroused suspicions in Scott's Tory mind of scant respect for 'ancient property' and 'private rights, for the protection of which government itself is instituted'.[33] Moreover, the flat country of Picardy, for all its rich and sedulously cultivated soil, offered 'no picturesque beauty' with its sluggish rivers, uninteresting banks, and total absence of hedges and hedge-row trees complemented by groups of cattle, sheep, and horses, 'which add so much in reality, as well as in painting and descriptive poetry, to the beauty of a country'. In France, on the contrary, these domestic animals were chiefly fed in large farm-houses, or grazed in distant tracts of open pasture; while the other French practice of cultivating large woods or masses of plantations, 'solely for the axe and never for ornament', could not supply 'the variety of landscape afforded by detached groves' and solitary farm-houses with their 'little dependencies of cottages'.[34] Above all, the fortifications of the towns 'are of the modern kind', like those of Bergen-op-Zoom, 'and consequently more formidable than picturesque'. Not a single specimen of 'those feudal castles which add such a venerable grace to the landscape of England and Scotland' was visible to Scott, 'either ruinous or entire'.[35] He recognised, on the other hand, that all the appealing castles of England and Scotland had originally drawn their inspiration from France, following the Norman Conquest of Britain, precisely like his beloved Gothic cathedrals.

In attributing the absence of feudal castles from the landscape of Picardy to 'the policy of Louis XI', who had allegedly called up the French nobility from their estates to the court, thereby rendering them dependent as far as possible on the crown instead of on their local property and on the loyalty of their peasantry, Scott did much more than throw out a hint of his increasing interest in Louis XI and his period of history, which was to culminate in *Quentin Durward*, with Louis as its principal character. For, in going on to deplore the absence of 'a *noblesse campagnarde*', or of 'a mild and beneficent aristocracy of landholders', who 'found their importance, their power, and their respectability dependent on the attachment of the peasants among whom they lived, and over whom their interest extended',[36] Scott outlined his ideal of a benevolent feudal order of society based upon 'a spirit of harmony between the proprietors of land and the occupiers', who knew and loved each other.[37] In that context the feudal castle constituted for Scott much more than an object of picturesque beauty; it stood as a symbol of a way of life that he was himself to achieve to the full as laird of Abbotsford in virtue of the rapport that he was to establish with his own retainers and cottagers. One of the best spokesmen for this ideal in the Waverley Novels was to be Caleb Balderstone in *The Bride of Lammermoor*:[38] 'these times are not like the gude auld times, when authority had its right, yet ... we of the House of Ravenswood do our endeavour, in keeping up, by all just and lawful exertion of our baronial authority, that due and fitting connexion betwixt superior and vassal, which is in some danger of falling into desuetude'.

Needless to say, the decline, if not the destruction, of the authority and estates of the French country aristocracy, which, following the policy of Henri IV, had been accelerated by the civil wars of religion between the Catholics and Huguenots at the Reformation,[39] had come to a climax in Scott's lifetime, when 'the furious patriots of the [French] Revolution denounced war against castles',[40] and the nobility had fled abroad, many of them to England. Only in one part of France had a really formidable stand been made 'in behalf of the ancient proprietors, constitution, or religion' of the country, namely, in La Vendée, which lay well outside the bounds of Scott's journey. Nevertheless, in the *Life of Buonaparte*,[41] which he was to open with a survey of French society at the time of the Revolution, he was to hold up La Vendée as the classic embodiment of his own ideal of a resident country nobility and gentry who 'united their interest and their fortune with those of the peasants who cultivated their estates'.

Foremost among the French nobility who had fled abroad was the Duke of Bourbon, the descendant of the great Princes of Condé, whose ancestral seat was Chantilly, which was the last notable town on Scott's route to Paris. Its environs seemed to him to have 'more picturesque beauty' than he had so far observed in France.[42] He reached it with his fellow-travellers after surviving a terrifying carriage drive over a road broken up by the cavalry and artillery of the invading armies, but which he described with an extraordinary mixture of high spirits and vivid imagery.[43] The road ran for 10 miles through the celebrated forest of Chantilly, which drew out Scott's interest as an amateur tree planter.[44] It also appears to have reminded him of the striking description of it in the *Autobiography* (1764) of Lord Herbert of Cherbury, who, as ambassador to France, had travelled through the forest when the whole extent of it had served as 'the chase of the princely family of Condé'.[45]

The forest's fame had also been spread in England by the distinguished statesman, the 1st Earl Bathurst, whose enthusiasm for landscape garden-ing had made him plant Oakley Park, his country house at Cirencester in Gloucestershire, in the style of Chantilly.[46] Bathurst's taste, good sense, and patronage of the poets and wits of the age of Queen Anne and George I had drawn a celebrated 'Moral Essay' in verse from Alexander Pope, with which Scott was, of course, perfectly familiar. Moreover, as editor of Swift's works, Scott had handled the correspondence exchanged between Swift and Lord Bathurst,[47] whose descendant, the 3rd Earl Bathurst, was Minister for War in the ruling Tory cabinet of Lord Liverpool at the time of Scott's journey to Paris, so that it was to him that Wellington had addressed the 'Waterloo Despatch' from Brussels.[48]

On the way to Chantilly Scott's party passed through several towns which had only lately been stormed by British and Prussian troops, assisted by supporters of the newly restored King of France. Scott, in fact, described France as 'neither at peace nor war' in the letter that he sent to the Duke of Buccleuch from Cambrai, near which his party changed horses at a solitary post-house.[49] Many of the Prussian troops were young militia men, in whom Scott took a particular interest not only as himself an ex-volunteer but because he had come to know that the *landwehr*—as the Prussian militia was called[50]—was the special creation of Blücher's late chief of staff, General Scharnhorst. He had built it up into a powerful national force in Prussia's War of Liberation of 1813 against French occupation. Scott was to praise Scharnhorst in the *Life of Buonaparte*[51] as 'one of the best staff officers in Europe'.

Scharnhorst's successor in the same post under Blücher was the tal-ented, even if somewhat arrogant, General Augustus Gneisenau, who, as Scott explained in *Paul's Letters to his Kinsfolk,*[52] had organised the pursuit of the French army by moonlight after the battle of Waterloo. Blücher called Gneisenau 'the brains' of the Prussian army, to which Scott was himself to attest several years later in a letter to his elder son Walter. For, on obtaining a recommendation to Gneisenau for Walter, when the latter was to visit Berlin as an army captain, Scott was to describe Gneisenau as the man who 'formed the plan of all the veteran's campaigns'.[53]

Gneisenau had passed through Cambrai on the march to Paris the month before Scott's party entered it and found it partially damaged by the shelling.[54] Scott himself had long known of Cambrai from Froissart's *Chronicles* for the siege that Edward III of England had laid to it in his war with Philip VI of France. It was best known, however, to English travellers as the former see of Archbishop Fénelon, whose *Les Aventures de Télémaque* (1699) was then a standard text-book for students of French in Britain. Accordingly Scott's party went to see the church containing Fénelon's tomb, but found that the congregation were just beginning to sing *Te Deum* for the restoration of the King, and were told that they could not have admittance.[55] Instead, they toured the extensive ramparts, particularly the points that had recently been scaled by English troops, who were sharing the garrison duties with the Belgians. Scott's description of the assault on Cambrai and other frontier towns pointed to his talent for describing sieges, which he was shortly to demonstrate in more detail and more dramatically in *Old Mortality* with the siege of Tillietudlem, followed by that of Torquilstone in *Ivanhoe* (1819).

The most formidable defences that Scott's party saw were those of Péronne on the river Somme, which had earned it the epithet of *Péronne la Pucelle*, 'the Virgin Fortress, because it had never been taken'.[56] The Duke of Wellington, however, as Scott was to explain in a note to *Quentin Durward*,[57] had destroyed Péronne's proud reputation, for he had taken it on the march to Paris. Scott was already familiar with Péronne's earlier history from the *Mémoires* of Philippe de Comines, who had witnessed there the celebrated encounter between Louis XI and his great rival, Charles, the Duke of Burgundy. Accordingly Scott was not only to make that encounter the most sustained dramatic highlight of the plot of *Quentin Durward*[58] but he was to introduce Comines into the narrative precisely at Péronne.[59] He was also to invoke Fénelon in defence of his own characterisation of King Louis XI in *Quentin Durward*.[60]

Scott was gratified to find that, as at Cambrai, the feeling of the people at Péronne 'was decidedly in favour of the legitimate monarch'.[61] Their appearance contrasted with the dejected looks of the inhabitants of Valenciennes, which was threatened with bombardment by its Prussian besiegers after a long blockade. For its French governor, having sued for an armistice, was still refusing to admit the Allied troops into the town,[62] the name of which had long been familiar to Scott as the birthplace of Froissart, when Valenciennes had formed part of a Flemish countship in the Middle Ages. On being admitted into the town as non-combatants, Scott's party found it to be 'dark, ill-built, and dirty', and still in possession of a hostile soldiery, so that they felt it unsafe to walk about the streets after they had been forbidden to go upon the extensive ramparts.[63] They simply contented themselves with breakfasting at an inn, where they gathered from the landlady that Valenciennes had served as a centre for English prisoners of war in the early years of the French Revolution when an Anglo-Austrian army had first besieged and captured it,[64] but had afterwards been forced to evacuate it as part of a general withdrawal from Flanders.

Whereas the tricolour still flew over the ramparts and batteries of Valenciennes, Scott observed the white flag of the Bourbons waving from every house at Chantilly, whose inhabitants had lately refitted in haste a small château for the reception of the restored Duke of Bourbon,[65] who was a cousin of Louis XVIII. The duke's old, magnificent palace, which 'might well have accommodated the proudest monarch in the world', had been 'destroyed by the revolutionary mob of Paris' shortly after the storming of the Bastille.[66] The palace itself had been built by a descendant of 'the Great Condé', as Louis II, Prince of Bourbon, was commonly called in recognition of his military genius. Accordingly, when Scott and his party arrived at Chantilly, they found that only 'the superb stables' of the palace of Chantilly had escaped the fury of the mob. But these stables, 'which pride, rather than an attention to utility, had constructed for the stud of the Prince of Condé', were on such a scale and so magnificently ornamented as to impress Scott's mind with an idea of 'the power and consequence of the prince by whom it [the palace] was planned and executed'. At the same time he found the town of Chantilly crowded with riotous Prussian soldiers who were wrecking the superb stables 'as if in studied insult'.[67] At seeing this barbarity, Scott fell into another of his favourite reflections on the revolutions of time and fate, and the irony of history. But this time he perceived a *double* irony. For he first wondered what the mortification of the princely builder of the palace would have been if he had witnessed, as Scott did, the spacious range of the stables and all its ornaments broken down and defaced, 'while its high and echoing vault rung to the shouts, screams, and gambols of a hundred or two of the dirtiest hussars and lancers that ever came off a march'. Then it occurred to Scott that, whatever the feelings of the Bourbon builder of the stables might have been to witness such pollution, 'they would have been inferior to those with which his ancestor, the Great Condé', who had inflicted such resounding defeats on invading German armies, 'would have heard that the Sarmatian partizans who occupied Chantilly formed part of an invading army, which had marched almost without opposition from the frontiers to the capital, and now held in their disposal the fate of the House of Bourbon and the Kingdom of France'.[68]

Scott's train of reflections formed part of an agreeable evening that he spent with his party wandering in the park and the remains of the palace, accompanied by an old domestic of the Condé family, who acted as their guide, and gave full vent to his indignation at 'the domineering insolence of "these northern [Prussian] barbares"'. He showed them the site of a magnificent theatre formerly communicating with the palace, where the plays of Molière and Racine had been performed. For the Great Condé had gathered round him a brilliant circle of men of genius in his hours of

Louis II, Prince of Bourbon, 'the Great Condé', by Teniers the Younger. (Condé Museum, Chantilly)

leisure and retirement. The site, like other wasted and desolate patches of ground, was intersected by the canals which had been constructed for the palace's ornament and defence, supplemented by a broad, artificial lake.[69] The canals had drawn praise in the celebrated *Travels in France* (1792) by Arthur Young,[70] who was among the last contemporary English travellers to see Chantilly in its glory on the eve of the palace's destruction.

Scott's guide also pointed out to them a house which had been built for the late and much-lamented Duc d'Enghien,[71] who was the young, handsome, and gallant heir to the title of Prince of Condé. His seizure, on Napoleon's orders, from his private house in a neutral, foreign country, and his transfer to the castle of Vincennes near Paris, where he was summarily tried by court martial at dead of night, and condemned to death by firing squad, had outraged public opinion in Britain and throughout Europe. Although Scott had already expressed his feelings on the murder of the Duc d'Enghien in a letter to Southey before his departure for Brussels,[72] he was to make them even more explicit in public and at much greater length in forceful narrative in the *Life of Buonaparte*,[73] complete with the setting of 'the ancient Gothic castle' of Vincennes and the burial of the Duc d'Enghien 'by torchlight' in its ditch. For Scott had long been aware, from his knowledge of the history of Louis XI, who had turned Vincennes into a state prison, that the castle, particularly its keep or dungeon, where the Duc d'Enghien had been held before his burial 'by torchlight', was the French counterpart of the Tower of London in respect of antiquity and history. Scott, in fact, was to couple the two fortresses in *Paul's Letters to his Kinsfolk*[74] shortly after his arrival in Paris from Chantilly on hearing that the commandant of Vincennes was behaving even more defiantly than his colleague at Valenciennes. Although the commandant had hoisted the white flag, he 'will neither receive a Royalist nor an Allied soldier within the castle', even though it was 'of no more strength than the White Tower of London, or any other Gothic keep'.

As for the castle of Vincennes itself, it was so inextricably associated in Scott's memory and imagination with the execution of the Duc d'Enghien, particularly with his burial in the ditch 'by torchlight', that that image had at once surfaced from Scott's subconscious the year before his journey to France, when he had first heard, with shock and dismay, of Napoleon's escape from Elba and of his rapid and triumphant march on Paris. 'This cursed news turns the very cream upon my stomach;' Scott had exclaimed, 'I trust they will put down this Apollyon [Napoleon] and make short work with him. The castle of Vincennes and a burial by torchlight would be my doom for him.'[75]

CHAPTER III

First Fortnight in Paris

Scott's belief that no other age had witnessed so many, so rapid, and such profound political and military vicissitudes as his own received full confirmation shortly after his travelling party entered Paris in warm weather and lodged at the Hôtel de Bourbon in the splendid quarter adjoining the royal palace (the Tuileries). For the quarter, which no other capital could rival for its boulevards and for 'so many and such magnificent public edifices within the same space of ground', was redolent of the history of the Bourbon kings, the French Revolution, and, above all, of Napoleon, whose monuments, designed to commemorate his 'mighty actions', rose on every side as 'most resistless evidence that the hand which placed them there had once at its arbitrary disposal the fortunes of the civilized world'.[1] Accordingly Scott felt 'an awful solemnity in the reflection' that 'the possessor of this mighty power is now the inhabitant of a distant and sequestered islet, with hardly so much freedom as entitles him to claim from his warders an hour of solitude, even in the most solitary spot in the civilized world'.[2]

This reflection tempered 'the natural feelings of elation' that Scott, 'as a Briton', had felt at seeing British troops in the Allied army of occupation of Paris. Most of them were encamped near his hotel in the splendid Rue de Champs Élysées, 'which was planted and laid out in regular walks like those of Hyde Park', and where the Duke of Wellington's headquarters was also situated. Scott first sighted it when the duke happened to be receiving visits from the Emperors of Austria and Russia and the King of Prussia, whose armies, together with those of Britain, had turned Paris into 'one great garrison of foreign troops'.[3] Thus Scott, on walking back to his hotel at night in full enjoyment of 'the pure and delicious summer air', found himself 'challenged by a dozen centinels in half the languages of Europe'. In contrast, all the French people of fashion had left the city, and few of any rank were to be seen in the public walks or places of entertainment. Their spirits seemed to Scott quite broken and

43

Napoleon Bonaparte by Robert Lefèvre. (Wellington Museum, Apsley House. By permission of Victoria and Albert Museum, London)

humiliated.[4] The glimmer of English camp fires and the music of Scottish airs prompted his historical sense to recall that 'an English drum has not been heard in the capital of France since 1436, when the troops of Henry VI were expelled from Paris'. It had seemed unbelievable to him and to so many of his generation that they would ever live to see what had come to pass, considering that France had for so long 'predominated as arbitress of the continent', and that there had been 'periods when Britain seemed to continue the conflict only in honourable despair':[5] hence the significance of the moral lesson of 'constancy in the good cause' with which Scott rounded off the envoy to *The Field of Waterloo* for instant despatch to his publishers in Edinburgh and London. For that poem was written during his three-week stay in Paris[6] in the intervals of intense sight-seeing, theatre-going, and invitations to receptions, balls, and excursions of the highest-ranking English society attached to the army of occupation.[7]

The speed and frequent interruptions marking the composition of *The Field of Waterloo* were openly admitted by Scott in an introductory note printed on the title-page as an 'apology' for its 'imperfections'. Later, in his private correspondence, he pleaded for an indulgent reading of the poem on the ground of 'the difficulty of a theme unmanageable in proportion to its magnificence'.[8] His plea recalled the argument he had initially advanced, several years before, on repeatedly failing to celebrate, in a poem on its own, the death of Nelson at the moment of victory in the battle of Trafalgar. The fate of that hero, Scott had argued, 'is almost too grand in its native simplicity to be heightened by poetical imagery'.[9] In the course of time, however, he had managed to pay due tribute to Nelson in the Introduction to the first canto of *Marmion*.[10]

Scott also explained, in his private correspondence about *The Field of Waterloo*, that, although he had picked up many anecdotes of the battle, it was not his intention to append 'copious notes' to his poem,[11] as he had done for his earlier verse romances, and as he was to do for the Waverley Novels. His patriotic gesture in forgoing the profits of the first edition of *The Field of Waterloo* for the benefit of the dependants of the fallen and disabled in the battle was in line with the action he had taken with the royalties from *The Vision of Don Roderick* for the relief of the dependants of the dead and injured in the Peninsular War. In fact, a reprint of *The Vision of Don Roderick* was going through the press of his publishers jointly with *The Field of Waterloo* in a fresh volume as complementary poems.[12] Together with the Introduction to the first canto of *Marmion* and the stirring war song that Scott had written for the regiment of Edinburgh Light Dragoons, they constituted his principal contribution to the wealth of war poetry as a feature of the narrative and lyric verse of the Romantic Age. Perhaps the finest lyric contributor to it was Scott's friend, Thomas Campbell, whom Scott himself had quoted in Flanders, in his remarks on the fortifications of Bergen-op-Zoom.[13]

Scott dedicated *The Field of Waterloo* to the Duchess of Wellington, who was not in Paris with her husband at the time of Scott's visit, but in England with their children. Scott had been presented to her the previous spring in London, and his impression of her was that she had 'simple and unaffected manners'.[14] She had told him that 'she was impressed with a presentiment almost to superstition, that whenever her husband met Bonaparte, he would destroy him at ONE blow', which was a variant of the prediction that Scott himself had made in the concluding lines of *The Vision of Don Roderick*. Accordingly, when Scott, on returning to Edinburgh from London shortly after his meeting with the Duchess of Wellington, had first heard the news of Wellington's defeat of Napoleon at Waterloo in one of the streets of his native city amid unforgettable public rejoicing and bell-ringing, he had related the duchess's presentiment as prophetic to the first friend that he had come across.[15]

As for his party's sight-seeing of Paris, the first public building to claim their attention for artistic inspection was the Louvre, because they heard on arrival that the Allied Powers were insisting with the new government of Louis XVIII on the return of hundreds of masterpieces by Europe's greatest artists, which had been plundered on Napoleon's orders from the galleries of Italy, Spain, Holland, Belgium Austria, and Germany.[16] 'The day of reckoning is at length arrived,' Scott, therefore, wrote in *Paul's Letters to his Kinsfolk*,[17] after he had hastened to the Louvre, just *before* the return had started, in order to share with thousands of visitors 'the most magnificent *coup d'oeuil* in the world', for 'the gallery is near[ly] a quarter of a mile in length, and was then crowded with paintings, all of the very first order'.[18] By the time Scott's party left Paris, after several visits to the Louvre, 300 of the masterpieces had been packed off. They included the *Venus de Medici*, the *Transfiguration of Christ* by Raphael, Titian's *St Peter Martyr*, and Domenichino's *Communion of St Jerome*.[19] At the same time, outside the Louvre, the celebrated Venetian bronze horses, which Napoleon had put up on a splendid triumphal arch, were to be taken down and returned to Venice the month after Scott's departure. The arch lay in 'the superb square' called Place du Carrousel, where Napoleon had reviewed his army previous to marching out of Paris to meet his fate at Waterloo.[20]

The Louvre itself had originally been a royal palace of 'Le Grand Monarque', Louis XIV, the most flamboyant of the Bourbons, but Napoleon had enlarged it and turned it into a museum, precisely to house 'this surpassingly magnificent display of human genius', as trophies and 'precious spoils of victories gained and abused in every country of Europe'. Accordingly Scott, while conceding to Napoleon 'the highest praise that military achievement alone, abstracted from the cause in which it was accomplished, could be entitled to', denounced him, with particular reference to the Louvre, for having 'proceeded from battle to plunder, less like a soldier than a brigand or common highwayman, whose immediate object is to rifle the passenger whom he has subdued by violence or intimidation'.[21] At the same time Scott represented the

Louvre as perhaps the most striking of the many grand monuments which Napoleon had been bent to complete or perfect on the lines, or following the plans, of his predecessors with a view to 'establishing his own reputation as heir of the monarchy as well as of the revolution'.[22] Thus, in crediting Napoleon with 'great ability and dexterity' in his public works, particularly 'in availing himself of that taste for national display, which is a leading feature of the French character',[23] Scott disagreed completely with Byron's perception of Napoleon's character. For Byron, as he was to allege in *Childe Harold's Pilgrimage*,[24] attributed a 'just habitual scorn' for 'men and their thoughts' to Napoleon, which was a judgement that perhaps applied more to Byron himself than to Napoleon. Scott was, therefore, to take issue with Byron on this subject in his review of *Childe Harold's Pilgrimage* for the *Quarterly Review*,[25] and to argue that, 'far from being deficient in the necessary branch of the politician's art, which soothes the passions and conciliates the prejudices of those whom they wish to employ as instruments, Buonaparte possessed it in excellent perfection'.

Despite the extreme mortification felt by the Parisians at the removal of the stolen masterpieces from the Louvre, which they had come to associate with 'national glory', Scott regarded their return to their original owners as 'a lesson of retributive justice'.[26] He even questioned the wisdom or magnanimity of the Allied Powers, who, following Napoleon's *first* abdication in 1814, had not stipulated in the Treaty of Paris for the return of the plundered treasures. Neither was he unsparing in criticism of the new government of Louis XVIII over their refusal to co-operate with the Allies in the restitution of the plunder, out of fear of incurring unpopularity, or to ingratiate themselves with 'their new subjects as good Frenchmen'.[27] Consequently Wellington and Blücher had to resort to physical force to ensure the removal of the stolen masterpieces, especially the Venetian bronze horses, the dismantling of which, as Scott himself reported, at first 'excited such a mob that they were forced to turn out the guards'.[28] Scott compared the acquiescence of Louis' government in the plunder they had inherited from their imperial predecessor to that of a notorious character in *Gil Blas* by Le Sage,[29] which had long been one of his favourite books as arguably the most famous picaresque romance in European literature. It abounded in the kind of 'dubious characters of borderers, buccaneers', banditti, smugglers, outlaws, and gypsies, to which Scott had confessed 'an unfortunate propensity', first, as creator of Highland robbers in *Waverley*, and, more recently, of smugglers and gypsies headed by Meg Merrilies in *Guy Mannering*.

It was significant, therefore, that on his several visits to the Louvre with his fellow-travellers, the picture that he was reported to have looked at most often was the celebrated *Witch of Endor* by Salvator Rosa.[30] For the Witch of Endor was a quasi-supernatural woman with 'a familiar spirit', and was gifted with prophecy, exactly like Meg Merrilies, and like Scott's other notable future creation: Old Alice Grey in *The Bride of Lammermoor.* On the other hand, the Witch of Endor had also been traditionally equated, in a pejorative context, with a common sorceress, which explains why Scott was to represent the accusers of Rebecca, the Jewish heroine, in *Ivanhoe*[31] as calling her 'a second Witch of Endor' for having allegedly cast a spell upon the Christian knight, Brian de Bois Guilbert.

As for Salvator Rosa, he was the artist *par excellence* who had fired the imagination of English Romantic poets and of prose writers of 'gothic' romances with groups of banditti and other 'dubious characters' in dark, wild, rocky settings, on which Scott had modelled himself in *Waverley* and *Guy Mannering*, complete with explicit allusions to the Italian master.[32] Salvator Rosa, moreover, had also painted battle scenes, one of which Scott was also reported to have looked at with keen interest.[33] He himself referred to it in *Paul's Letters to his Kinsfolk*,[34] principally for an amusing comment on it that he overheard from two English dragoons, who formed part of the 'moving picture of all the nations of Europe in their military dresses' that the Louvre exhibited 'besides its other striking beauties'. For every soldier in Paris had a free entrée there.[35]

Scott's taste for battle pieces was served less extensively by Salvator Rosa than by the Dutch artist, Philip Wouwerman,[36] many of whose pictures belonged to the stolen paintings from Holland and Belgium that were earmarked for return to the new Kingdom of the Netherlands. They were headed by Rubens's *The Descent from the Cross* and thirteen more by the same artist,[37] many of which, as Scott had already observed at Antwerp, had originally been designed as altar pieces or for specific places in chapels, churches, cathedrals, and private residences. Scott complained, therefore, that they suffered from having been torn from their local associations,[38] as had already been observed by contemporary travellers to Paris,[39] whom Scott also echoed in his condemnation of the 'unawed audacity' with which the French art restorers 'have in several notorious instances undertaken to repair, and even to alter, the master-pieces which conquest and rapine had put within their power'.[40] (Perhaps the two most 'notorious instances' were Raphael's *The Transfiguration of Christ* and Titian's *St Peter Martyr*.)

One of the best-known contemporary travellers who had voiced these and other criticisms was Scott's namesake, John Scott, the London journalist, who had recently published *A Visit to Paris in 1814* (1815). Scott had made a point of reading it on the way to Brussels,[41] and towards the end of *Paul's Letters to his Kinsfolk*[42] he recommended 'the very spirited and acute work of Mr John Scott' to readers who wanted the kind of 'general view of French manners, or habits of society' that was outside the scope of his own travel book. At the same time, however, he hinted at John Scott's 'severe' treatment of 'the French vices and follies' and at his failure to do full justice to 'the gallant, amiable, and lively disposition' by which the French were still widely distinguished from other European nations.

Although John Scott afterwards questioned the accuracy of Scott's use of the word 'amiable' as he had applied it to the French, and although Scott graciously conceded his namesake's objection,[43] there is no doubt that Scott, in *Paul's Letters to his Kinsfolk*, put his finger on the excessive anti-Gallican spirit running through and marring John Scott's book. On that and other accounts it is much less readable, and certainly much less informative, than the journal about Paris by an 'ingenious friend' that Scott also recommended towards the end of *Paul's Letters to his Kinsfolk*.[44] Its author was none other than the young Edinburgh advocate called James Simpson, who had lately inscribed Scott's concluding lines of *The Vision of Don Roderick* on the walls of the farm-house of La Belle Alliance at Waterloo. Simpson was also the friend to whom Scott, on first hearing, in one of Edinburgh's streets, of Wellington's defeat of Napoleon at Waterloo, had related the Duchess of Wellington's 'prophetic' presentiment that, 'whenever her husband met Bonaparte, he would destroy him at ONE blow'. Simpson, who had excellent connections and was well furnished with letters of recommendation, again ran into Scott—this time in Paris, at different places—in the course of their sight-seeing in separate parties as well as at the receptions to visiting English 'fashionables' at the British Embassy and elsewhere. As Scott himself attested, Simpson's 'extreme assiduity in collecting information' about Paris, as he had already done about Flanders and Waterloo, could not 'fail to make his journal interesting'. In fact, his *Paris after Waterloo* (1853), which he published many years after his extremely popular *A Visit to Flanders and the Field of Waterloo* (1815), is invaluable as a record of Paris under Allied occupation as well as for its 'live' references to Scott in a fast-moving narrative against a background of grand buildings, international celebrities, and military pageantry.

Both Simpson and Scott observed that the greatest sufferer in the way of art losses at the hands of Napoleon's armies had been Italy, especially the Vatican, for which reason Pope Pius VII had sent the celebrated sculptor, Antonio Canova, from Rome to supervise the removal of the plundered treasures from the Louvre.[45] These included perhaps the three most renowned pieces of sculpture in all Europe: the *Apollo Belvedere*, *The Flying Gladiator*, and the *Laocoon*, the first-named of which appealed most to Scott for 'the sublime simplicity' of Apollo's attitude and 'the celestial expression of his countenance'.[46] Scott reacted with characteristic good sense to a widely circulated report that the *Apollo Belvedere* might end up in England. However strong its appeal as an 'exquisite specimen of ancient art', Scott sincerely hoped that 'neither by purchase, nor gift, or otherwise, however fairly, will Britain possess herself of that or any other the least part of those spoils, since the French would eagerly grasp at such a pretext for alleging that we sought the gratification of our own selfish ends while we affected to render justice to others'.[47] That allegation, in fact, had been precisely behind the report about the *Apollo Belvedere*, which had been a fabrication deliberately spread to cast odium on the

British authorities, particularly Wellington, for the part they had played in enforcing the restoration of the works of art to the rightful owners.[48]

Scott welcomed Canova's presence in the Louvre as an act of justice, bearing in mind that 'that eminent artist' had 'remonstrated formerly against the transference of the works of art from Italy'.[49] On the other hand, Canova himself had executed works of art for Napoleon, including the colossal statue of the ex-emperor which is now in the Wellington Museum at Apsley House in London. Scott himself was shown a bust by Canova in a private collection representing Napoleon's son,[50] whom he had proclaimed King of Rome, and whom, on his second abdication, after the battle of Waterloo, he had nominated as his successor, but without having secured recognition for him from the Allied victors. For the latter had insisted on the principle of legitimacy, which meant the restoration of the Bourbons in the person of King Louis XVIII under a Constitutional Charter or Bill of Rights.

Scott and his generation esteemed Canova's statues as the touchstone of beauty, so much so that, when Scott was to write *St Ronan's Well* (1824), he was to make one of the characters say of Clara Mowbray, the heroine of that novel: 'I thought she might have rivalled one of Canova's finest statues'.[51] Scott's admiration for Canova, however, did not imply that his own taste for sculpture was other than very limited. In fact, at the Louvre he preferred the picture gallery to the halls of sculpture, even though his party fell in with Sir Thomas Beechey, the distinguished court painter, in their circuit of the halls of sculpture, and he pointed out to them some of the more technical aspects of the statues.[52]

Beechey himself was accompanied by another traveller to Paris, to whom Gala referred as 'Mr Hoppner', but without explaining his exact relationship to the late John Hoppner, the famous portrait painter and author of *Oriental Tales* (1805), of which Scott had been keen on obtaining a copy through John Murray.[53] 'Mr Hoppner' was almost certainly one of the sons of John Hoppner: either Lascelles, the second son, who was himself a minor painter, or, more likely, Richard, the youngest son, who was the newly appointed British Consul at Venice, where he was to become an intimate friend of Byron.[54]

Scott attributed his limited taste for sculpture chiefly to 'there being few good statues to be seen in England and scarcely any in the northern part of the island'.[55] He had not yet seen any of the statues of Francis (later Sir Francis) Chantrey, who was then rising steadily to the top of his profession. Chantrey, in fact, had travelled to Paris only a few weeks before Scott, precisely to see the renowned pieces of sculpture in the Louvre before their dispersion. There he had made the acquaintance of Canova, and a few years afterwards he was to become friendly with Scott, of whom he was to execute a celebrated bust in marble.[56]

As for Scott's taste for painting, it too was, on his own confession, unpretentious. 'With respect to the arts,' he wrote in *Paul's Letters to his Kinsfolk*,[57] 'I pretend to no skill in the province of the amateur,' using 'amateur' in the sense of 'connoisseur' or 'dilettante'. His criterion for appreciating and judging pictures was essentially based on 'sensibility', so that he counted himself among 'those who love the art for the noble and enthusiastic feelings by the excitement of which it is best applauded'.[58] He followed convention in regarding historical painting as the highest branch of art, and in looking upon the Renaissance as the supreme period of art in Europe, especially as it had manifested itself in Italy.[59] As himself a historical novelist, he constantly looked at portraits of the Renaissance for information about 'period costume', which he regularly incorporated into his own descriptions of the dress of his characters, particularly of royalty, military leaders, and courtiers. His own generation's taste for Renaissance art had been moulded by Sir Joshua Reynolds's lectures at the Royal Academy in London, commonly known as *Discourses* (1769–90), which explains the quotations from them in the journals of Scott's fellow-travellers on their visits to the Louvre.[60] Scott, for his part, besides exploiting the Italian Renaissance artists and craftsmen in several ways in his future novels, made clear in the Louvre his preference for 'the dignity and simplicity of feeling' of the Italians, in contrast to the alleged 'flutter and affectation' of the French painters,[61] such as Boucher and Fragonard. Although he excepted Poussin from this censure, he was curiously silent about Claude Lorrain, traditionally the idol of English lovers of 'the picturesque'.

Even Scott's high regard for historical painting did not inhibit him from criticising the 'greatest living artist' of France, Louis David, 'whose figures, though often nobly conceived and disposed, have a hardness of outline resembling statuary'.[62] This judgement was perhaps not uninfluenced by political prejudice, for David, as one of the earliest and most rabid revolutionaries, had given his vote in the National Convention for the execution of King Louis XVI. Moreover, as a member of the notorious Committee of Public Safety, he had instigated or condoned the beheading by the guillotine of thousands of innocent royalists in the Reign of Terror. Consequently he was looked upon by his political opponents inside and outside France, including Scott, as the artist of 'the blood-stained brush'. '"Let us grind enough of the Red"'—to quote Scott's scathing words about him in the *Life of Buonaparte*[63]—'was the professional phrase of which he made use, when sitting down to the bloody work of the day.' Having been banished to Brussels after the first restoration of Louis XVIII, David was still in exile at the time of Scott's visit. There seems to have been no truth, therefore, in the story related by Lockhart,[64] and repeated by one or two of Scott's editors and biographers,[65] that Scott was presented at a dinner by a French host to an ugly-looking stranger, whom he afterwards found with disgust to be the regicide David.

Scott's host was a distinguished traveller and classical archaeologist, Jean-Baptist Le Chevalier, who proved an invaluable cicerone. He took Scott's party on tours of Paris and obtained access for them to the private collection that included Canova's statue of Napoleon's son, the King of Rome. The collection was celebrated for its Egyptian antiquities as well as for its paintings, coins, and medals. It was owned by the great *savant*, Baron Dominique Denon,[66] who had accompanied Napoleon on his expedition to Egypt. Denon's book on the expedition afterwards served Scott as one of his sources for the *Life of Buonaparte*,[67] in which he was to pay a handsome tribute to Denon's pioneering work in Egyptology. For that and other services to scholarship Denon was one of the most distinguished members of the Royal Academy (formerly the *Institut National*), which was the French equivalent of the Royal Society of England. Le Chevalier obtained admission to one of its meetings for Scott's party, at which several leading scientists were present.[68]

Le Chevalier also recommended Scott to the royal bookseller, from whom he purchased 'a noble folio collection of French historians' by the Benedictine monks of Paris.[69] There was then no parallel to it in English historiography, as Scott himself was to observe in the introductory epistle to *The Monastery* (1820), in which he was to praise the scholarship represented by the collection.[70] His praise complemented the observation he had already made in *Waverley*,[71] that the French had produced 'an almost exhaustless collection of memoirs', which in his time were primary documents in historiography, exactly like the chronicles of Comines, Brantôme, and other historians that Scott already possessed in his library. Thus Le Chevalier contributed indirectly to the great library of thousands of volumes that Scott was gradually to build up at Abbotsford after his return to Scotland, and in which French books, predominantly historical, were to be very numerous. Moreover, these later acquisitions of his included French historians who still practised his favourite method of 'producing an effect by dialogue', as he was to call it in the *Life of Buonaparte*.[72] His earlier phrase for it was 'colloquial history', which he had first used in a review article in praise of Froissart's *Chronicles*.[73]

Scott was principally indebted to Le Chevalier's good offices for the impression that he took away with him, that 'of all the capitals in the world, Paris must afford the most delightful residence to a mere literary lounger'. He attributed much of this advantage to 'the liberality of the French nation, in affording every possible means to the public of enjoying the collections of curiosity, or of scientific objects, made for their behalf'.[74] These national collections, 'accessible in the easiest manner', could not be matched by London, where the National Gallery had not yet been founded, and where 'the various departments of St Paul's [Cathedral] and Westminster Abbey', which had monuments and treasures of public interest, 'are secured by a dozen of petty turnpikes and tax-gatherers'.[75] Nor could any other city rival the grand botanical garden, zoo, and museum of natural history, to which Scott and his party were taken by Le Chevalier, who showed them specimens of the great work that had lately been done by the celebrated naturalist, Georges Cuvier,[76] the forerunner of Charles Darwin. Even when they visited on their own the magnificent Royal Library, where Scott expressed a wish to see the more valuable manuscripts, everything most worth noticing was immediately shown them with civility. Accordingly, Scott, for all his repeated criticisms of French national vanity, had the good sense to admit that 'if there be in this open display of the treasures, which they [the French] possess, some traces of national pride, it is in this case an honest and fair pride, and those who derive so much benefit from its effects ought to be the last to question its motive'.[77]

Scott found Le Chevalier equally useful as a source of political and historical information for *Paul's Letters to his Kinsfolk*, particularly about the origin of the French Revolution, the state of Paris under siege from the Allied armies, and about the contending political parties in the French National Assembly at the time of Scott's visit. For Le Chevalier, who was an old bachelor, 'a decided royalist', and an enthusiastic anglophile,[78] had lived, like Scott, through the whole of the French Revolution and the Napoleonic Wars, apparently in Paris most of the time, although he had paid a long visit to Edinburgh as travelling tutor before the outbreak of war between Britain and France.[79] It was precisely to this visit to Edinburgh that was largely attributable Le Chevalier's special cordiality and hospitality to travellers from that city, including James Simpson, who left the fullest and warmest record of him in his Paris journal.[80] For Le Chevalier had been 'devoured by kindness' from several of its leading academics, when both Scott and Simpson had been students there. Both of them, in fact, had attended the classes of Le Chevalier's two closest friends, namely, the famous Professor of Philosophy, Dugald Stewart, and the Professor of Greek, Andrew Dalzell,[81] who had translated into English an important paper that Le Chevalier had read to the Royal Society of Edinburgh on the topical subject of the Plain of Troy, with special reference to Homer. Thanks to Dalzell's translation, which had appeared in the widely read *Transactions of the Royal Society of Edinburgh*, Le Chevalier's work had become better known among classical scholars on the continent.[82]

Le Chevalier took Scott to the Place de la Bastille, and showed him the very spot on which he had stood when it had been attacked on 14 July 1789—the historic day of the commencement of the French Revolution. Le Chevalier's observations—from a royalist point of view—on the alleged unfortunate errors on the part of the Governor of the Bastille and of his superiors at the court of Louis XVI were carefully heeded both by Scott and his fellow-traveller, John Scott of Gala, for the latter recorded them in his journal,[83] while Scott reproduced them many years later in his own account of the fall of the Bastille in the *Life of Buonaparte*[84]—without, however, mentioning Le Chevalier by name. Scott merely referred to him as 'a spectator who could be trusted'. He then went on to explain how, in the aftermath of the fall of the Bastille, when 'the popular [republican] fury' had set about destroying 'all the remembrances of royalty', and had sacked and pillaged churches all over the country, including the tombs of 'princes, legislators, and heroes', an 'ingenious collector' called Monsieur

Le Noir had saved from ruin a very large number of objects invaluable for history and art.[85] Having selected them and transported to Paris, Le Noir had set them up in the church, convent, and gardens of the Augustinians in chronological order, spanning the various periods of French history, literature, and philosophy. (For the *Monuments Français*, as the museum was called, contained even 'the tombs of Abelard and Heloise, with those of Des Cartes [*sic*], Moliere [*sic*], La Fontaine, Boileau, and others dear to French literature'.[86])

Foremost among the sepulchral monuments seen by Scott in the museum were those that Le Noir had rescued from the Abbey of St Denis, a suburb of Paris, through which Scott's party had passed on the way from Brussels. St Denis had from time immemorial been the burial place of the French royal family.[87] Le Noir himself was in Paris at the time of Scott's visit, and had lately been introduced to Lady Frances Shelley, who was newly arrived from England with Sir John Shelley, and was staying in Scott's hotel at Rue de la Paix, formerly Rue de l'Empereur.[88] It is not clear, however, if Scott was introduced to Le Noir by Le Chevalier, and indeed if it was Le Chevalier who took him to Le Noir's museum (which was a kind of unofficial national mausoleum), but he particularly recommended it in *Paul's Letters to his Kinsfolk*[89] to all who shared his antiquarian taste.

It was certainly Le Chevalier who showed Scott and his party the national mausoleum that had been established to honour the heroes and sages of the French Revolution, including Voltaire and Rousseau. It lay in front of the handsome apartments where Le Chevalier lived in the mediaeval district of Paris as librarian of a large school, which had formerly been the famous College of St Geneviève, founded by Henri IV,[90] the first and most popular of the Bourbon kings. Scott called the national mausoleum 'a magnificent new church of Grecian architecture'. For it was—and still is—the celebrated Pantheon, crowned by the loftiest dome in Paris.[91] Its chequered history, and even more, the extraordinary reversals of fortune of several of the regicide chiefs whose remains had been deposited in it, prompted not only Scott's usual reflections on the vicissitudes of time but also some of his most cutting comment in *Paul's Letters to his Kinsfolk*.[92] For, after recalling how the Pantheon had originally been built by Louis XV as a Christian church dedicated to St Geneviève, and how it had been 'polluted by the appellation of the Temple of Reason', when the revolutionaries had abjured religion and had persecuted the clergy, and how, more recently, it had been restored as a Christian church by Bonaparte but without taking away its character as 'a general mausoleum for departed worth', Scott remarked wryly that 'the honours of those who received this distinction were not always permanent'. Accordingly he cited the fate of the first chief to be buried in the Pantheon, who, of course, had been Mirabeau, whose corpse had afterwards been removed to make way for that of the notorious Marat, whose remains, in turn, had soon after been 'dragged from the church, and thrown into the common sewer of the Rue de Montmartre'.

The Pantheon's commanding view of Paris from its high dome was nearly matched by that from an observatory attached to Le Chevalier's apartments in the College of St Geneviève, and to which Scott was led after an examination of the college's magnificent library.[93] His great interest in military topography and sieges was drawn out when Le Chevalier explained to Scott's party that he had witnessed from the observatory the two sieges of Paris before its capitulation to the Allied armies in 1814 and 1815. Besides pointing out the defences of the city to Scott, with particular reference to the celebrated heights of Montmartre, which Scott had first seen on entering the city from that direction on the road from Brussels,[94] Le Chevalier recalled the preparations that had been made to meet the expected Allied attacks. These, in fact, had taken place in 1814, although not in 1815, because Blücher and Wellington had been able to approach and threaten Paris from its vulnerable southern side, as a result of which they had succeeded in forcing its defenders to surrender without bombarding and destroying it.[95] Le Chevalier himself, however, had distinctly seen from the observatory the first entry of the Allied troops in the spring of 1814. Thus he had lived through the same suspense that Scott's party had heard that the citizens of Brussels had experienced before and during the battle of Waterloo.

In Scott's account of the second siege of Paris in *Paul's Letters to his Kinsfolk*,[96] which was somewhat more detailed than the later version in the *Life of Buonaparte*,[97] he provided further evidence of his good sense and moderation as a product of the Scottish Enlightenment. For he took sides against the 'fervid politicians', who, 'in the energy of patriotic hatred', had wished that Paris 'had been burnt to the ground' in revenge for the wars and atrocities associated with the French Revolution and the Napoleonic campaigns throughout Europe.[98] Accordingly Scott conjured up a vivid picture of the horrors that would have befallen Paris if the Prussian and British soldiers had been given free licence to sack the city, and he enhanced the picture's cautionary effect with his usual technique of drawing on 'the emphatic language of Scripture',[99] which he had also employed for his moral reflection on the reversal of fortune that had overtaken Napoleon.[100] Then he attributed the averting of the destruction of Paris, 'when it appeared almost inevitable', to the Duke of Wellington, 'to whose wise and powerful intervention was chiefly owing the timely arrangement of the articles of capitulation, in consequence of which the King of France again obtained possession of his capital, and the allied armies became the peaceful garrison of Paris'.[101] Even after the Allied armies' entry into Paris, Wellington had saved the celebrated bridge of Jena from destruction. For the name of that bridge had stirred resentment in the Prussian army at 'the almost total annihilation' that their kingdom had suffered, following one of Napoleon's greatest victories, so that Blücher had made preparations to blow up the bridge; but Wellington had successfully pleaded with him for a delay, pending the arrival of King Friedrich of Prussia, whom Wellington had afterwards persuaded to repeal Blücher's 'hasty and vindictive order'.[102] Thus, in stressing that these *statesmanlike* acts had 'added to the glories which the Duke of Wellington has acquired in this immortal campaign', Scott implicitly recognised that Wellington had reached a turning-point in his life: his military career was at its zenith, but also at its end, following the pacification of Europe which his and Blücher's victory had achieved. His *political* career, as a European statesman delegated by his country to enforce the decisions of the Congress of Vienna, had begun, and it was to culminate in his becoming Prime Minister of Britain within thirteen years and in Scott's remaining lifetime. As Wellington himself had lately admitted to Lady Shelley, his confidante in Paris, following her arrival at Scott's hotel: 'I hope to God that I have fought my last battle ... I never wish for any more fighting', partly in view of the campaigns he had been conducting for nearly twenty years, first, in India, then in Spain, and lately in Flanders, but, even more, in view of the losses of men, especially of his best friends, that he had suffered at Waterloo. 'I always say,' he had added, 'that, next to a battle lost, the greatest misery is a battle gained. Not only do you lose those dear friends with whom you have been living, but you are forced to leave the wounded behind you.'[103] This remark was almost identical to a passage put in Wellington's mouth by Scott in his own account of the battle of Waterloo in *Paul's Letters to his Kinsfolk*.[104] Scott also echoed Wellington's remark in *The Field of Waterloo*,[105] in the lament rounding off the stanza containing the names of the outstanding heroes who had fallen in the battle.

In his eulogy of Wellington's recent acts of statesmanship Scott was faced with the difficulty of justifying Wellington's approval, seconded by Lord Castlereagh, of King Louis XVIII's retention of the notorious Fouché in the newly formed French ministry.[106] Fouché was Napoleon's former minister of police. While fully acknowledging that 'it is pitiable to think how dependent the legitimate government is on the good faith of such a fellow',[107] and while well aware of 'the attacks upon Fouché in our English newspapers', Scott wrote an apologia in *Paul's Letters to his Kinsfolk*[108] setting out the reasons, based on grounds of internal security and political expediency, for Fouché's *temporary* appointment by the new royal government. For he predicted that, once the royal authority was fully established, Fouché would not keep his place in Louis XVIII's ministry—which was, in fact, what happened a few days after Scott's departure from Paris.

In his apologia, and with a view to showing that 'the conduct of Fouché is by no means singular' in times of 'frequent and hasty changes', such as those of the French Revolution and Napoleonic Wars, Scott again drew on the English Restoration of the Stuarts in 1660 for parallels to the turncoats and time-servers who had marked recent French political history, and of whom Fouché was only one of many—admittedly the most iniquitous.

In that context, Scott took great delight in going through an extremely popular satiric book that he picked up in Paris shortly after its publication. It was called *Dictionnaire des Girouettes*, 'in which we find the names of almost all the men distinguished for talents, or influence, now alive in Paris with a brief account of the changes of their political lives'.[109] Scott might well have been given a copy of the book by Le Chevalier or by one of the officers with whom he made friends after he called on Wellington.

His first meeting with Wellington took place shortly after Scott had renewed his acquaintance with one of Wellington's early and intimate friends, Sir John Malcolm, the distinguished Scottish general, Indian administrator, and former envoy to Persia. His brother, Admiral Sir Pulteney Malcolm, was staying in Scott's hotel.[110] Scott had originally described Sir John—on meeting him in Scotland three years before their reunion in Paris—as 'a really fine fellow', principally in recognition of Malcolm's extraordinary oriental knowledge, which had culminated in the publication of the classic *History of Persia* (1815) the month before he again met Scott in Paris. Scott, moreover, had taken an immediate liking to Malcolm's 'frankness and sound ideas of morality and policy',[111] which partly meant that he shared Scott's Tory politics, so much so that in his review of canto three of *Childe Harold's Pilgrimage* for the *Quarterly Review* Scott was to avail himself of some 'admirable letters' of Malcolm and another like-minded author to round off his reflections on Waterloo.[112] He was also to refer to the *Dictionnaire des Girouettes* in his observations on the alleged inconsistencies in Byron's politics.[113]

As for Malcolm's naval brother, Sir Pulteney, he had lately been in command of a squadron off the North Sea in co-operation with Wellington's army in Flanders during the so-called 'hundred days', which covered the period of time from Napoleon's escape from Elba to his defeat at Waterloo. Sir Pulteney was still attached to Wellington's headquarters, so that Scott was to say that 'I saw him often in Paris'.[114] He was as old and intimate a friend of Wellington's as his brother John, for he had taken Wellington to India in his ship as a lieutenant-colonel at the start of his military career. Shortly after Scott's departure from Paris, Sir Pulteney was posted to St Helena in command of another squadron specially appointed to blockade that island and prevent another escape by Napoleon. In that capacity, in fact, Sir Pulteney was afterwards to supply Scott with valuable information for the last volume of the *Life of Buonaparte*,[115] which covered the ex-emperor's exile and death at St Helena.

Scott was already in Sir John Malcolm's debt as one of the earliest contributors to the 'cabinets of curiosities' that complemented his collection of weapons and armour for his projected Scottish baronial manor at Abbotsford in the antiquarian tradition of Monsieur Le Noir and Baron Denon. Scott's curiosities included the manuscript collection of French songs picked up from the field of Waterloo and presented to him by Mrs Pryse Lockhart Gordon at Brussels; while the centre-piece of his collection

Major-General Sir John Malcolm by Sir George Hayter, engraved by J C Armytage

of weapons and armour was a superb jewelled sword that King Charles I had given to the Marquess of Montrose, his most faithful servant in Scotland and the hero of *A Legend of Montrose*. At the time of Scott's first meeting with Malcolm the tomb of Charles I in St George's chapel at Windsor, where the King's body had been hastily buried after his execution, had been opened and his body identified. Scott had acquired 'a lock of the hair cut from the head of Charles at the late discovery of his lowly grave'.[116] Sir John Malcolm had given Scott some valuable Persian gold coins, which he meant to convert into 'a ring for enchasing King Charles' hair' for one of the 'cabinets of curiosities' at Abbotsford.[117] (It was a fashionable practice then to preserve and display locks of celebrities.)

Abbotsford itself lay only a few miles from Burnfoot in Dumfries, where Malcolm had been born in surroundings of striking natural beauty, which Scott had first celebrated in *The Lay of the Last Minstrel* and, more recently, in *Guy Mannering*. In fact, the strongest personal bond between him and Malcolm was that they were fellow-borderers.[118] Malcolm even appears to have hinted to Scott in Paris that he might settle with his family on the Scottish border, following the termination of his service in India. Accordingly Scott afterwards wrote to him of 'a handsome villa' that was on the market at a reasonable price near 'my cottage' at Abbotsford. 'I long for some opportunity,' he added, 'of talking over ... Border anecdotes with you.'[119]

Malcolm's versatile accomplishments included a love of poetry, which he had put to good use in the form of oriental translations for his *History of Persia*. Although Scott had not yet read the *History of Persia*, he had described the translations as 'very splendid' on hearing Malcolm read extracts from them at their first meeting in Scotland.[120] It is likely, therefore, that Scott reciprocated with extracts from, if not with a reading of the whole text of, *The Field of Waterloo*, and that he told Malcolm of the 'large notes' that he was making for *Paul's Letters to his Kinsfolk*, particularly as he had made no secret of those literary projects when he had been in Major Gordon's company at Brussels.[121] Although Malcolm had not himself taken part in the battle of Waterloo, he was in touch with the highest-ranking officers on Wellington's staff, who were newly arrived in Paris from the battlefield. These included the Commandant, Sir Colin Campbell, about whom Malcolm was to write to Scott that, on the appearance of *Paul's Letters to his Kinsfolk*, 'Sir Colin Campbell, who, you know, was well acquainted with the Scene [of Waterloo] told me yesterday that he considered the account of the Battle of Waterloo—as given in the production of *an unknown author*—to be the best and most correct that had been yet published'.[122]

With such an excellent person as Malcolm to present him to Wellington, Scott hardly needed to make use of the letter of introduction from the Duchess of Buccleuch that he had brought with him to Paris from Brussels. He did write, however, to the Duke of Buccleuch before he called on Wellington with Malcolm, partly to send his noble patron an accurate map of the battle of Waterloo to complement the account of the fighting that he had already sent him from Cambrai,[123] and partly to inform him of the latest news of an alleged conspiracy, of which Scott had heard from Le Chevalier and other royalist circles. The alleged plot was connected with the arrest of General Charles de La Bédoyère by the government of Louis XVIII, which had taken place on Scott's arrival at Paris. La Bédoyère had been found guilty of treachery to Louis XVIII by having been the first to desert with his army to Napoleon as soon as the latter had landed in south France on escaping from Elba.[124] Scott's information from Le Chevalier, who apparently was known to the Duke of Buccleuch from his old visit to Edinburgh,[125] was that La Bédoyère had 'made confession of a desperate conspiracy which must have laid this capital in blood and ashes'. It would allegedly have served as a signal for a popular uprising against the Allied sovereigns and their generals, including Wellington and Blücher, 'as well as the Bourbons and their adherents'.

In point of fact, it was the Allied Powers—as Scott learned shortly afterwards on going to Wellington's headquarters—who had insisted with the government of Louis XVIII on the arrest and 'exemplary punishment' of the so-called 'traitors',[126] namely, the ringleaders of the French army, who had gone over to Napoleon, following his escape from Elba. The 'traitors' were excepted from the general amnesty granted by the Allied Powers in the articles of capitulation.[127] Accordingly La Bédoyère was tried and condemned to death, as Scott hastened to inform the Duke of Buccleuch in a postscript to his letter,[128] which he followed up in *Paul's Letters to his Kinsfolk*[129] by casting doubt on the credibility of 'so wild and impracticable' a project against the Allied sovereigns and their generals as that originally put out by Le Chevalier and the royalists. At the same time Scott argued that the royal authority of Louis XVIII could only be established by bringing to justice traitors of 'superior countenance' than La Bédoyère,[130] the most notorious of whom was Field Marshal Ney, who, on Napoleon's re-emergence from Elba, had assured Louis XVIII that he would bring 'the usurper' to Paris in an iron cage, but had paved the way for Napoleon's triumphant entry into the capital by deserting to him with his troops.

Scott and his fellow-travellers observed that 'Ney's letter to the Duke of Otranto in defence of his conduct during the campaign, was in everybody's hands' in the streets and cafés of Paris.[131] This celebrated letter to Fouché,[132] whom Napoleon had created Duke of Otranto, was not in Ney's defence as a turncoat, in which rôle he was certainly cut out for inclusion in the *Dictionnaire des Girouettes*, but in reply to the severe accusations that had been made against his military conduct by the French after their defeat at Waterloo. For Ney had first led the French attack on the British positions in the battle of Quatre Bras, and afterwards had commanded the imperial guards in the battle of Waterloo. Needless to say, therefore, he was prominent in Scott's account of the two battles in *Paul's Letters to his Kinsfolk*,[133] but it was precisely to this letter of Ney's in defence of his own conduct that Scott mainly related his references to Ney, because the latter had rounded on his critics by alleging grave errors of judgement on Napoleon's part, and holding him responsible on that account for the final French rout. Thus Scott drew on Ney's letter to discuss the more controversial aspects of Napoleon's tactics,[134] which, on the whole, he tended to justify despite Ney's strictures. Significantly Scott, who had celebrated loyalty so splendidly in *Waverley* and other works, ended his references to Ney's letter with a censure of 'the tone the mareschal [*sic*] assumes to his fallen master, and the reproaches which he permits himself to cast upon him'.[135] Equally significant of Scott's genius for hitting on the right quotation from Shakespeare was his clinching his censure of Ney with Wolsey's reproach of the Earl of Surrey in *Henry VIII*:

> Within these forty hours Surrey had better
> Have burned his tongue than said so.

As for the trial and condemnation of General de La Bédoyère to death, Scott himself does not appear to have attempted, unlike James Simpson, to attend the trial, but he was present at a distance for La Bédoyère's public execution by firing squad, which was followed, as he predicted in his letter to the Duke of Buccleuch, by that of Ney shortly after Scott's departure from Paris.[136] Before La Bédoyère's execution Scott witnessed a dramatic scene in front of the royal palace, when La Bédoyère's wife threw herself at Louis XVIII's feet to beg mercy for her husband. According to Scott, the King had answered her that 'if the crime had been against himself alone he would have forgiven it but justice and the safety of the Kingdom demanded an example'.[137]

As La Bédoyère was very good-looking, Scott alleged in *Paul's Letters to his Kinsfolk*[138] that 'the handsome sufferer finds the usual degree of favour in the eyes of the fair', so much so that 'one lady talked of his execution as *un horreur*, an atrocity unequalled in the annals of France'. An unnamed royalist, but not Scott himself, asked her: '"Did Bonaparte never order such executions?"—"Who? the Emperor?—never."—"But the Duc D'Enghien, madam?" continued the persevering querist.—"*Ah! parlez moi d'Adam et d'Eve*" was the reply.'[139]

La Bédoyère had compounded his treachery by declaring for Napoleon's son—the King of Rome—following the emperor's second abdication after Waterloo. He had done so in a stormy debate in the National Assembly, the impotence of which—in the face of the victorious Allied advance on Paris—Scott incisively evoked with a celebrated couplet from Swift,[140] who appears to have been eminently congenial to Scott, as they both belonged to the old tradition of combining literature with politics. On the other hand, it was not on Swift's 'simple' prose style and short, even sentences that Scott modelled himself for *Paul's Letters to his Kinsfolk*. He

Brigadier-General Count Charles de La Bédoyerè. From a miniature after Pierre Guérin.
(Private Collection)

favoured the heavier, Latinate, and more modulated form of composition usually associated with Dr Johnson and the eighteenth-century orators.

In consequence of the public agitation arising out of La Bédoyère's arrest and execution, as well as of the rumours of plots against the restored Bourbon government and the Allied emperors and their generals, special precautions were in force when Scott accompanied Sir John Malcolm to Wellington's headquarters in the Champs Élysées.[141] A general order to that effect had gone out from the Prussian military governor of Paris, General Count von Müffling,[142] whom Scott was to cite as 'an eye-witness' in his chapter on the battle of Waterloo in the *Life of Buonaparte*.[143] For Müffling had served on Wellington's staff as liaison officer before and during the battle, about which he afterwards published 'the best account of the campaign',[144] complete with observations on the strengths and weaknesses of the British army as well as with discussions of issues disputed by military historians: hence Scott's other reference to him as 'an unquestionable judge'.[145]

Müffling's orders for special precautions against the rumoured plots at the time of Scott's first call on Wellington were complemented by a doubling of the National Guard for the security of the public places, especially around the Tuileries. Scott was reminded by the National Guard's dress and appearance of the blue regiment of the Edinburgh Volunteer Cavalry,[146] in which he had served as quarter-master during the war with Napoleon. He had brought his own uniform to Paris with him. He observed that the National Guard, which was responsible for the internal order of Paris, together with the fine-looking household troops of Louis XVIII, formed the only French military force to be seen in Paris.[147] The remnants of the old imperial army of Napoleon were being disbanded and reorganised for the King's service beyond the river Loire by one of the great marshals of France whom Scott had particularly wished to meet because of his Scottish descent and Jacobite ancestors. He was Marshal Macdonald, whom Napoleon had made Duke of Taranto. Although Scott would not now have the good fortune to meet him in Paris, he paid a warm tribute to Macdonald's 'military skill and loyalty' in *Paul's Letters to his Kinsfolk*.[148] For, although Macdonald had originally served Napoleon ably and faithfully, he had not followed the example of La Bédoyère, Ney and the other 'traitors' to King Louis XVIII, when Napoleon had returned to France from Elba. On the contrary, Macdonald had remained faithful to the King, to whom he had sworn loyalty after Napoleon's first abdication. Accordingly Scott represented him as 'now one of the most respectable characters whom the French army list presents to us'; and bearing his Scottish readership in mind for *Paul's Letters to his Kinsfolk*, Scott appended a short sketch of Macdonald's Jacobite ancestors, with special reference to the rôle that Macdonald's father had played in the insurrection which Scott had himself related in *Waverley*.

Macdonald, for his part, was in correspondence with his kinsmen in the Isle of Skye, which Scott had visited the year before on his memorable

Field Marshal Alexandre Macdonald, Duke of Taranto. After a portrait by Baron François Gérard. (Private Collection)

voyage by yacht to the northern and western coast of Scotland.[149] It was from these kinsmen of Macdonald's that Scott had brought a letter of introduction with him to Paris for presentation to Macdonald, of which he would not now be making use.[150] Macdonald himself had never set foot in Scotland, and did not speak of word of English,[151] but he had been contemplating a visit to the land of his father for some time, and intended to travel for that purpose on completing the task of reorganising the French army. He had, in fact, already declared, in a letter to Sir John Sinclair, a well-known advocate and baronet, and an acquaintance of Scott's, that he considered it 'an honour' to be 'the countryman of the Scots Highlanders', [who] are known for their fidelity, their courage, and their determined loyalty'. Macdonald, whose letter was afterwards translated into English and published in *The Scotsman*[152] just as Scott was returning home from Paris, felt proud not only 'to have imitated them [the Highlanders] in the career which I have chosen', but 'to bear a name and belong to a family, who, in all times, have been renowned, in common with the other highland clans of Scotland, as the *élite* among the brave of a generous and hospitable nation'.

Macdonald's loyalty to King Louis XVIII had earned him the respect of Wellington,[153] whose headquarters in the Champs Élysées Scott found to be a large, handsome building, with a court or *porte-cochère* intervening between it and the street, which Scott had already observed to be characteristic of the houses of Paris belonging to 'persons of importance'.[154] Although he was certainly partial to the aristocracy, especially the *old* aristocracy of Scotland and England, among whom he already had so many friends, to whom he was now every day adding more in Paris, it was significant of Scott's habit of moving freely and easily among all classes of society that he did not quite approve of this style of building, by which the great of Paris 'thus sequestered their mansions'. While granting that they 'do indeed deprive the shop-keeper or *roturier*, who lives opposite, of the powers of looking upon the windows of his neighbour the duke, count, or marquis', he complained that 'mansions constructed upon this unsocial and aristocratic plan, by which the splendour of the habitations of the noble and wealthy is reserved and veiled as too dazzling and precious to form a part of the public street, cannot contribute to the general beauty of the city in which they are placed'.[155]

Scott's idea of beautiful urban street fronts appears to have approached that represented by the architecture he had seen in Antwerp and Brussels, which was marked by variety and decoration, in contrast to the allegedly 'tame uniformity of modern streets', such as Portland Place in London or George Street in Edinburgh, where Scott had first resided on marrying Charlotte Carpenter.[156] He did not indicate, however, if his objection to *porte-cochères* applied also to them as a style of building for stately homes in the country. That style, in fact, had recently been introduced even in Britain by the distinguished immigrant Italian architect, Joseph Bonomi, for the country seats of the aristocracy and gentry. Indeed Bonomi's most

The Duke of Wellington's Headquarters on the Champs Élysées in Paris. From a water-colour by Jean Pierre Berthault in the possession of the 8th Duke of Wellington. (Stratfield Saye House)

famous work in that style was to be seen precisely in Scott's own country, namely, at Roseneath on the river Clyde, which was one of the seats of the Duke of Argyle, where Scott himself was to set the scene of the latter part of *The Heart of Midlothian*.[157]

Apart from his general objection to *porte-cochères*, Scott had no criticism to make of the building occupied by Wellington, which was beautified by a garden overlooking the encampments in the Champs Élysées.[158] Its name was the Hôtel de la Reynière after a celebrated gourmet who had originally lived in it, and to whom Scott referred as 'some wealthy courtier of Napoleon', who had furnished it 'most elaborately'. Although this description of Monsieur Grimod de la Reynière appears to have been incorrect, Scott was on firmer ground in calling the hotel 'Marshal Junot's palace',[159] for its latest occupant before Wellington had been one of Napoleon's generals. On entering it, Scott first met Wellington's aide-de-camp, Colonel James Hamilton Stanhope, who was the youngest son of the 3rd Earl Stanhope.[160] His half-sister was Lady Hester Stanhope, the oriental traveller, who had been instrumental in giving Scott great pleasure at the time of his rise from obscurity to fame with *The Lay of the Last Minstrel*. For her uncle, William Pitt, the great Prime Minister, had asked her to find out more about the identity and personal circumstances of the author of that poem, the opening of which had particularly impressed him. Accordingly Lady Hester Stanhope had resorted, for the desired information, to a friend of Scott's, who had communicated Pitt's praise to him, with the implied prospect of high ministerial patronage.[161]

On meeting Colonel Stanhope at Wellington's headquarters, Scott appears to have at once established very friendly relations with him, which he followed up after his return to Scotland, for he was to consult Stanhope over the military career of his elder son Walter. Besides, Stanhope was to be Scott's guest at Abbotsford after marrying a Scottish lady of Scott's acquaintance in the person of a daughter of the Earl of Mansfield.[162] 'I lived much with him at Paris,' Scott later wrote about Stanhope, 'and always held him to be one of the most sensible and agreeable men I knew.'[163] As an officer in the Foot Guards, Stanhope had served at Wellington's side in the Peninsular War and in the battle of Waterloo, so that he may well have been Scott's source for further anecdotes of Wellington, one of which Scott incorporated into his letter to the Duke of Buccleuch.[164] Stanhope was also believed to have been the donor to Scott of the pair of ornamented pistols that had been found in Napoleon's carriage after its capture near Waterloo.[165]

Whether it was also Stanhope who repeated to Scott the celebrated remark that Wellington had lately made to Lady Shelley, namely, that 'the finger of God was upon me' in the carnage of Waterloo, is a matter of speculation, but Scott certainly echoed it in a long letter that he wrote to Joanna Baillie shortly before his departure from Paris.[166] In it he also stated to her that 'a friend told me that the scene' at Waterloo the day after the battle had reminded him 'strongly of the field of battle in *Ethwald'*, which was the play of Joanna Baillie's that Scott himself cited, as has already been explained, in his own description of the battle in *Paul's Letters to his Kinsfolk*.[167] The 'friend' might have been Stanhope, who appears to have had several literary and other qualities in common with Scott, on the evidence of Lady Shelley who saw him frequently in Paris. She represented him in her diary[168] as witty, an excellent raconteur, gifted with 'a wonderful memory' for poetry, including *Childe Harold's Pilgrimage* (the published cantos one and two), which he recited on excursions outside Paris in Watteau-like settings. Altogether, therefore, Stanhope might have served as a model for Scott in his confession, at the end of *Paul's Letters to his Kinsfolk*,[169] to 'an inherent partiality' to the military class 'when they add gentle manners and good information to the character of their profession'. The confession itself complemented Scott's remark, in an earlier letter to Southey, that 'my mind has naturally a strong military bent, though my path in life has been so very different'.[170]

As Scott's meeting with Wellington took place at an early hour before a full day of sight-seeing by Scott and John Scott of Gala in Le Chevalier's company,[171] Scott at first only had time to report to his wife that 'the Duke has been distinguishingly civil to me', so much so that he was about to meet Wellington again—this time for dinner—on the night that he wrote his letter to Mrs Scott, which he sent to England under cover of Lord Castlereagh's diplomatic bag. For the Foreign Secretary 'has also been extremely civil to me as well as his lady who gives all sort [*sic*] of invitations general and special',[172] by which Scott meant that, besides an open invitation to the British Embassy, he was being asked to Lady Castlereagh's private tours to historic and literary places outside Paris.[173] She was, therefore, renewing—but on a much more generous scale—the hospitality that she had first extended to him in London, after he had achieved fame with *The Lay of the Last Minstrel* and *Marmion*, and when he had secured an introduction to her on hearing that she owned 'a numerous collection of original letters of Swift written to her ancestress Mrs Howard, the favourite of Queen Caroline'.[174] He had sought to obtain access to these valuable autograph letters of Lady Castlereagh's ancestress for his projected edition of the works of Swift. It was then that, at his first meeting with her at a party, he had described her in a letter to his wife as 'a fat good-humoured, laughter-loving Dame'.[175] As for 'her ancestress Mrs Howard, the favourite of Queen Caroline', she was better known as Lady Suffolk, the mistress of King George II, whom Scott was to recreate in a celebrated scene, complete with Queen Caroline, in *The Heart of Midlothian*.[176]

In his brief letter to his wife about Wellington, Scott confirmed the general impression of him as natural, straightforward, and unpretentious in society, for he assured her that 'he is the most plain and downright person you ever knew'.[177] Wellington's well-known 'detestation of all sort [*sic*] of foppery' had earned him the nickname of 'the beau'; but Scott referred to it, not in his letter to Mrs Scott, but later, in his long letter to Joanna Baillie before his departure from Paris.[178] In it he also referred to Wellington's celebrated 'nonchalance and coolness of manner', to which Scott himself certainly did full justice both in *The Field of Waterloo* and in his account of the battle in *Paul's Letters to his Kinsfolk*. In informing Joanna Baillie, however, that 'all our young men [meaning 'officers'] pique themselves on imitating the Duke of Wellington in nonchalance and coolness of manner', he could not refrain from admitting that by wandering about everywhere 'with their hands in the pockets of their long waistcoats or cantering upon cossack ponies, staring, whistling, and strolling to and fro as if all Paris were theirs', they were incurring the hatred of all the French for 'the hauteur of their manner and pretentions'. Fortunately 'these grounds of dislike against us are drowned in the actual causes of detestation afforded by the powers', notably the destructive habits of the Prussian troops, of which Scott continued to see examples even in Paris.[179] His observations on this subject and on the contrast provided by 'the most orderly and regular manner' of living of the British troops, for which he gave much of the credit to Wellington's 'strong sense and firmness' as a disciplinarian, were fully confirmed by his fellow-travellers in their journals. Wellington and his senior officers had received King Louis XVIII's personal thanks for their troops' 'humanity'.[180]

Scott enlarged on his brief report to his wife about his first meeting with Wellington, and gave an idea of the veneration with which he had approached him, only after he returned home from Paris. For he was then asked by his old school-fellow, James Ballantyne, the printer of the Waverley Novels, what general impression had been left on his mind by Wellington. He answered that, although he could say that he had seen and coversed with all classes of society, from the palace to the cottage, 'he had never felt awed or abashed except in the presence of one man—the Duke of Wellington. He said he beheld in him a great soldier and a great statesman—the greatest of each'. When Ballantyne suggested to Scott that Wellington, on his part, might have seen before him 'a great poet and novelist', Scott smiled, and said, 'What would the Duke of Wellington think of a few *bits of novels*, which perhaps he had never read, and for which the strong probability is that he would not care a six pence if he had?'[181] Scott's comment foreshadowed his unconcealed distaste for the self-importance of fellow-authors as well as implied his long-held belief that courage in active life, including war, was the highest of virtues together with love of truth.[182] As for his self-confessed feelings at his first meeting with Wellington, they seem to have served as model for his later description of the introduction of Roland Graeme to the Regent Moray in *The Abbot* (1820), in which the former 'felt overawed in the presence of the eminent soldier and statesman, the wielder of a nation's power, and the leader of her armies'.[183]

Scott's feeling for Wellington, which was shared by his travelling party and by so many English visitors to Paris after Waterloo, reached a climax

The Duke of Wellington by Sir Thomas Lawrence. (Wellington Museum, Apsley House. By permission of Victoria and Albert Museum, London)

two or three days after his first meeting with the Duke, when he was invited to 'a grand ball' at Wellington's hotel in honour of Blücher (whom he had not yet seen) and of the Prussian, Austrian, and Russian generals, on whom the Prince Regent had conferred the Order of the Bath for their outstanding services leading to peace in Europe. The ball was attended by the Prussian royal family and by practically all the most senior British and Allied heroes of Waterloo, including the Prince of Orange, who was still pale and with an arm in a sling from his recent wound in the battle.[184] Also present were all the Foreign Ministers and leading diplomats of the Great Powers, including Lord Castlereagh, Prince Metternich of Austria, and Wilhelm von Humboldt of Prussia, who had signed the Treaty of Paris or had attended the Congress of Vienna. Their French counterpart, to whom Scott afterwards referred in a letter to his wife, in view of the key rôle he had played at the Congress of Vienna, was Prince Talleyrand. His powdered, beau-like appearance at the ball belied his character of a wily politician.[185]

Scott arrived for the ball in a large party led by Sir John Malcolm and his brother, Sir Pulteney, the admiral. Both of them wore the insignia of the Order of the Bath, which was the oldest order of chivalry in Britain after those of the Garter and the Thistle. Their party was later joined by James Simpson, who shared Scott's pleasure in 'the easy and agreeable company' of the Malcolm brothers.[186] The guests were first received by Wellington's Commandant, Sir Colin Campbell, and other officers, including Colonel Stanhope, through whose kindness John Scott of Gala had received a separate invitation. Among Wellington's more personal guests was Lady Shelley, who apparently had not yet been introduced to Scott. She was accompanied by Sir John Shelley, an old friend of Wellington's. A seasoned society lady, speaking excellent French (like Wellington), she was honoured with much cordial talk by King Friedrich III of Prussia after Wellington had formally received him and his splendid entourage.[187] Lady Shelley adored Wellington,[188] who was 'the observed of all observers'. Dressed in field marshal's uniform, and with his breast covered with orders, he walked in high spirits from room to room, conversing with many in a frank and easy manner.[189]

Both Simpson and Gala (particularly the former) kept a full record of this event, which was the highlight of Scott's visit to Paris in respect of personalities, pageantry, and romance. When prince after prince was announced in the saloon, followed by nobles, statesmen, generals, and marshals, resplendent in uniforms, and wearing stars, crosses, and ribbons, Scott remarked to Simpson that 'the romance of the Round Table is probable in comparison. No romance ever came up to this'. According to Simpson, Scott was 'moved to tears' when Blücher—a venerable-looking, seventy-year-old figure, with fine silver hair, and a beautiful countenance—was announced to the assembled company and, having been met by Wellington half-way down the saloon, shook hands with him as heartily as they had done near the ridge of La Belle Alliance at the victorious conclusion of the battle of Waterloo. 'Look at that!'

Field Marshal Prince Gebhard Von Blücher by George Dawe. (Wellington Museum, Apsley House. By permission of Victoria and Albert Museum, London)

Scott exclaimed to Simpson, 'A few weeks ago these two men delivered Europe.'[190] He summed up the significance of the scene for himself at the end of *Paul's Letters to his Kinsfolk*,[191] in the passage referring to the Hôtel de la Reynière as Wellington's headquarters: 'It is a great thing to remember, that I have seen in that hotel ... the greatest and the bravest whom Europe can send forth from [St] Petersburgh to Cadiz, assembled upon the invitation of the British general, and yielding to him, by general assent, the palm of military pre-eminence.'

Scott deliberately included 'Cadiz' for Spain in this geographical pointer to the range of European heroes that he saw at the hotel, because General Miguel Alava, Wellington's faithful companion through much of the Peninsular War, was also frequently observed beside his chief at the ball.[192] Scott picked up a typical anecdote of a 'feat of personal strength and valour' credited to Alava at Waterloo for insertion in his account of the battle in *Paul's Letters to his Kinsfolk*.[193] Alava himself had written a spirited, eye-witness account of the battle in Spanish immediately after Wellington's victory for publication in the Madrid Gazette, whence it had been distributed throughout Spain as the official version.[194] It complemented Scott's account in drama, heroism, and moving personal touches about Wellington. Although Scott did not mention Alava by name in the stanza in *The Field of Waterloo* describing how Wellington's staff 'fell man by man around him', he was to refer to Alava in later life as 'a man who alone of the Duke of Wellington's suit[e] escaped horse and man from the storm of Waterloo'.[195]

Alava's appeal to Scott's imagination, however, was less powerful than that of the celebrated chief of the Cossacks—the Hettman, as he was called—Count Platoff, whom Scott had declared to be 'a great favourite of mine' ever since Napoleon's campaign of 1812 against Russia.[196] In view of his own love of horses, his wartime service in the Edinburgh Volunteer Cavalry, and his celebration of courage, Scott had been so taken with the conduct of Platoff and his Cossack cavalry during Napoleon's disastrous retreat from Moscow that he recalled it graphically in one of the stanzas that he wrote in Paris in *The Field of Waterloo*.[197] He focused the stanza on the Cossacks' devastating pursuit of Napoleon's army in the crossing of the river Beresina, which he combined with the parallel Prussian onslaught on the rear of Napoleon's routed troops at Waterloo:

> List! frequent to the hurrying rout
> The stern pursuers' vengeful shout
> Tells that upon their broken rear
> Rages the Prussians' bloody spear.
> So fell a shriek was none,
> When Beresina's icy flood
> Redden'd and thaw'd with flame and blood,
> And, pressing on thy desperate way,
> Raised oft and long their wild hurra
> The children of the Don.

This stanza foreshadowed the poetic imagery that Scott was to employ for Platoff and his Cossacks in the long, gripping, prose narrative of Napoleon's Russian campaign in the *Life of Buonaparte*.[198] Moreover, these Cossacks, as Scott explained in *Paul's Letters to his Kinsfolk*,[199] were not the regular, disciplined troops of the Russian guard, but 'the irregular Cossacks and light troops of a similar description', including the Tartar tribes, whom Scott saw encamped outside Paris. They were 'children of the desert, savouring of the earliest state of society', and owning absolute allegiance to their patriarchal chieftain, such as Platoff. Scott looked upon them, therefore, as the counterparts of the Vendeans in France ('children of the soil', as he was to call them in the *Life of Buonaparte*)[200] and of the Highland clans in Scotland, whose manners, loyalties, superstitions, weapons, and language he had attempted to recreate in *Waverley*. He had done so in the knowledge that this 'old culture', savouring of 'the earliest state of society', and exemplifying his long-standing general interest in 'primitive communities', had almost died out, or had given way to a 'new culture' within the lifetime of one or more generations of his ancestors: hence *Waverley*'s sub-title: *'Tis Sixty Years Since*.

It was in this context of the so-called 'clash of cultures', which Scott was to make his theme as a historical novelist,[201] that, shortly before the composition of *Waverley*, his imagination having been fired by the exploits of Platoff and his Cossacks, Scott had requested 'a print or drawing of Platon [*sic*] the celebrated Hettman of those grand fellows the Cossacks' from a senior British officer, whom he had heard to be *en route* for Russia. He had also secured a promise from the same officer to obtain 'a Cossack pike weilded [*sic*] by one of his [Platoff's] warriors' for his own collection of weapons at Abbotsford.[202]

Although Scott does not appear to have been introduced to Platoff at Wellington's ball, he was hoping to have that honour presently through Lord Cathcart, the British ambassador to Russia, with whom Scott had become acquainted in Scotland,[203] and who was assisting Lord Castlereagh and Wellington in the negotiations for the signing of the Second Treaty of Paris. On the other hand, Platoff does not appear to have spoken French, which was Scott's only foreign language in non-British company; and even in that language he just managed to make himself understood and to maintain a little conversation.[204] Platoff was much less well equipped linguistically than the other Russian general, Barclay de Tolly, who was also at the ball,[205] and in whom Scott was certainly interested not only because Barclay de Tolly had first commanded the Russian armies against Napoleon's advance on Moscow but also because he was of German birth and Scottish extraction.[206] The Scottish guests, in fact, at Wellington's ball as well as Scottish travellers elsewhere in Paris looked for, and professed to have identified, the marks of Barclay de Tolly's Scottish origin in his countenance.[207] He provided, therefore, an example of the many Scottish officers in foreign service, in which rôle Scotland had traditionally been surpassed only by Switzerland. Scott had a large store of knowledge of these Scottish mercenaries, many of whom were real 'characters', as he was himself to prove by creating the unforgettable Captain Dugald Dalgetty in *A Legend of Montrose*.[208]

Platoff and Barclay de Tolly's sovereign was the only absentee from Wellington's ball. He had sent an excuse for his absence. Brilliant and handsome, but wayward, the Emperor Alexander I of Russia was reported by Scott to be called 'the imperial dandie [*sic*]' by 'our military jokers'.[209] He was occupying the splendid Élysée Bourbon Palace opposite one end of the Champs Élysées, where, as Scott knew very well, Napoleon had lodged during 'the hundred days'.[210] Scott had first observed it after one of his walks along the Seine, which he had found to have a less majestic appearance than the Thames, 'being diminutive both in depth and breadth, and strait-waistcoated by a range of ungraceful quays'. Moreover, the river militated against Scott's conception of 'the picturesque' as a disciple of Uvedale Price. For it was divided at intervals by small islands, completely occupied by buildings, as a result of which Nature was allegedly 'subjugated and tyrannized over by the despotic authority of human art'. On the other hand, Scott agreed with Gala that the view of the Tuileries and the façade of the Louvre from the Quai de Voltaire was magnificent.[211]

Inevitably Scott found material even at Wellington's ball for an observation on the subject of the vicissitudes of fortune. The material was in the form of a celebrated portrait of Napoleon, to which Scott himself referred in the passage extolling Wellington in *Paul's Letters to his Kinsfolk*.[212] The portrait was by François Gérard, a disciple of David, and the most fashionable artist of the time in high society. Scott had not yet seen the portrait, but had been recommended to do so, possibly by Stanhope or Sir John Malcolm, with whom Scott was seen at one stage by Gala in conversation beside the celebrated naturalist and traveller, Friedrich Humboldt, a brother of the diplomatist.[213] Gala had also heard of the portrait as reputed to be the best likeness of Napoleon. Scott walked up to Gala and asked him to walk with him through the crowded rooms in search of it. 'A singular errand indeed,' Scott said, as he took Gala's arm, and led him through the crowd, 'who could have imagined that we should ever, by any possibility, have been engaged in looking for a picture of Buonaparte in the hotel of one of his marshals, while occupied by the Duke of Wellington?'[214]

When eventually the portrait was found, Gala had apparently got separated from Scott, but his place was taken by Simpson, who was certainly interested in art, on the evidence of the very full notes in his journal about the pictures in the Louvre. The portrait had been left leaning against the wall in one of the rooms. Simpson noticed the King of Prussia and one or two other personages stand for a few seconds before it and make a couple of remarks on the fidelity of the likeness. It struck Simpson, who also fell into a reflection similar to Scott's, that at that moment the original of the portrait had barely arrived at St Helena, 'discrowned and a prisoner, while here was one of his palaces occupied in triumph by his conquerors ... who were employing themselves in criticising his portrait, which was all that remained of him'. Scott, for his part, was still under the emotional influence of the spectacle around him. He observed to Simpson that 'if he should venture, in fiction, to depict such a scene as was here presented to our eyes, with all its circumstances and associations, brilliant, noble, and affecting, he should be charged with unpardonable exaggeration'.[215]

In the meantime the banquet had been announced, and Scott walked back to a small room close to the *grande salle-à-manger*, in response to what he afterwards wrote to his wife was 'a special invitation', thanks to which 'I had the honour of sitting next [to] the Duke' at supper,[216] but without explaining how exactly and from whom this 'special invitation' had originated. For it was precisely when he had been making his way with Gala through the crowded rooms for Gérard's portrait of Napoleon that they had observed Wellington in company with some ladies, standing at a window of a room towards the court of the hotel, listening to a military band. In this room several tables had been laid out for the banquet. One of the ladies had advanced towards Scott, and had invited him to sup at Wellington's table, which was near the window where the band was stationed on a calm, starry night.[217]

The source of this information was Gala, but he did not give the name of the lady who had invited Scott to Wellington's table. Nor since then has any of Scott's biographers, from Lockhart to Professor Edgar Johnson, given the lady's name or related the circumstances of this incident, so that it deserves to be explained in a little detail. As far as Gala was concerned, he simply contented himself with adding that, when Scott returned to partake of the banquet shortly after the anonymous lady had given him the 'special invitation', Gala had 'the satisfaction to see my distinguished friend seated in the place of honour, and evidently affording that pleasure to his illustrious entertainer and his friends, which his conversation never failed to impart, and which, I may add, he was always desirous that it should impart, whatever might be the rank or situation of those with whom he was in company'.[218]

The anonymous lady was either Lady Frances Wedderburn-Webster or Lady Caroline Lamb, both of whom sat at the table with Wellington and Scott, which explains why Gala stated that he had the satisfaction of seeing Scott entertaining Wellington 'and his friends' (not 'a friend') with his talk. Their names were given (printed in innuendo form, as was the convention) by James Simpson, whose own account of the incident more or less starts where Gala left off. For he recorded that, after he had seen Gérard's portrait of Napoleon, and had strayed into the beautiful garden of the Hôtel de la Reynière to counter the excitement generated by the scene indoors, he re-entered the *grande salle-à-manger* expecting 'to see the Duke presiding over monarchs and princes at the banquet'; but, although the room was full, there was no sign of Wellington. In disappointment,

Simpson went to the small adjoining room to take his seat at one of the round tables on which supper was spread. At the next table where he was seated, he noticed 'two very beautiful English women of high fashion', Lady Frances Wedderburn-Webster and Lady Caroline Lamb, keeping a chair vacant between them. In a few minutes Wellington looked into the room, and the ladies called to him that they had kept a place for him. He joined them, passing so close to Simpson that the latter rose to let him pass, for which Wellington thanked him. Simpson could not help observing, when Wellington had taken his seat, that over his head, by mere accident, was a bust of Napoleon, which apparently was quite striking, for Scott too coupled it with Gérard's portrait in *Paul's Letters to his Kinsfolk*[219] as 'most excellent'. What followed afterwards was that, in Simpson's words, 'the *trio* were presently joined by Walter Scott, and the *four* formed a very merry supper party. I could not help hearing their conversation, for it was rather loud, but there were no state secrets in it. Lady C[aroline] L[amb] startled us by an occasional scream. What became of the crowned heads and *their* supper, I never heard or inquired'.[200]

It was significant that even in this 'very merry supper party' Scott, who believed so much in the *oral* transmission of literature, and had reaped such inexhaustible stores of balladry, folklore, and antiquarian traditions by this method for his poetry and novels, attempted to ask Wellington about 'his campaigns and particularly about the Battle of Waterloo' for *Paul's Letters to his Kinsfolk*, as he had already done with his military acquaintances in Brussels. Afterwards he reported to his wife that Wellington 'told me all I could ask him' about these subjects,[221] which could not have been much in the circumstances of the supper party, at which Scott, far from being a listener, appears, on Gala's evidence, to have lost no time in establishing himself as principal contributor to its mirth with his anecdotes, humour, and miscellaneous erudition. It was not at this stage of Scott's acquaintance with Wellington but several years later, by which time a closer personal and political relationship had developed, that Scott was to become directly and more substantially indebted to Wellington as a source of information for one of his publications. For Wellington was to offer to assist him with information for his *Life of Buonaparte*, particularly with a memoir in his own hand about Napoleon's Russian campaign of 1812. Wellington was also to be asked then what he thought of Scott in society; 'I thought him a very agreeable man,' he was to reply, 'full of anecdote.'[222]

As for the two ladies among whom Scott, in his veneration of Wellington, and in pursuit of authentic material for *Paul's Letters to his Kinsfolk*, found himself at the supper party, they were not particularly savoury characters, however aristocratic their credentials. For Lady Caroline Lamb was, of course, as Simpson seemed to notice, the highly excitable and wayward, however clever and pretty, daughter of the Earl of Bessborough. Formerly Lady Caroline Ponsonby, she had married, ten years previously, William Lamb (later Lord Melbourne), the future

Prime Minister; but her patient, long-suffering husband had already attempted to separate from her, as he was eventually to do after several reconciliations. Her brother, Colonel (later Major-General Sir) Frederick Ponsonby, had been very badly wounded in the battle of Waterloo, and had been left for dead on the field, but had miraculously survived, and was recovering in a hospital at Brussels, where Wellington had made a point of visiting him before marching on to Paris.[223] She too had hastened to see him,[224] and at Brussels had fallen in with Lady Frances Wedderburn-Webster and her husband, a captain in a hussar regiment and a future baronet. From Brussels she had travelled to Paris, where she had apparently resumed her friendship with the Websters. Her cousin, Sir William Ponsonby, had died heroically at Waterloo, for which reason he drew a memorable tribute from Scott in *The Field of Waterloo*,[225] followed by a lament at his loss in *Paul's Letters to his Kinsfolk*.[226] At the time of her meeting with Scott and Wellington she was aged thirty. Scott had never met her before, but had certainly heard of her scandalous affair with Byron three years previously, particularly of her extraordinary conduct at a ball in London when Byron, who had originally been enchanted with her, but had come to be repelled by her indiscretions, had passed her with some dry remark, at which she had attempted to stab herself. On hearing of this incident, Scott, brought up as he had been in a strict Presbyterian household, and leading an impeccably virtuous domestic life in Edinburgh and Abbotsford, had written to his informant: 'As for Lady Caroline Lambe [*sic*], I suppose she will prove what Shakespeare calls 'a laced mutton [a loose woman of high society]'.[227]

Shortly after Byron had rejected Lady Caroline Lamb, he had flirted with Lady Frances Wedderburn-Webster, who had passed love notes to him under the nose of her conceited, philandering, and jealous husband. Byron's head had been full of Lady Wedderburn-Webster during the composition of *The Bride of Abydos* (1813) and the well-known lyric, 'When we two parted'.[228] Formerly Lady Frances Annesley, she was a daughter of an Irish peer, the Earl of Mountnorris, who was distantly related to Wellington. Scott had never met her before, although they seemed to have missed each other by a few weeks in Brussels, where she had first met Wellington, and where she was rumoured to have flirted with him once or twice in public before and during the ball of the Duchess of Richmond.[229] It was afterwards alleged of her that she was 'vain to an excess', and that her great ambition was 'to attract people of celebrity'. She was aged only twenty-four (nearly half Scott's and Wellington's age), and when they met at Wellington's ball she was pregnant by her husband, who was about to write to Byron in London to ask if they could name the expected son after him. Byron, in his reply, was to give his assent at once, and at the same time to warn Webster, who had apparently made advances to Lady Caroline Lamb at Brussels, to '*keep clear of her*—I speak from experience—she is a villainous intriguante'.[230]

It is not clear to what extent, if at all, Scott was aware, when he was invited to share Wellington's supper table with Lady Frances Wedderburn-Webster and Lady Caroline Lamb, that Wellington had been observed, ever since his military service in India, to have 'a very susceptible heart', particularly towards married women. Moreover, he made no secret of his relish for the female adulation in Spain, Flanders, and Paris that had followed his victories in the Peninsular War and at Waterloo.[231] Nor is it clear if Scott knew that Wellington and his wife—a plain-looking, homespun woman, formerly Catherine Pakenham, a daughter of an Irish peer, Lord Longford—were an ill-assorted couple, and that he suffered from what he called 'domestic annoyances'.[232] Following the long years of his separation from her on account of his campaigns abroad, he had come to recognise that she was cut out much less for international high society than for a quiet, retired life at home with their children. Wherever he went, he was lionised, whereas, when she appeared with him in Paris as ambassador's lady the year before Scott's meeting with him, she had not been treated at all as a lioness, nor had she quite measured up to that high station. Scott himself, at his one and only meeting with her in London before his trip to Paris, appears to have formed the impression that, devoted as she was to Wellington as a hero, and simple and natural in manners, she was rather lacking in 'liveliness'.[233]

What is certain is that Scott observed Lady Wedderburn-Webster often in Wellington's company after the ball at the Hôtel de la Reynière, and that even James Simpson saw her riding beside him at a review of all the British troops that had joined his army since the battle of Waterloo, and at which the salute was also taken by Emperor Alexander I of Russia. It is true that at another review Wellington asked Lady Shelley, not Lady Wedderburn-Webster, to ride beside him, this time in sight of all the imperial sovereigns of Prussia, Austria, and Russia.[234] (For, as Scott explained in *Paul's Letters to his Kinsfolk*,[235] 'the pomp of war must of course be displayed in its full glories; we have reviews of many thousands every morning from six o'clock until ten or eleven'.) It is also true that Wellington, recognising Lady Shelley's excellent horsemanship, asked her again to ride beside him at other reviews,[236] one or two of which were watched by Scott, who was afterwards to declare her to be 'the boldest horsewoman I ever saw', and to write about her to his elder son (who shared his love of horses) that 'I saw her at Paris ride like a lap-wing in the midst of all the aid[es]-de-camp and suite of the Duke of Wellington'.[237] But Lady Shelley, although an 'enthusiast' for Wellington, was happily married, committed to her family, prudent and disciplined in society; nor was she pregnant like Lady Wedderburn-Webster. The gossips and scandal-mongers, therefore, fixed on the latter to circulate stories in Paris, and spread them to England, about her relationship with Wellington. In consequence, a few months after Scott's return home from Paris, a report, allegedly emanating from 'the first Parisian circles', was published in London in the fashionable *St James's Chronicle*, insinuating 'criminal conversation'—the legal phrase then for adultery—between 'a distinguished commander' and 'the beautiful wife of a military officer of high rank'. More insinuations followed in subsequent issues. Wellington, who usually professed indifference to what was said about himself, was deeply annoyed, and denied that he had ever seen Lady Wedderburn-Webster alone,[238] while Lady Shelley, having seen him with her at a ball, was convinced it was all platonic—at least on his side: 'his manner is the most paternal of any I ever saw'; he was 'simple and kind' to her in public, that was all.[239] The upshot was that the Wedderburn-Websters, husband and wife, brought an action for libel against Baldwin, the proprietor of the *St James's Chronicle*, who made no defence, offered reparation, and, on conviction by a jury, was ordered to pay substantial damages by the presiding judge.[240]

Scott naturally appears to have followed this case—which, needless to say, caused a sensation in both England and France—with keen interest. Shortly afterwards he heard that James Wedderburn-Webster was considering buying a house that was up for sale at Melrose near Abbotsford. Accordingly he wrote to a close friend that 'in that case, we may hope to see the Duke of Wellington, for despite the verdict of the jury against the *St James's Chronicle* man, he had greatly the appearance of *l'ami de maison*'.[241] In view of this remark, and of Lady Wedderburn-Webster's alleged ambition 'to attract people of celebrity', she herself, rather than Lady Caroline Lamb, might well have been the anonymous lady in John Scott of Gala's record of Wellington's ball, who had originally given Scott the 'special invitation' to sit at Wellington's supper table with herself and Lady Caroline Lamb. In any event, Scott was never to meet either of these two ladies after his return home from Paris, although he continued to refer to Lady Caroline Lamb as 'a laced mutton' when news occasionally reached him of her indiscretions. His other name for her was that of 'Calantha',[242] which she adopted for herself in a sensational and extremely fashionable novel called *Glenarvon* (1816), which she published a few months after her meeting with Scott in Paris on hearing that Byron, having formally separated from his wife, Annabella Milbanke, after only a year's marriage, had left England for good for Italy via Brussels and Waterloo. She shadowed her 'fatal passion' for him in the novel, complete with extracts of his love letters to her.

CHAPTER IV

Second Fortnight in Paris

A few days after Wellington's ball Scott was invited by Lady Castlereagh to join a large party for an excursion to the celebrated Château de Montmorency north of Paris. The party included Colonel James Hamilton Stanhope and Lady Shelley, who appears to have been first introduced to Scott on this occasion, for she made her first reference to him in her journal.[1] She knew of him, of course, as a celebrity, but as a poet, not as a novelist, because of the anonymous publication of *Waverley* and *Guy Mannering*, both of which she had read without being in the secret of their authorship,[2] and without tracing parallels and links in them with *The Lay of the Last Minstrel*, *Marmion*, *The Lady of the Lake*, and Scott's more recent verse romances. His first appearance, she noted, was 'not prepossessing: a club-foot, white eye-lashes, and a clumsy figure'. Nor did he have any expression when his face was in repose; 'but upon an instant, some remark will lighten up his whole countenance, and you discover the man of genius'. His conversation reminded her of his poems: 'the same ideas and images recurring', which was also true of *Paul's Letters to his Kinsfolk*, in the sense that its imagery provided an excellent cross-section of the sources—Shakespeare, Cervantes, the Bible, Swift, *The Arabian Nights*, *Gil Blas*, ballads, and Restoration Comedy—on which he repeatedly drew for figures of speech, quotation, and allusions for other publications. As for his mode of expressing his ideas and imagery, Lady Shelley detected the 'carelessness' that critics of his poetry, while marvelling at its energy, movement, colour, variety, and profusion, had agreed to be his principal weakness.

Scott, for his part, did not record his own impressions of Lady Shelley, but four years later, when she was his guest at Abbotsford without having seen him again since their visit to Paris, he acknowledged his liking for her 'perfectly feminine' manners,[3] by which he implied that, although she was well read, highly cultured, widely travelled, and an excellent correspondent like the court ladies of old times, she was not a blue stocking, to whom he was, in general, not drawn.[4] He also credited her with 'good sense', and, bearing in mind that he had by then written *Rob Roy* (1817), in which he had created his most popular female figure, Diana Vernon, who is renowned, among other skills, for her horsemanship, he suggested that Lady Shelley's riding, as he had observed it at one of Wellington's reviews, had served him as model for his own heroine's accomplishment.[5]

Lady Shelley shared Scott's sense of 'the picturesque', which was drawn out by the situation of the Château de Montmorency, overlooked as it was by a wooded mountain setting, and commanding a fine view of a deep valley, which led to a lake and extensive plains beyond it. The effect of the view was enhanced by the tints it derived from the setting sun, as in a Claude Lorrain painting. For, although Scott had been silent about Claude Lorrain in the Louvre, he was fully alive to that master's colouring in his treatment of mountain scenery.[6] The view also drew out his historical sense, as the plains were those of Clichy, where the battle had been fought the year before between the Allied troops under Blücher and the French garrison of Paris under Napoleon's marshals, who had afterwards capitulated to the Allies, thereby bringing about Napoleon's first abdication. The plains of Clichy and the adjoining heights of Montmartre had first been pointed out to Scott by Monsieur Le Chevalier from the observatory of St Geneviève.[7] Moreover, the Allied army had included the Russian troops under General Barclay de Tolly, whom Scott had seen at Wellington's ball. Accordingly all this topographical and military detail was to be incorporated by Scott into his account of the Allied attack on Paris in 1814 in the *Life of Buonaparte*,[8] together with an explanation of how the defence of Paris had been materially weakened by the defection to the Allies of one of the French marshals called General Auguste Marmont. Scott hinted even in *Paul's Letters to his Kinsfolk*[9] that the citizens of Paris could still not forgive Marmont for his alleged treachery, although at the time of Scott's visit Marmont was in command of the royal guard of Louis XVIII, who had created him a peer of France.

Both Scott and Lady Shelley's warm response to the view of Montmorency gave way to utter shock and revulsion when Lady Castlereagh's party reached the château, the original owners of which— the Montmorencies—claimed kinship with mediaeval kings, including Henry I of England, and had traced their descent to an even more ancient line than that of the Condés, whose seat Scott had seen at Chantilly. Moreover, the château was where Rousseau had partly composed *Émile* (1762). On entering it, Scott and the rest of the party saw that the Prussian troops quartered in it had completely wrecked it. The devastation he witnessed seemed to be worse than that at Chantilly, judging by the language he used to describe it and by his referring to it twice afterwards: first, in the same letter to Joanna Baillie before his departure from Paris,[10] and, second, in *Paul's Letters to his Kinsfolk*.[11] 'In the fine chateau of

Montmorency,' he wrote to Joanna Baillie, 'the most splendid apartments, highly ornamented with gilding and carving, were converted into barracks for the dirtiest and most savage hussars I have ever seen—imagine the work these fellows make with velvet hangings and embroidery. I saw one hag [a camp follower] boiling her camp-kettle with part of a picture-frame.'

The irony connected with this destruction, as Scott explained in *Paul's Letters to his Kinsfolk*, was that the latest owner of the château had been attached to Napoleon, 'had fled upon Napoleon's first exile, and had returned to share his triumph. The brief interval before the battle of Waterloo, which compelled him to a second retreat, had been employed in refitting the château with painting, panelling, and sculpture, in the most expensive style. The Prussians were now busily undoing all that he had commenced, and the contrast between recent repair and the work of instant destruction was very striking'. Significantly, in the rest of this passage Scott made a specific reference—the only reference in his letters and other writings of Paris date—to Colonel James Stanhope as 'one of my friends, who had been long in the Spanish [Peninsular] war'; and he cited, not only in this passage but also in his letter to Joanna Baillie, the military jargon that Stanhope had used for the destruction that was going on at the château. Moreover, in drawing on Rabelais and *The Arabian Nights* for figures of speech with which to describe, both in the letter to Joanna Baillie and in *Paul's Letters to his Kinsfolk*, the 'gargantuan' powers of eating and drinking of the young Prussian soldiers, Scott provided a further example of the 'recurring' imagery in his poetry, prose, and conversation.

In repeating in a letter to his wife, towards the end of August 1815, that the Prussians 'have the stomachs of devils and eat from four in the morning till twelve at night',[12] Scott, who certainly was himself no spartan in regard to food and drink at home, did not imply that he was not doing full justice to the renowned French *cuisine*, especially as he had found the cost of living in Paris cheaper than in London. 'I always go to the very best restaurateurs,' he wrote to Mrs Scott, 'and drink a bottle of Champagne or Burgundy every day instead of Porter and Port wine.'[13] In fact, he humorously claimed to her in another letter shortly afterwards, that 'I am quite a Frenchman in eating and drinking and turn up my nose at roast beef and port wine—fricasses and champagne are much better—then you have the most delicious fruit—huge bunches of grapes peaches and nectarines for nothing at all'. Scott trusted that in quieter times his wife too would travel to France and go to Switzerland, as two of his fellow-travellers, Alexander Pringle and Robert Bruce, would soon be doing, thus leaving him and Gala on their own for the return journey. The only objection to travelling in August was 'the extreme heat', which had been making him feel 'listless and inactive' at mid-day, but lately the weather had turned cooler. Nothing, he believed, gave 'such a fillip to the imagination', as travel.[14]

As the harvest had been gathered in from the large parts of the country unaffected by the Allied invasion, Scott was evidently impressed by the fertility of the soil and the 'animated industry' of the inhabitants, as reflected in the abundance and cheapness of the food in the restaurants, and as observed in his excursions outside Paris. The impression was supplemented by the vast granary of Paris—the Halle au Bled—which not only mirrored the agricultural richness of the country but also exhibited its mechanical advances.[15] Therefore, Scott confidently declared shortly afterwards, in his letter to Joanna Baillie before his departure from Paris, that France had the natural means of recovering from the numerous losses she had suffered in the Napoleonic Wars, and, worse still, from the crippling burdens she now had to endure under the conditions imposed on her by the victorious Allies, if only the people would renounce the militarism that the Revolution and Napoleon had instilled into them, and resolve to live in peace with their neighbours. For Scott was perfectly aware of the economic consequences for France of having to maintain an Allied army of occupation, numbering nearly three quarters of a million and at the same time paying an indemnity of billions of francs.[16] Drawing on his poetic imagery, in a passage smacking of the periods of Dr Johnson and the eighteenth-century orators, he declared that 'France is at present the fabled giant struggling or rather lying supine under the load of mountains which have been precipitated on her but she is not and cannot be crushed—remove the incumbent weight of six or seven hundred thousand officers and she will soon stand upright, happy, if experience shall have taught her to be contented to exert her natural strength only for her own protection and not for the annoyance of her neighbours'.[17]

Although Scott did not spell out, in his letter to his wife about French food, the names of 'the very best restaurateurs' that he was frequenting, they can be easily ascertained from the journals of his fellow-travellers and of James Simpson, all of whom were responding to French food with as much gusto as himself. Moreover, the restaurateurs were to re-appear in the extraordinarily popular poem called *The Fudge Family in Paris* (1818) that Scott's future friend, Tom Moore, was to write in ridicule of certain groups of English travellers in Paris after the Bourbon Restoration.

The best-known restaurant, patronised by most visitors to Paris, was called Véry's, which Scott was to recall several years later in *Quentin Durward*[18] as particularly notable for its '*Bifstiks de Mouton*'. It lay near his hotel, off the Rue de Rivoli, which he described in *Paul's Letters to his Kinsfolk*[19] as a 'magnificent' boulevard, even though it was still unfinished. His party had started going to Véry's since the first night after their arrival in Paris, followed by calls at other well-known restaurants, such as Beauvilliers' in the Palais Royal, and the Quadron Bleu in the Boulevard du Temple, which was the oldest and one of the best.[20] Their cicerone, Le Chevalier, had taken them to a couple of the smaller restaurants—then known as *cabarets*—on the Seine.[21] One of them faced the celebrated gardens of the Luxembourg Palace, in whose beautiful gallery Scott, besides seeing, as has already been mentioned, Rubens's pictures commemorating the life of Marie de' Medici, looked at many masterpieces on a par with those in the Louvre.[22]

One of the pictures was evidently of special appeal to Scott, as he recalled it many years later in the *Life of Buonaparte*[23] in his highly personal and moving account of the counter-revolution of the Vendeans against the republicans, which had culminated in their virtual annihilation in the Terror, following their unsuccessful siege of Nantes. The picture, representing that siege, was by Carle Vernet, who, although himself a republican, and, on that account, a glorifier of the defenders of Nantes, earned Scott's approval, and indeed praise, for having depicted the Vendeans 'in all their simplicity of attire and devoted valour', precisely as 'primitive soldiers' or 'patriarchal warriors', like the irregular Cossacks of Count Platoff and the Highland clans led by their chieftains in the Jacobite rebellion of 1745.

The most notorious surviving symbol of the French Revolution and of the massacre of the Vendeans by the republicans was, of course, the guillotine, or 'Mme Guillotine', 'Saint Guillotine', and even 'Holy Mother Guillotine', as it had been variously 'canonized' in the Reign of Terror. Scott, who was no stranger to public executions on the scaffold (for they were still a common spectacle in his home town and other parts of Scotland), was apparently curious to see the guillotine. His curiosity sprang not only from that instrument's notoriety but from the fact that, as a historical novelist, he had already given the first proof of his remarkable talent for creating execution scenes by writing a brilliantly imaginative and dramatic chapter at the end of *Waverley*[24] connected with the trial and beheading of the Jacobite Highland chieftain, Fergus Mac-Ivor. Accordingly, when he heard, apparently from James Simpson, on information from the Hôtel de Ville, that the guillotine could still be seen in Paris, he declared to Simpson that he was resolved to see it before he left the city. In the event, however, he found himself so caught up in the festivities of the English 'fashionables' that he appears to have given up his resolve. Thus it was left to Simpson to ride out on his horse from his hotel in search of 'the murderous instrument', and on discovering it behind a large door in a sort of coach-house near the vast corn market, to conjure up the kind of vision of its victims[25] that Scott himself would undoubtedly have evoked, as he was indeed to do, several years later, in his chapter on the Reign of Terror in the *Life of Buonaparte*.[26]

Simpson's hotel in the Rue Vivienne lay exactly opposite the famous bookshop and reading-room that had been opened by an enterprising Italian immigrant called Galignani and his English wife for British residents and travellers.[27] At the time of Scott's visit Galignani published a Paris guide in English and German, on opposite pages, for the use of officers of the Allied troops, and the year before he had begun to publish *Galignani's Messenger*, which was to become the standard newspaper for

English travellers throughout Europe. Both as publisher and bookseller Galignani was to become a significant figure for Scott as far as the distribution and sales of the Waverley Novels on the continent were concerned. For Galignani, who had lived in London before emigrating to Paris, was in the process of building up a bookselling and publishing empire on the continent comparable to that of John Murray in England by selling books cheaply and undertaking to deliver them in London, paying the import duties himself, and undercutting his English competitors, while not paying royalties to the English authors in an age when the law of international copyright was not yet established. At this stage of the development of his business, however, he does not appear to have entered Scott's life personally or professionally. Even though Simpson wrote enthusiastically about the various facilities Galignani offered to English travellers, including up-to-date information about what was going on in Paris, there is no evidence to suggest that Scott's sight-seeing included 'the old pirate's den', as he was himself to call Galignani's bookshop on his second visit to Paris.[28]

Nor does it appear that any of Scott's fellow-travellers made use of Galignani's reading-room for the English newspapers that they certainly represented themselves in their journals as reading regularly before setting off on their sight-seeing, as they had also done at Brussels.[29] Although both they and Scott may well have heard of Galignani's reading-room from Simpson and other sources, they seem to have preferred to follow the practice of using the coffee-shops for reading the principal London newspapers, where they also had breakfast *al fresco* or under an awning, and met other travellers, including Simpson. Their hotel, moreover, was close to the best coffee-shops in the boulevards and the Palais Royal. One of their favourites was in the Boulevard des Italiens, where Scott's love of animals led him to form a quick intimacy with the dog of a blind beggar, who used to station himself in the street, while his rough mongrel held up a wooden cup in his mouth for charity from pedestrians. Scott could not resist saying a word to the dog, and depositing a trifle in the cup.[30] He deplored the lack of adequate protection for 'the aged, the timid, the infirm', including the blind beggar, in the streets of Paris owing to the absence of 'the safe pavements and foot-paths of an English street or road'. The risk of accidents had been multiplied at the time of his visit by 'the numerous accession of strangers' from all over Europe, 'who drive in their own way, and give their own mode of warning, which the pedestrian must construe rightly upon his own peril'.[31]

All the boulevards were lined with attractions of various kinds, including print-shops, where Scott and his party were surprised at the large number of caricatures of Napoleon and his friends, including ballads, skits, and epigrams on the fiasco of his hundred days and on his alleged poorness of spirit in adversity at Waterloo. Scott bought a portfolio of these and other caricatures to take home with him. Naturally the national characteristics, costume, and manners of the Allied army of occupation were favourite targets of the French caricaturists, particularly 'the singular dress of our Highlanders', as represented, for instance, in a popular print reading 'The Highland Soldiers on a Windy Day'.[32] Scott himself overheard in a café a French lady say to her companion after she had passed two of these mountaineers: *'Aussi j'ai vu les sauvages Americains'*.[33]

Undoubtedly the most celebrated coffee-shop in Paris was the Café de Mille Colonnes in the Palais Royal. Even royalty called there, so much so that Scott's visit to it had been preceded the night before by one from King Friedrich of Prussia. The café, with its Corinthian columns and numerous mirrors, which seemed to multiply themselves as well as the company of native and international customers, provided a showy *coup d'oeuil*, which surpassed that of most ballrooms. But its chief attraction was the so-called *La Belle Limonadière*, a beautiful matron, who had been patronised, it was said, even by Napoleon, principally to worm state secrets from ambassadors. Every coffee-house in Paris had a woman seated on an elevated dais to superintend the business of the establishment, but *La Belle Limonadière* was a real 'Parisian lion'.[34] Although she had become 'rather large and *un peu passée*' at the time of Scott's visit, she was still a striking personage, albeit heavily made up and bejewelled. Few individuals presumed to address her without formal presentation. It was precisely when Scott had happened to be sitting at the right hand of her 'throne' that James Simpson had first run into him shortly after his party's arrival at Paris, and, on joining him and his companions, had been 'delighted to hear Mr Scott's remarks on the truly Parisian scene in which we sat, and his commentaries on the singular personage who solemnly, brilliantly presided—sparkling with diamonds, multiplied, front, back, and profile in mirrors, and intrenched in *arrondisements* of sugar, peaches, and nosegays'.[35]

Unfortunately Simpson did not record what exactly Scott had said about 'this truly French scene', although Gala did confirm, briefly and in mock-heroic style, in his journal that 'we of course paid our devoirs to the celebrated deese, seated on her burnished throne ... gorgeously attired' and 'gracefully doing the honours of the establishment'.[36] Scott himself did not refer to her in *Paul's Letters to his Kinsfolk*, but it is tempting to speculate if 'this truly French scene' at the Café de Mille Colonnes, and 'the flutter and affectation' of the French paintings that he had seen in the Louvre, combined with the gambling dens in the Palais Royal, the best known of which was called the *Salon des Étrangers*, and which he had the curiosity to visit,[37] might not have been behind the remark he afterwards made in his travel book, which suggested an ambivalent attitude on his part to Paris. 'There is so much in Paris', he wrote, 'to admire and so much to dislike, such a mixture of real taste and genius, with so much frippery and affectation, the sublime is so oddly mingled with the ridiculous, and the pleasing with the fantastic and whimsical, that I shall probably leave the capital of France without being able to determine which train of ideas it has most frequently associated in my mind.'[38]

Although Scott initially reported his own visit of curiosity to the *Salon des Étrangers* light-heartedly to his wife, and even admitted that he had gambled 'for two or three Napoleons and gained seven or eight',[39] he adopted a highly censorious attitude to the place in *Paul's Letters to his Kinsfolk*,[40] particularly as he appears to have observed or learned that the gaming houses in the Palais Royal were also notorious dens of prostitution.[41] Although he evidently disapproved in principle of the State running a gambling house, which was the case with the *Salon des Étrangers*, he stressed that everything in 'the bank', as he called the *Salon*, 'seemed to be conducted with perfect fairness', thanks to the enormous extent of the funds, 'by which it is enabled to sustain any reverse of fortune; whereas most of the individuals who play against the bank are in circumstances to be ruined by the first succession of ill luck'.[42]

However indeterminate Scott might have felt over the predominant associations evoked by Paris, there was one fashion of all good Parisians which could only have excited pleasing trains of ideas in his mind, namely, the practice of going to the theatre after dinner. His party had started doing so since the night of their arrival—after dinner at Véry's.[43] The most famous theatre then was the Théâtre Français (the former Comédie Française), the London counterparts of which were Covent Garden and Drury Lane Theatres. But whereas both London theatres, having been destroyed by fire in quick succession a few years previously, had been rebuilt to an enormous size, to which Scott was implacably opposed on several grounds, the Théâtre Français, he was delighted to find, answered exactly to his own idea of the style of building proper for a theatre. Therefore, he was to write, in criticism of the new Covent Garden and Drury Lane, that 'whoever has seen the interior of a Parisian theatre, will, and must admit, that they manage things better in France'.[44]

It was fortunate for Scott and his party that at the Théâtre Français they were able to see the celebrated Talma and Mlle George, followed by performances by the other leading actress, Mlle Mars, who excelled in comedy and was playing the part of Elmire in Molière's *Le Tartuffe* (1669) with grace and ability.[45] Her male opposite number was the veteran Fleury, and their combined talents demonstrated to Scott's party how unrivalled the French theatre was in the kind of drama represented in England by the plays of Cibber, Steele, and Goldsmith, and commonly known as 'sentimental or genteel comedy'.[46]

Scott seems to have been attracted to Molière of all the French playwrights. He bought an edition of Molière's collected works for his library at Abbotsford, and afterwards he reviewed a *Life of Molière* with self-confessed feeling for it as 'a gallant subject'.[47]

As for Talma and Mlle George, they were the counterparts of John Kemble and Mrs Siddons, whom Scott had come to know well at the Theatre Royal in Edinburgh,[48] of which he was an influential

François Talma. From a contemporary engraving

supporter. It was there, in fact, that he had played a key rôle in the triumphant success of Joanna Baillie's *The Family Legend* (1810), followed by her earlier play, *De Montfort* (1798), with Mrs Siddons in the principal part.[49] Scott was now hoping that, on his return from Paris to England, he might have an opportunity of urging Byron, as a member of the Committee of Management of Drury Lane Theatre, to produce one of Joanna Baillie's plays in London.[50] In that event both he and Joanna Baillie would be able to count on the active assistance of his close friend, Daniel Terry, the actor, who, as Scott probably read in Paris in one of the London newspapers, was then playing, 'with great applause', the principal part of the extremely popular comedy, *The Man of the World* (1781), at the Haymarket Theatre.[51] Scott had first seen Terry on the stage in the Edinburgh production of *The Family Legend*, after which Terry had acted in *The Lady of the Lake*,[52] the first of Scott's works to be adapted for the stage.

Inevitably Scott and his fellow-travellers had John Kemble in mind when they went to the Théâtre Français to see Talma play the leading rôle in Racine's *Britannicus* (1669), for they were curious to see how he compared with Kemble in his celebrated Shakespearean parts. They were not disappointed, for although they found Talma's countenance and features much less handsome than those of Kemble, 'his figure, dress, manner, and voice' were pronounced 'highly impressive and forcible' by Gala, who summed up the effect of Talma's performance on his mind as having been 'fully as deep and lasting as any I have witnessed, not excepting the Wolsey or Coriolanus of Kemble'.[53]

Talma, who was a long-standing friend of Kemble, had told him an anecdote of a fellow-actor, when Talma and Kemble had once been together behind the scenes of the Comédie Française. Kemble, in turn, had repeated the anecdote to Scott in one of their conversations in Edinburgh, when Kemble and Mrs Siddons had been performing *The Family Legend* at the Theatre Royal. The point of the anecdote, as related by Kemble to Scott, was to complain that in England 'we have not, as on the better regulated stage of Paris, respectable French actors who, finding their talents inadequate to fill the first rate rank in their profession, wisely content themselves with applying their powers to parts within their reach'. In other words, in France there was 'a race of actors who never aspire to more than secondary parts', whereas in England these parts were 'filled upon our stage because they must be filled, but it is with discontented Hamlets and Richards and Romeos, who revenge themselves upon the public by *walking through* characters better suited to their powers than to their ambition'.

This criticism had been repeated by Scott to Joanna Baillie[54] the year before his visit to the Théâtre Français to see Talma and Mlle George, but without mentioning either Kemble or Talma as his sources. When, however, after Kemble's death, he reviewed a life of him in the *Quarterly Review*,[55] he repeated the complaint and anecdote more fully, naming

Kemble and Talma as his authorities, and rounding off his observations with the general criticism that the 'Parisian theatre presents a company so completely drilled to work together', in contrast to the more individualistic and egocentric English actors. So imbued did Scott become with admiration for 'the discipline' of the French actors in achieving 'a general harmony and correspondence' in all the parts of a play, contrary to 'the intolerable, contemptuous, and wilful negligence' of English actors in 'the subordinate parts', that he returned to this subject in the important essay on drama that he contributed to the *Encyclopaedia Britannica* a few years after his return from Paris.[56]

He also never forgot, on the evidence of the *Life of Bonaparte*,[57] the other piece of information about Talma that Scott had gathered from Kemble. This was to the effect that Talma had attended in early life the same military college at Brienne to which Napoleon had gone, and that several years later, when Napoleon, as a young artillery officer, had turned up in Paris from Toulon in search of employment and unfriended, Talma had assisted him at what had afterwards proved to be a turning-point in his extraordinary career. In return for this service, Napoleon, who 'forgot neither benefits nor injuries', had always, 'during the height of his grandeur, [been] particularly kind to Talma, and honoured him even with a degree of intimacy', apart from the universal acclaim that Talma had earned in his own right with his pre-eminent dramatic gifts.

Although Talma was best known as the greatest actor of his day for tragedy, he was versatile enough even for comedy. In fact, he delighted Scott at the Théâtre Français with his brilliant acting in a comedy which in several ways was after Scott's heart, for it had historical characters, a pastoral setting, a ballad already known to Scott, sparkling dialogue, and a plot partly taken from a familiar English story by Robert Dodsley called *The King and the Miller of Mansfield*. The comedy, which was the *chef d'oeuvre* of Charles Collé, was called *La Partie de Chasse d'Henri IV*, and it delighted not only Scott but also Gala, who was himself familiar with the ballad sung in French by the actors. Besides writing a fairly full analysis, in his journal,[58] of Talma's performance in the comedy, Gala stated that Scott often told him, well after his return to Scotland, that 'he never received greater pleasure from any theatrical exhibition'. It appears, therefore, that Scott afterwards brought up the comedy in his conversation with others, including Lockhart, who seems to have given, in the *Life of Scott*,[59] a highly confused version of the circumstances connected with the comedy. For Lockhart cited a stanza of the ballad, which referred to the celebrated mistress of Henri IV, Gabrielle d'Éstrées, commonly known as *La Belle Gabrielle*, in whom Scott had long been interested for historical and romantic reasons. Indeed, on going to the Royal Library with Gala, and on asking to be shown its more valuable manuscripts, his attention had been arrested by 'several letters of Henri Quatre to the Fair Gabrielle',[60] whom Scott afterwards represented in *Woodstock*[61] as the French counterpart of 'Fair Rosamond Clifford', the mistress of Henry II of England. But Lockhart, instead of relating the ballad about *La Belle Gabrielle* to the comedy seen by Scott and Gala at the Théâtre Français, connected it with an excursion organised by Lady Castlereagh for a large party, including Scott, to the Château d'Ermenonville outside Paris, which was, of course, where Rousseau had died after passing the last years of his life in retirement, writing his *Rêveries d'un Promeneur Soliteur*. As for this so-called 'excursion to Ermenonville', Lockhart might also have confused it with the excursion, already mentioned, to the Château de Montmorency, where, as again already explained, Rousseau had written *Émile*.

Lockhart made no mention of 'an immense to-do at Versailles', as Scott called it, which took place on the last Sunday of August 1815 in the form of a spectacular water-works display in the celebrated gardens of Louis XIV's grandest palace. Scott went to see it 'with Lady Castlereagh and her suite' after one of the attendants at his hotel had assured him and his fellow-travellers that this sort of spectacle had not been set in motion for many years, and that it would be 'something magnificent'. 'All Paris seemed to be assembled' for it, according to Gala, who averred that the advance notice that they had received of its excellence had not been overrated, so much so that he wrote an enthusiastic description of it in his journal, complete with a dramatic sketch of the splendid setting of the palace and gardens and the gaiety of the spectators.[62] Scott, on the other hand, tempered his report of it in a letter to his wife with the remark that, although the effect of the water display, culminating as it did in 'a thousand streams' shooting out of the fountains of Versailles, was 'very fine', he could not say that it quite justified 'the immense expense', which he had been told ran to thousands of francs.[63]

The great designer of the gardens at Versailles was, of course, André Le Nôtre, who, as Scott himself was to recall in *Peveril of the Peak*,[64] had also been employed by Charles II for the garden and artificial lake of St James's Park in London. Le Nôtre's genius, however, was for the so-called 'formal' style of landscape gardening, whereas Scott, or rather, his aesthetics masters led by Price, championed the so-called 'natural' style, as was evident enough from Scott's remarks in criticism of the French countryside on his way to Paris for the alleged absence of 'the variety of landscape afforded by detached groves'. His enthusiasm for the 'natural' style was even more specifically worded in his other charge that Nature was 'subjugated and tyrannized over by the despotic authority of human art' in the case of the buildings that completely occupied the small islands of the Seine. His later writings, in fact, represent him as even hostile to the artificial lakes, canals, and 'most things of the kind', associated with the 'formal' style.[65] His central interest being tree-planting, he took his cue for landscape gardening from the English manor houses, 'embosomed among old woods'.[66] In this context he highly respected—besides the eighteenth-century writers on 'the picturesque'—the earlier English authority on plantations, namely,

John Evelyn, whose *Sylva* (1664) Scott was to call in *Kenilworth*[67] 'still the manual of British planters'.

Besides reporting his excursion to Versailles in his letter to his wife, Scott informed her that he had 'dined with all the Emperors and great folks', thanks to an invitation from Lord Cathcart to a dinner in honour of Alexander the Tsar, and the Russian generals, including Platoff and Barclay de Tolly. Although Scott limited himself to saying that 'the dinner was quite Russian in complement to the Emperor' ('we had first brandy—then cake—then oysters—then cheese—then brandy again—then a world of other things'), and that 'old Platoff was presented to me and we said a world of pretty things to each other by signs',[68] he enlarged on these details afterwards, first, to his fellow-travellers, Gala and Pringle, just before the latter's departure with Robert Bruce for Switzerland, and then to his family and friends, including Lockhart, after his return to Scotland. Happily, therefore, Gala was able to record that Scott had sat next to Platoff at Lord Cathcart's dinner, and that he had 'received much attention' from Platoff in spite of the language barrier. 'The Het[t]man', said Scott, 'addressed several sentences to me in a very obliging manner, to which I replied in English, taking care to make my answer nearly of the same length, as his own speech; and with this I was glad to perceive he was perfectly satisfied.'[69] The tenor of Scott's response had apparently been explained to Platoff by some of Lord Cathcart's guests in the neighbourhood, such as the Russian ambassador to France, Count Pozzo di Borgo, who was fluent in languages, including English. Scott had lately come across his name in Wellington's 'Waterloo Despatch', for Pozzo di Borgo had taken part in the battle[70] as one of Napoleon's bitterest political enemies, although they were both of Corsican origin.

Pringle, for his part, was able to confirm to Lockhart the other piece of information about Platoff in Scott's letter to his wife, namely, that 'apparently he [Platoff] took me into great friendship, for meeting him the other day on horseback, he dismounted, gave his horse to one of his cossacks, embraced me with great affection, and then mounted, and galloped away'.[71] Scott, according to Lockhart's information from Pringle, had been walking with Pringle in Rue de la Paix (the street of their hotel), when Platoff had jumped off his horse, and running to Scott, had kissed him on both cheeks with extraordinary demonstrations of affection, and then had made him understand, through his military interpreter, that he wished Scott to ride beside him and his staff at an impending great Russian review (exactly as the Duke of Wellington had been asking Lady Shelley and Lady Wedderburn-Webster to ride beside him at the British reviews), and that he [Platoff] would take care to mount Scott on the gentlest of his Ukraine horses.[72]

Although Scott was certainly looking forward to seeing the Russian review, in which he had heard that 'some 150,000 men' would be taking part,[73] and which was due to take place on 2 or 3 September 1815, he did not, in the event, avail himself of Platoff's invitation to ride beside him. He had, however, observed Platoff's appearance carefully at Lord Cathcart's dinner for creative purposes in novel writing, so that when, several years later, he wrote *St Ronan's Well* (1824), he acknowledged in a note[74] that he had drawn on his memory of Platoff's face for his description of one of the characters, Mr Touchwood, in the novel. He also acknowledged, at the end of *Paul's Letters to his Kinsfolk*,[75] the hospitality of Lord Cathcart, 'whose situation as ambassador to the Russian court gave him opportunities of gratifying the curiosity of his countrymen by presenting them to the emperor' and to the other heroes of Russia, 'where the spear of the mighty was first broken', by which Scott, of course, meant that the decline of Napoleon's military and political fortunes had started in 1812, following the failure of his Russian expedition.

As for Scott's presentation to the Emperor Alexander by Lord Cathcart, Lockhart immortalised it in the *Life of Scott*[76] with a hilarious retelling of Scott's own version of his dialogue with the Tsar. For Scott had turned up for the dinner wearing his old uniform of the Edinburgh Volunteer Cavalry, at which Alexander, having also observed Scott's limp, had assumed that he had been wounded on active service, and, despite Scott's attempts to explain in French that he had only served in the home militia without injury, the Tsar had persisted in his mistaken belief and in plying him with questions, which Scott had cleverly parried with mock-heroic answers.

The Tsar and his fellow-sovereigns called on King Louis XVIII at the Tuileries on 25 August to congratulate him on his sixtieth birthday, which was marked in the streets of Paris with flags and garlands and with a general illumination and fireworks at night. Although Scott's party observed sincere public rejoicing and dancing in front of the royal palace, Scott wrote to his wife that 'the royal family are unpopular and suffer all the odium of the burdens imposed to maintain the foreign troops' and to pay the heavy indemnity.[77] Louis himself had an amiable temper, dignity, and good sense, especially in his resolve to rule as a constitutional monarch, but he was wearied by adversity, following his long years in exile and dependence on royal courts in so many countries of Europe. Old and infirm, he suffered increasingly from gout and obesity,[78] as Scott and his fellow-travellers had an opportunity of seeing for themselves a few days after the King's birthday, when they obtained admission to the Tuileries. They happened to be in the magnificent hall called *Salle des Maréchaux*, which was adorned with portraits of the marshals of France, including an excellent one of Field Marshal Macdonald, in whom they were most interested. As they were admiring the hall and the portraits, the King and the royal family passed through it on their return from morning service in the private chapel of the palace. Louis looked 'extremely infirm, and walked with much difficulty', although these personal disadvantages were atoned for by the calm and intelligent expression of his face.[79]

King Louis XVIII by Baron Antoine Jean Gros. (Private Collection)

Scott himself had informed his wife that 'I have declined being presented to the King of France, referring it to some more quiet day', in view of 'the perpetual whirl wind and tempest of gaiety going on among the strangers—that is among *us*'. 'The poor man', Scott had added about Louis, was alleged to be too much under the influence of the English in the persons of Wellington and Lord Castlereagh: 'The French call him *Le Préfet d'Angleterre* and *Louis l'Inévitable*'.[80] Louis himself had acknowledged his immeasureable indebtedness to the English for his restoration to the throne of France in 'the very good reply' that Scott had heard that Louis had given to some of his attendants at the Tuileries who had proposed shutting his apartments to keep out the throng of people. 'Open the door,' he had said, 'to John Bull; he has suffered a great deal in keeping the door open for me.'[81]

Louis' regiment of guards, in their handsome uniforms of blue and red, richly laced with silver, drew praise both from Scott and Gala for the great loyalty they had shown 'in the late trying crisis', when they had gone into exile with Louis at Ghent in Flanders, following Napoleon's return to Paris on his escape from Elba.[82] The special appeal of this *Gardes du Corps* to Scott sprang from the fact that he looked upon them as the modern representatives of the so-called 'Scottish guards' who had formed the royal bodyguard of the mediaeval French kings, as Scott was himself to explain in *Quentin Durward*.[83] Accordingly he was to make the hero of that novel a member of Louis XI's Scottish guard.

At the Tuileries Scott particularly admired 'the chivalrous feeling' with which the *Gardes du Corps* conducted themselves towards the crowd. Indeed he went so far as to hint in *Paul's Letters to his Kinsfolk*[84] that 'my infirmities [presumably his lame foot] perhaps claimed a little compassion, and it is no discredit to them that I have seen Messrs Les Gardes de [*sic*] Corps feel the claim, and make a little way, by the influence of voice and authority, for one who was not so able to make it for himself'.

Scott's party observed at the Tuileries that the King's brother, Charles, the Count of Artois, provided a complete contrast, in appearance, to Louis. Although only a couple of years younger, he still retained 'the grace and elegance' for which he had been formerly celebrated as 'an ornament of the court of Marie Antoinette', his sister-in-law, in the days of the *ancien régime* before the outbreak of the French Revolution.[85] Scott had first seen him as far back as 1794, after his brother's and sister-in-law's execution, when, having gone into exile with countless *émigrés*, he had lived at Holyrood Palace in Edinburgh at the invitation of the British government. He had then seemed to Scott 'one of the most elegant men in address and exterior whom I ever saw'.[86] Charles was now the heir to the throne, as Louis XVIII was a widower and childless. He was the leader of what Scott called in *Paul's Letters to his Kinsfolk*[87] 'the faction of *royalistes purs*', by which he meant the so-called 'Ultras', the extreme royalists, the reactionary party, who favoured the restoration of the ancient rights and property of the *émigrés*, the aristocracy, and the Catholic Church, whose estates had been confiscated, following the French Revolution.

These circumstances explain to a considerable extent why Scott reported to his wife that 'the royal family are unpopular'. For the *émigrés*, the ultra royalists, were opposed by 'the *Liberalists*', who were supported by the old Jacobins of the Revolution, by the army or 'the imperialists' (the old followers of Napoleon). Scott, therefore, wrote, in a perceptive analysis of the contemporary political situation in France towards the end of *Paul's Letters to his Kinsfolk*,[88] that 'it must be owned that the general rallying point of the *Liberalists* is an avowed dislike of the present monarch and his immediate connections', by which Scott meant not only Charles, the Count of Artois, but also his niece, the Duchess of Angoulême, the only surviving member of the family of Louis XVI and Marie Antoinette. She was the Princess Royal of France, and had lived in exile in England till the fall of Napoleon. A strong character, who had survived imprisonment and all sorts of trials and vicissitudes,[89] she shared the zeal of her two uncles, King Louis XVIII and the Count of Artois, to re-establish religion in France, and, together with her husband, favoured the clerical or Catholic party,[90] to the alarm of the peasants, the *bourgeoisie*, and the French Protestants or Huguenots. For the peasantry and the *bourgeoisie* had benefited from the Revolution by becoming the proprietors of the confiscated church lands, as had happened in England during the Reformation, while the Huguenots, who were particularly numerous in the south of France, had benefited from Napoleon, who had proclaimed universal religious toleration, and had guaranteed the full exercise of their religion, contrary to some of the ancestors of the restored Bourbon royal family, who had persecuted the Huguenots in the wars of religion during the Reformation.[91]

In view of these circumstances, Scott explained in *Paul's Letters to his Kinsfolk*[92] that the French Liberals, who formed the main opposition to the royalists in the new ministry of Louis XVIII, 'will sacrifice, they pretend, so much to the general inclination of Europe [by which Scott meant the victorious Allied Powers] as to select a king from the Bourbon race; but he must be one of their own choosing', not one imposed on them by the Allies, particularly Britain, which explains why Scott informed his wife that the French had nicknamed Louis XVIII *Le Préfet de l'Angleterre* and *Louis l'Inévitable*, even though Louis was bent on observing the constitution, exactly as the Liberals or 'constitutional royalists' wanted. Accordingly Scott admitted that, in keeping with the Liberals' wish to have 'a king of their own choosing', Louis-Philippe, 'the Duke of Orleans is most familiar to their mouths'.[93] His father, also named Louis-Philippe, had, at the outbreak of the Revolution, when he was only sixteen, identified himself with it, for which reason he had been popularly known as 'Philippe *Égalité*'.

This idea, however, of an *elected*, instead of a *hereditary*, monarch, or, as Scott put it, of 'a king whose title should be connected with the Revolution, and who might owe his crown more to their [the Liberals'] courtesy than to his own right', was absolutely anathema to Scott as a Tory and as a disciple of Edmund Burke, who had defended the principle of hereditary succession in *Reflections on the Revolution in France*. Scott, therefore, condemned 'the doctrine now held in France', on the ground that 'it strikes at the very foundation of hereditary right', which, together with the majority of his generation in Britain, he regarded as 'the fundamental principle of a limited monarchy',[94] the advantages of which he was to spell out in the *Life of Buonaparte*.[95] Bearing in mind King Louis XVIII's intention to pursue a prudent, conciliatory, and constitutional policy, Scott argued that the doctrine of the Liberals was 'founded on no overt act of the sovereign tending to affect the liberties of his subjects, but upon jealousies and fears that he has, or may call, evil counsellors around him, who, at some time or other, will persuade him to attempt the reestablishment of the feudal rights of the nobility and the domination of the church'. In developing his criticisms, Scott again drew on the parallel of the Civil War and the Stuart Restoration in England, in order to explain that, when the English Whigs (who corresponded to the French Liberals) had wanted to exclude the Catholic James II from the succession, and had drawn up the Exclusion Bill, even they had ultimately dropped it as 'a dangerous innovation on the constitution'.[96] It was not surprising, therefore, that, several years later, Scott was to write to his friend, Robert Southey, 'how easy it would be for a good historian to run a parallel betwixt the Great Rebellion [of 1688 in England] and the French Revolution', and 'what an instructive comparative view may be made' in such a study.[97]

Scott's good sense, moderation, and balanced judgement as a product of the Scottish Enlightenment was nowhere better displayed than in his remarks in *Paul's Letters to his Kinsfolk* on the ruling Bourbon family's attempts to re-establish religion, which, in general, he welcomed in view of the 'empty and neglected' churches he had found in Paris, in contrast to the full and devout congregations he had observed in Flanders.[98] He insisted, however, that this re-establishment should not be based purely on 'external observances', or on a revival of obsolete ritual and mediaeval superstition, but on sound doctrine, 'common sense and reason', and proper education, particularly of the rising generation in moral duties. 'The Catholics of this age,' he affirmed, 'are not excluded from the lights which it has afforded, ... and all the mummery of barbarous ages is far from meeting the enlarged ideas which the best and most learned of them have expressed.' Although the time, therefore, was ripe for 'rebuilding the Gallican church on a more solid basis than ever, by leaving room for the more gradual and slow reformation introduced by the lapse of time', Scott set his face firmly against any attempt to 'force back the nineteenth century into the rude and degrading darkness of the ages of excommunications and crusades'.[99]

As for 'the ancient enmities' between the Catholics and the Huguenots, that Scott had heard with regret had been revived since the restoration of

Louis XVIII, particularly in the south of France, where 'the angry passions of both parties are understood to be at full tide', and, worse still, were 'envenomed by political hatred' (for the Catholics were pro-Bourbon, and the Huguenots pro-Napoleon), Scott ardently deprecated 'a renewal of those savage and bloody wars, which, founded on difference of religious opinion, seem to convert even the bread of life itself into the most deadly poison'.[100] Accordingly the more 'philosophical' side of Scott was struck by 'the singularity of human affairs' in a wider survey of these 'ancient religious enmities' in Europe. For in Flanders he had found the Catholics complaining, because in the new Kingdom of the Netherlands William of Orange had proclaimed universal toleration, even for his Protestant subjects; whereas in Ireland severe discontents existed among the Catholics for not possessing the privileges of their Protestant compatriots; and now in France he had found that 'in the south ... the sword is nearly drawn, upon the footing of doubts, jealousies, and apprehensions of mutual violence, for which neither party can allege any feasible ground, except mutual dislike and hatred'. Scott wished that 'all of them would qualify their zeal for the doctrinal part of their religion with some part of that meekness of spirit which would be the best proof of its purity'.[101]

Naturally Scott, as a Protestant himself, was particularly interested in the Huguenots of South France, especially in the province of Languedoc, where they were said to number as many as 2 million, and who, in return for the universal toleration and special privileges that Napoleon had granted them, had welcomed him back to France on landing at Cannes after his escape from Elba.[102] On the other hand, Scott, with his knowledge of French history, particularly of the period of Henri IV, knew that it was the latter who had first granted toleration to his Protestant subjects through the Edict of Nantes after the terrible Massacre of St Bartholomew's Day, when some 50,000 Protestants had been slaughtered, first, in Paris, and then in the provinces. The special merit of Napoleon, therefore, with regard to his Protestant subjects, as Scott pointed out in *Paul's Letters to his Kinsfolk*,[103] was that he had reversed the policy of King Louis XIV, who had revoked the Edict of Nantes, which explained the distrust of the Huguenots of South France towards the ruling Bourbon family of Louis XVIII, 'by the bigotry of whose ancestors they had suffered', even though all parties admitted 'the sound judgment and humane disposition' of Louis XVIII himself.

What appealed most, however, to Scott's historical imagination about these Huguenots of South France was that they were 'the descendants of the ardent men who used to assemble by thousands in the wilderness' in the old days of persecution,[104] which had culminated in the Massacre of St Bartholomew's Day in 1572. The mere reminder of those ancestral heroes and martyrs, however bigoted the times they lived in, drew out the creative artist in Scott with particular reference to Jacobite history. For these ancestral Huguenots were precisely the French counterparts, as Scott put it, of 'the Calvinistic heroes of moor and moss [in Scotland] in the days of the last Stuarts', who had persecuted them.[105] Herein, therefore, was the earliest hint, or, at any rate, one of the earliest hints, of the theme that was to take shape in *Old Mortality* within a year of Scott's return home from Paris. The very title of that novel was to be taken from the adopted name of a most singular Calvinist, who, having suffered imprisonment and oppression, had made it his lifetime's practice to wander, like the ancient Huguenots of South France, in the remote parts of Scotland seeking and repairing the graves of his fellow 'Whig martyrs', complete with the inscriptions recording their sufferings.[106] His real name was Robert Paterson, and Scott had met him for the first and last time in the churchyard of a castle, engaged in the very same task, many years before, during one of Scott's memorable Highland excursions.[107]

Possessed as he was of a wonderful memory, Scott was not the man to let so historic a date as that of the Massacre of St Bartholomew's Day pass unnoticed in his correspondence from Paris. For its anniversary, namely, 24 August, nearly coincided not only with the rumours that had linked General La Bédoyère with the plot to assassinate the visiting Allied sovereigns and their generals, including Wellington, but also with another invitation that Scott had received to 'a great ball', in which the visiting sovereigns and their generals would all be again assembled together at the British Embassy, and would be potentially vulnerable to any plot that might be hatched by 'the Bonapartists' in the cafés, gaming houses, and the underworld of the Palais Royal, which he stigmatised in *Paul's Letters to his Kinsfolk*[108] as the original breeding grounds of the Revolution and of the successful plot for Bonaparte's escape from Elba and triumphant return to Paris. Therefore, in replying to his printer, James Ballantyne, who was seeing *The Field of Waterloo* through the press in Edinburgh for publication in October 1815, Scott informed him on 30 August that 'tonight Lady Castlereagh gives a great ball to the Emperors, King of Prussia, etc, etc', and then added: 'Were the French half so devoted as they pretend to be, they might make a St Bartholomew of some of these shines'. But, as always, Scott quoted a snatch of a ballad to reassure Ballantyne that the Allied troops and the National Guard of Louis XVIII's government were on the alert against any conspiracy.[109]

Scott also informed Ballantyne that he would be sending no more material for the press, because he could not prudently risk miscarriage of the politically sensitive topics dealt with in some parts of *Paul's Letters to his Kinsfolk*. 'I only wait to see the grand review' of the Russian army, he added, although he had already informed Mrs Scott that 'the great Russian review', involving 'some 150,000 men', had been put off to 10 September, by which time he and Gala would have left Paris.[110] The review that he would shortly be seeing would not involve so large a number of troops, although it would still be 'grand', and would be held inside Paris, unlike the larger one, which would be at Vertus, many miles outside the city.[111] For, as Scott explained in *Paul's Letters to his Kinsfolk*,[112] whereas the regular Russian troops were 'very fine men, and under good discipline', the wilder Tartar tribes, who wore little more than 'cloaks of sheep-skin, bows and arrows, and shields made of dried hides ... were judiciously kept at a distance from Paris, where the splendour and wealth of the shops formed rather too strong temptations for Tartar morality'. Scott had seen 'one man who had come with his tribe from near to the Great Wall of China, to fight against the French under the walls of Paris! The poor fellow was in the hospital from a very natural cause, the injury which his feet had sustained in so long a march'.

Scott had also walked past a sentinel near a spot held by the Prussian troops, who had provided him with a fresh insight into his long-standing interest in gypsies, which he was to follow up in *Quentin Durward*.[113] For he had happened to be in the company of a British officer, who had been smoking a cigar when they had walked past the sentinel. The officer, in compliance with a general regulation, had been about to take the cigar out of his mouth on approaching the sentinel, but the latter had astonished both Scott and the officer by exclaiming to them in German: 'Smoke away; may the Prussian service be damned!' On looking at the sentinel more closely, they had found him to be a true gypsy of the indolent, undisciplined, vagrant type known in France as 'Bohemian' from the belief that his tribe had originally wandered into Western Europe from Bohemia. The sentinel had taken that method of expressing his dislike of the duty imposed on him, even at the risk of incurring the punishment of a severe lashing. It was this type of Bohemian that Scott was to create as a treacherous character in the service of King Louis XI in *Quentin Durward*,[114] complete with a knowledge and practice of palmistry at a time of widespread belief in astrology and occult sciences. For *Quentin Durward* was to be set in France and Flanders in the late Middle Ages, precisely when the first great migrations of gypsies had taken place into Western Europe from the Balkans and the neighbouring countries bordering the Danube.

Although Scott did not give the name of the British officer with whom he had encountered the German-speaking gypsy, he might well have been Sir John Malcolm, who himself made two or three references to Scott in his journal as an occasional companion in his sight-seeing of Paris. In one of the references he represented himself and Scott as having paid a call on François Gérard, the fashionable painter, accompanied by one Mackenzie, whom Malcolm described as having 'long been a public character in this country',[115] possibly as a diplomat. Although they had found Gérard unwell, his wife had shown them his studio, which contained 'pictures of all the great men of the day', including a portrait of Wellington. (Lady Shelley had called specially to see it before Scott and Malcolm.[116]) Although Gérard's likenesses were good, and although Scott had seemed so keen at Wellington's ball to see Gérard's portrait of Napoleon, he appears to have agreed with Malcolm that, on the whole, Gérard ranked well below the Old Masters.[117]

As for the 'great ball' at the British Embassy, it went off without mishap. All the sovereigns, generals, statesmen, diplomats, and ministers whom Scott had seen at Wellington's ball were there, with the addition of the Emperor of Russia and a large entourage of the Emperor of Austria's Hungarian guards, set off by their white uniforms. Scott judged them to be 'unquestionably, in point of exterior appearance, the handsomest of the Allied troops'. As their emperor's hotel in the Place de la Madeleine lay near Scott's lodging, he and Gala had sometimes walked to it to hear the celebrated military band that played in front of it every morning.[118]

Scott again met Colonel Stanhope and Lady Shelley at the embassy ball, which she described as 'charming' in her journal, thanks not only to the company but to the dancing, particularly the waltzing at a time when a 'mania' for it was seizing polite society after its introduction from Germany into France at the end of the eighteenth century, and into England a couple of years before Scott's visit to Paris.[119] Although Scott himself, in his juvenile years, had not allowed his lameness to stop him from dancing in the grand, newly built Assembly Rooms at Edinburgh,[120] there is nothing to show if he still kept up the practice, and if he danced in the British Embassy. He certainly took pride that, as he was himself to put it, 'my early lameness considered, it was impossible for a man labouring under a bodily impediment to have been stronger or more active than I have been'.[121] (By 'early lameness' he meant that his disability had started at the age of eighteen months, following an attack of poliomyelitis.)

Whereas it had scarcely been possible to dance at Wellington's ball owing to the crowded rooms in the Hôtel de la Reynière, there was no space problem at the British Embassy, as it was larger. Wellington had bought it only the year before for the British government. Situated in the Rue de Faubourg St Honoré, it was—and still is—one of the historic stately homes of Paris. It had formerly been the palace of Princess Pauline Borghese, Napoleon's sister, as Scott himself explained towards the end of *Paul's Letters to his Kinsfolk*,[122] where he also gratefully acknowledged—even if in somewhat stilted diction—'the extended hospitality of the Duke of Wellington and of Lord and Lady Castlereagh, [which] has afforded rallying points to the numerous English strangers who have an opportunity of meeting, in their parties, with almost all the owners of those distinguished names, which for three years past have filled the trumpet of fame'.

The latest of these 'English strangers' in Paris to be welcomed by Lady Castlereagh to the British Embassy and to 'add much to the comfort' of Scott's society, to the extent of making him spend the greater part of his remaining time in Paris with herself and her two daughters, was Lady Alvanley, the widow of a Chief Justice and Tory politician. Although considerably older than Scott, who, like Wellington, was fond of female society, Lady Alvanley was a woman after his heart, for she was well-born, highly bred, and well-informed, but without affectation, pretentiousness, or pedantry.[123] She shared Scott's love of the theatre and literature, and had travelled widely and mixed freely in society.

Moreover, Scott had reason to be grateful to her, which explains why, in announcing her arrival at Paris in his latest letter to his wife, he referred to her as 'our friend Lady Alvanley'. For she had befriended Scott and his wife many years before, on their first visit to London from Scotland, shortly after their marriage, when—to quote Scott's own words—'we were then unknown to the world and she in the first rank—things not to be forgotten by honest minds'.[124] Since then Scott had corresponded with her from time to time, and had had the pleasure of meeting her again once or twice, together with her two daughters, the Misses Arden, at Rokeby Park, the Yorkshire mansion of their much-esteemed common friend, John Morritt. Lady Alvanley, for her part, had followed with warm interest Scott's rapid rise to fame as a poet since his first meeting with her. Her daughters shared her artistic interests, particularly painting and music.[125]

Lady Alvanley appears to have known Lady Castlereagh well, so that she was invited not only to the 'great ball' but also to the small supper parties that Scott had been attending at the British Embassy before her arrival. At one of them he had also met Lord Brooke,[126] whose ancestors included Robert Greville, the 2nd Baron Brooke, whom Scott had branded as 'fanatic Brook [sic]' in Marmion.[127] For he was the parliamentary general in the Civil War in England between the Royalists and Roundheads. His troops had stormed Lichfield Cathedral, one of whose royalist defenders had shot him dead. Accordingly Scott, at the conclusion of Marmion, had represented its hero, Lord Marmion, as having been buried in Lichfield Cathedral in a handsome tomb in the style of a knight of chivalry after his slaughter in the battle of Flodden in Scotland. But the troops of 'fanatic Brook' had desecrated the tomb exactly as the republican mobs of Paris had vandalised the graves of the Bourbon kings and their royalist followers in the French Revolution.

The Lord Brooke whom Scott met at the British Embassy was the son and heir of the 2nd Earl of Warwick, who owned Warwick Castle. Although Scott was afterwards represented by Lockhart[128] as having already seen Warwick Castle, there is no evidence that he had done so. He had indeed met Lord Brooke before, but not at Warwick Castle. They had both been the guests of Scott's early patrons, Lord and Lady Abercorn, at an Easter party in 1807 at Stanmore outside London; and as on that occasion Scott had written to his wife that he had met 'our old freind [sic] Lord Brooke',[129] it would appear that they had been introduced to him on their first visit to London, possibly by Lady Alvanley. But they had then gone nowhere near Warwick Castle. On the other hand, Scott had repeatedly read and heard of it as perhaps the most splendid and best-preserved specimen of the feudal castles the like of which he had not seen in the landscape of Picardy on the way to Paris.[130] Moreover, Warwick Castle was inextricably associated in his mind with Guy of Warwick, the reputed ancestor of Lord Brooke, whose legendary exploits in England, Germany, and Turkey during the

Crusades had been the theme of ballads and romances in English and French mediaeval literature.[131] Even Chaucer had referred to one of the versions of *Guy of Warwick* in *The Canterbury Tales*.[132]

Shortly after meeting Lord Brooke, Scott, who excelled in relating ghost stories, happened to be in the company of Lord Castlereagh and Colonel Stanhope, both of whom surprised him by attesting to 'supernatural appearances in their own evidence',[133] meaning that they believed in ghosts on evidence drawn from their own experience. Admittedly, at that time both Ireland, where Castlereagh had been born and bred, and Scotland, where Stanhope had lived for some time as a relation of the Earl of Haddington, were breeding grounds of myths, legends, superstitions, 'familiar spirits', banshees, and other supernatural appearances, all of which Scott himself had extensively exploited—and was continuing to exploit—as poet, novelist, and raconteur, following the central preoccupation of the Romantic Age with tales of 'the marvellous' in verse and prose, as the supernatural was then called. But neither Lord Castlereagh nor Colonel Stanhope was a poet or novelist, even though the latter was fond of reading and reciting romantic poetry. Lord Castlereagh, in particular, was then at the zenith of his fame not only as Britain's Foreign Secretary but as a European statesman on a par with Prince Metternich of Austria and Prince Talleyrand of France. Scott himself, in fact, bearing in mind Castlereagh's important rôle in the negotiations for the Treaties of Paris and Vienna, acknowledged his European standing in *Paul's Letters to his Kinsfolk*[134] by referring to 'our minister, whose name will be read with distinction in this proud page of our annals, and to whose determined steadiness in council much of the success of 1814 is unquestionably due'. Therefore, when Castlereagh told Scott, at the supper party in the British Embassy, of having seen a ghost in early life, when he had been stationed, as a military officer, in a large desolate country house in Ireland, Scott thought the story was 'a very extraordinary narrative from the lips of a man of so much sense and steadiness of nerve'. Castlereagh, however, related the ghost story with such vivid detail and conviction that Scott continued to repeat it after his return home from Paris, when Castlereagh, having sunk so low as he had formerly risen high in reputation, cut his own throat under the great strain of public life and in a condition of unbalanced mind. Scott then recalled his story of having seen a ghost as proof that Castlereagh, however *seemingly* sensible and steady of nerve, 'had been subject to aberrations of mind, which often create such phantoms', in environments of superstition.[135] Moreover, when Stanhope, a couple of years after Castlereagh's suicide, hanged himself in a fit of depression, following his wife's death, Scott again recalled the supper party in Paris. 'It is remarkable', he wrote, that Castlereagh and Stanhope 'were the only persons of sense and credibility who had attested on supernatural appearances in their own evidence, and both died in the same melancholy manner. I shall always tremble when any friend of mine becomes visionary.'[136]

It is unlikely that it was Castlereagh or Stanhope rather than Le Chevalier or some other Parisian who engaged Scott's interest in 'the marvellous' with the information that Napoleon too was said to be haunted by 'a familiar spirit' or supernatural apparition called '*l'Homme Rouge, or the red man*',[137] exactly like 'the grey spectre' that Scott had created in *Waverley*[138] for the superstitious Highland chieftain called Fergus Mac-Ivor. This *Homme Rouge* was said to have advised Napoleon 'in matters of importance', so that he had first appeared to him at Vilna to warn him against invading Russia. Afterwards, 'the visit of *l'Homme Rouge*' had been repeated—again as a warning—before the battle of Waterloo[139]—exactly like the appearance of 'the grey spectre' to Fergus Mac-Ivor on the eve of the battle that was to lead to his capture and execution outside Carlisle. Before *Waverley*, Scott had employed 'the fatal Banshee's boding scream' in *The Lady of the Lake*[140] for the same ominous purpose; and he was to repeat precisely that technique in *Peveril of the Peak*, part of which was to be set in the Isle of Man at a time of widespread superstitious belief. Accordingly Scott was to weave into the hero's mind, at the crisis point of his life, intimations of 'a Banshie, or female spirit who was wont to shriek, "foreboding evil times"'.[141] These and other instances accounted for the close attention that Scott had shown in the Louvre to Salvator Rosa's painting of *The Witch of Endor*,[142] the woman with 'a familiar spirit', consulted by the prophet Saul in a crisis.

Scott incorporated 'the legend' of Napoleon and *l'Homme Rouge* into *Paul's Letters to his Kinsfolk* with a view to showing that, 'if the French have no strong sense of religion or its precepts, [following the Revolution], they are not without a share of superstition'.[143] Napoleon himself, Scott was to allege, 'affected to despise superstition, [but] had a share of it in his own bosom', for it was well known that he had 'strange and visionary ideas on his own fated destiny', on which Scott was afterwards repeatedly to dwell in the *Life of Buonaparte*.[144] Indeed he was to represent Napoleon as 'confiding in his stars' even in his [Scott's] review of canto three of *Childe Harold's Pilgrimage* in the *Quarterly Review*.[145]

Napoleon shared this superstitious trait with other military leaders, of whom perhaps the best known to Scott's generation was the Austrian general, Albrecht Wallenstein, following Schiller's popularisation of him on the stage in his great historical trilogy. Schiller's *Wallenstein* had been translated into English by Samuel Taylor Coleridge, whose reputation at the time of Scott's visit to Paris was largely based on a handful of poems, notably *The Ancient Mariner*, perhaps the greatest ballad of 'the marvellous' in English poetry. Scott had already drawn on Coleridge's translation of Schiller's *Wallenstein* (1799–80) for *Guy Mannering* precisely because that novel's sub-title was *The Astrologer*, so that its plot largely hinged on a prophecy of an infant's destiny, based on a reading of the stars at its birth. Scott had cited an exquisitely beautiful passage from Coleridge's *Wallenstein* at the opening of *Guy Mannering*[146] in the act of launching the crucial prophecy of his plot, with particular reference to 'the influence ascribed to them [the stars] by superstition on human events'. As Schiller's drama of Wallenstein's life, with its emphasis on his 'strange and visionary ideas on his own fated destiny', which had precipitated his extraordinary rise and fall, 'seemed almost to trace the career of Napoleon', Scott again drew on Coleridge's translation to round off his remarks in *Paul's Letters to his Kinsfolk*[147] on Napoleon's alleged superstition.

Scott's 'man of destiny' was, of course, Wellington, who was in the *cortège* of the Allied monarchs on 31 August 1815, when they took their station in the splendid octagon of the Place Louis Quinze (nowadays the Place de la Concorde) for the long-awaited Russian review. Scott had set out with Gala for it from their hotel at an early hour, so that they succeeded in securing a stand immediately opposite the Allied sovereigns. The area where they stood was guarded by tall, handsome Cossacks in red jackets and blue trousers, armed with lances. On one side were the gardens of the Tuileries with the range of the royal palace; on the other, the broad avenue of the Champs Élysées, whence, at the appointed hour, Wellington, dressed in the scarlet uniform of a field marshal, and adorned with many decorations, notably the blue ribbon of the highest order of Russia, had been recognised by Scott trotting quickly to the reviewing stand. Immediately raising his hat and stout staff, Scott had given his hero a hearty cheer.[148] Wellington rode his famous chestnut horse, 'Copenhagen', which was the charger that had carried him through the battles in Spain, France, and Flanders.[149] Scott had left his own handsome, white charger called 'Daisy' at Abbotsford in the utterly dependable care of his beloved forester, Tom Purdie. High-spirited and 'with such a mane as Rubens delighted to paint',[150] 'Daisy' was Scott's last survivor of the troopers he had ridden as a volunteer in the Edinburgh cavalry militia during the war.

Scott observed Colonel James Stanhope among the numerous staff officers and generals in attendance on Wellington and the Allied sovereigns. Behind King Friedrich of Prussia stood Blücher, flanked by his adie-de-camp, Count von Nostitz, who had saved his old chief's life in an incident which Scott worked up dramatically into his narrative of the events preceding the battle of Waterloo in *Paul's Letters to his Kinsfolk*[151] as an outstanding 'feat of personal strength and valour'. For Blücher's horse had been shot under him at the battle of Ligny, and the French cavalry had ridden over him as he had lain on the ground. But his aide-de-camp had thrown himself down 'beside his general to share his fate; and the first use which the Prince Marshal [Blücher] made of his recovered recollection was to conjure his faithful attendant rather to shoot him than to permit him to fall alive into the hands of the French'.

The place where Blücher and his aide-de-camp, and all the other personages stood waiting for the Russian review to start, called up the usual intense historical associations in Scott's mind. For it was the very spot where Louis XVI had been publicly beheaded by the same guillotine that James Simpson had lately discovered lying on the ground in a sort of coach-house.[152] Louis' only attendant then had been his confessor, the Abbé Edgeworth, who, as Scott afterwards took care to explain in the *Life of Buonaparte*,[153] was an ancestor of his friend, Maria Edgeworth, the novelist, whose tales of Irish life had inspired his own 'Scottish tales', *alias* the Waverly Novels.[154] The octagon where Scott stood had originally been constructed to the memory of Louis' grandfather. Above the superb row of buildings behind Scott rose 'the bronze column erected by Napoleon to commemorate his victories over Russia, Prussia, and Austria, whose princes were now reviewing their victorious armies in what was so lately his capital'.[155]

For more than 2 hours the Russian troops, numbering between 15,000 and 20,000 men, defiled before the monarchs and the Duke of Wellington without a pause, in close column and with fixed bayonet, led by band after band, until the entire breadth of the avenue was filled with regiments of infantry, artillery, and cavalry. The rays of the morning sun struck the arms of the troops, including the burnished steel breastplates of the cuirassiers, with great brilliancy, so that the broad walk looked like 'a glowing furnace' to Scott, whose poetic imagery was fully drawn out by the grand spectacle, on the evidence of the description that he afterwards wrote of it, first to Joanna Baillie,[156] and then, more fully, in *Paul's Letters to his Kinsfolk*.[157] In both accounts he repeated the observation he had made to Gala, as they had walked back to their hotel after the troops had dispersed in different directions, that the spectacle, 'however magnificent for us', had drawn fewer than 'a hundred Frenchmen, and those of the very lowest order', out of so populous a city as Paris: 'This is the strongest sign of their feeling their present state of humiliation, and proves that the iron has entered into their soul'. It was 'sad indeed for *la gloire nationale*'.[158]

Scott followed up the historical associations of the Place Louis Quinze almost immediately after the review by going with Gala to see the mediaeval building known as the Temple, in the tower of which Louis XVI and his royal family had been imprisoned in conditions of barbaric cruelty until his execution. There he had been attended by his faithful *valet-de-chambre*, Cléry, who, after his execution, had published *Journal de la Captivité de Louis XVI à la Tour du Temple* (1798), which had been read all over Europe, including Scotland, and had had the effect of fixing in the hearts and minds of people throughout the continent the image of Louis XVI as the saintly, noble, martyred king.[159] Scott had read Cléry's *Journal*, and was to make it his principal source for his own chapter about Louis' imprisonment in the Temple in the *Life of Buonaparte*.[160] 'In the dungeon of the Temple', he was to write, for instance, 'misfortune threw around him [Louis] the glories of a martyr.' In the same chapter Scott was also to state that 'Clery [*sic*] we have seen and known, and the form and manners of that model of pristine faith and loyalty can never be forgotten'.[161] Scott did not explain, however, if he had seen and been presented to Cléry on

The Great Tower of the Temple in Paris. From an old engraving

his first or second visit to Paris, or perhaps, much earlier, in Edinburgh among the *émigrés*. He merely added that 'gentlemanlike and complaisant in his manners, his deep gravity and melancholy features announced that the sadness in which he had taken a part so honourable, were never for a moment out of his memory'.

The prison itself had been demolished by Napoleon several years before Scott and Gala went to see it, but they were shown the garden of a private house on which the square-shaped tower had stood, together with a plan of its four storeys. In the house was a model of the prison, complete with an inside view of the apartments, including the closet that Cléry had occupied, off King Louis' room.[162] Several figures represented the royal family, including the Princess Royal, the Duchess of Angoulême, whom Scott and Gala had seen in the Tuileries on Louis XVIII's birthday. She had been imprisoned in the Temple for three years, during which she had softened by every possible attention the severity of her parents' captivity. The Parisians now called her 'Antigone' in allusion to her sorrows and her piety. Her appeal to the imagination and sensibility of contemporary English poets, who shared Scott's Tory and royalist sympathies, had crystallised in an 'Ode to the Duchess of Angoulême' by a young Irish poet called Aubrey de Vere.[163] Scott had read it at Abbotsford on the eve of his departure for Brussels and Paris, and had judged it 'very good indeed', so that he had inquired about its author.[164] He himself conceived the Duchess of Angoulême as a latter-day specimen of the female warriors who used to accompany their husbands to the wars in the age of chivalry, and of whom Scott was to provide an example in *Count Robert of Paris* in the person of the Amazonian Brenhilda. For the Duchess of Angoulême had thrown herself, together with her husband, into the royalist stronghold of Bordeaux, following Napoleon's escape to France from Elba, and had heroically attempted to prevent its garrison from defecting to Bonaparte.[165]

As for the old, handsome house, where Scott and Gala were shown the model of the tower, where the Duchess of Angoulême had been imprisoned, it was marked off by one of the paved courts of Paris that Scott had observed on his first call at Wellington's headquarters. It led to the very rooms where Louis XVI and the royal family had first been lodged before their transfer to the tower. In these rooms Louis had been violently examined before his trial while the enraged mob had shouted insults from the court outside.[166]

Scott's guide provided him with further confirmation of Napoleon's proneness to superstition when he told him and Gala that Napoleon had demolished the prison house 'from a certain ominous feeling, that he himself might one day share the fate of the unfortunate Louis and become its inhabitant'. This precaution seemed to Scott not imprudent: 'It at least prevented, as I think, the possibility of anyone taking a fancy to make good the presentiment'.[167]

It was impossible for Scott to forget that an 'inhabitant' of the Temple, a few years before its demolition, was the British hero, Admiral Sir Sidney Smith, who had made a sensational escape from the tower by 'a daring strategem' in collaboration with a French royalist officer. The strategem, which Scott afterwards recalled in the *Life of Buonaparte*,[168] had also involved Smith in a secret telegraphic communication with a royalist lady, who had appeared at a window of a house adjoining the tower, which it was the guide's practice to point out to visitors in Paris, including James Simpson.[169] Sir Sidney himself had recently retired from the navy, and at the time of Scott's visit he was in Paris in the train of the British army from Waterloo;[170] but Scott, surprisingly, made no mention of him in his Paris letters, so that the conclusion must be that he missed him. Otherwise he would undoubtedly have mentioned him, bearing in mind that Scott admired him so much that, after his [Smith's] celebrated defence of Acre in Syria a couple of years after his escape from the Temple, Scott had put him on his list of heroes in one of the Introductions to the cantos of *Marmion*.[171] Indeed Scott had asked a Scottish genealogist if he knew 'anything of the descent of the mother of the Knight of Acre'.[172] For nothing would have pleased Scott more than to have linked Smith's 'descent to the Doughty Douglasses', perhaps the most renowned family of warriors in Scotland.

Scott was, of course, aware that the Temple had originally derived its name from the celebrated Knights of the Temple,[173] who had belonged to the richest and most powerful order of chivalry in the Middle Ages. In fact, the old house with the garden, on which the tower had stood, had originally belonged to the Grand Master of the Knights of the Temple.[174] Scott, therefore, found himself in the heart of what had been a state within a state, for the Knight Templars had owned property, privileges, and immunities all over Europe, including Scotland, and this district of Paris had been their headquarters. Scott was indebted to Froissart for his earliest knowledge of the Temple. His poetry included several English and Scottish Knight Templars, and he was to create many more in the Waverley Novels, notably the Grand Master of the Templars in *The Talisman* (1825), and the fiercest of all Templars, Sir Brian de Bois-Guilbert, in *Ivanhoe*.

As the Temple lay near the Bastille, Scott and Gala paid a second visit to the Place de la Bastille in order to see the model of a colossal elephant, which Napoleon had intended to cast in bronze and to serve as a fountain discharging enough water, through the elephant's trunk into a cistern, for all that quarter of Paris. They found the model exactly in size and figure what the bronze had been intended to be, and standing at the enormous height of 60 feet. Both Scott and Gala looked upon 'this gigantic grotesque' as another example of the French obsession with '*la gloire nationale*', in that, at a time of national poverty and distress, the new government of Louis XVIII had not yet 'ventured to avow' that they meant 'to dispense with erecting a monument, which, after being accomplished at enormous expence [*sic*], must appear *bizarre* and fanciful, rather than grand and impressive'.[175] On the other hand, Scott gave Louis XVIII's government credit for 'reclaiming for the Bourbons those public buildings, which by inscriptions and emblems, Napoleon had consecrated to his own dynasty'. Consequently 'N's are everywhere disappearing, or undergoing a conversion into H's and R's'.[176] For Scott was doubtless perfectly aware that even the Tuileries and the Louvre had first been erected by the mediaeval and Renaissance kings, including Henri IV, admittedly on a much smaller scale than their later remodelling.

Scott's knowledge of Henri IV's achievements was largely derived from the well-known *Mémoires* of the great statesman, Maximilien Sully, which had been translated into English by Charlotte Lennox, the novelist and friend of Dr Johnson. Her translation explains the familiarity of several visitors to Paris, including Lady Shelley and James Simpson, with Sully's *Mémoires*, which Scott appears to have read in the original.[177] He was to make its form the opening subject of discussion in *Rob Roy*.[178] For that novel was to purport to be the memoirs of its hero, Frank Osbaldistone, who acquires a knowledge of Sully from a residence in France.

Sully had been responsible for planning the great system of 'rectilinear' French highways, which Scott had found to be 'magnificent' but 'unpicturesque' on his journey to Paris from Brussels.[179] His regard for Sully as a statesman 'alike distinguished for severe integrity and for strong and unerring sagacity of mind', was to be best expressed in *Quentin Durward*.[180] Sully's 'severe integrity' had made him 'feared' by Henri IV himself, according to Scott in *Woodstock*.[181] As Henri IV's chief minister, Sully had been delightfully represented on the stage in the comedy by Collé that Scott had seen at the Théâtre Français with Gala.[182] Both of them had also walked past Sully's well-preserved house in the Faubourg St Antoine, where the armed mob had risen for the storming of the Bastille.

Scott's plans for his return journey from Paris with Gala were announced to his wife on 6 September 1815, on the eve of Alexander Pringle and Robert Bruce's departure for Switzerland. He confirmed that he was cutting out 'the grand review' of 150,000 troops at Vertus, because to go there would be 'attended with much difficuly', as it would take them north, near the Belgian border, contrary to his intention of travelling by the western route via Rouen and Dieppe to Brighton and London.[183] In this way he would be seeing Normandy and its ancient capital, where William the Conqueror had died, and where several of his kingly successors and nobles of England were buried, including the great Duke of Bedford, the former Regent of France. For Normandy had belonged to the English in the late Middle Ages, as Scott was himself to explain at the opening of *Quentin Durward*.

Scott had lately seen enough 'great shows' of the kind of the forthcoming grand review, for which the troops were beginning to break up from Paris, and to move to more distant quarters, although there were still more than 100,000 men in the vicinity of Paris. They were certainly needed, as 'there is more news of conspiracies and plots here', about which, however, Scott cautioned his wife against believing the wilder reports in the English newspapers. He had lately bade farewell to Sir John Malcolm on the latter's departure for the grand review, for which the Emperors of Russia and Austria, the King of Prussia, and the Duke of Wellington were also preparing to leave Paris, the last-named in a special carriage with Sir John and Lady Shelley.[184]

Among the latest arrivals in Paris on whom Scott reported to his wife that he had been calling, was her earliest and best friend, Sophia Dumergue, who was accompanied by 'Mrs Nickie', as Scott familiarly called Sarah Nicolson, the much-trusted and respected housekeeper of the Dumergues. Although they were staying 'at a great distance, quite another quarter of the city', he had offered to be 'their Cavaliere servante in as far as I can be useful', and in return for their kind hospitality to Mrs Scott and himself on all their visits to London.[185] In fact, Scott informed his wife that he was about to dine at Doyen's, a leading restaurant, with Sophia Dumergue and Sarah Nicolson as well as with the two grown-up sons of Robert Slade, the London barrister, who, many years before, had drawn up the marriage contract of Scott and his *fiancée*, Charlotte Carpenter, when she was a ward of Lord Downshire.[186] 'I assure you,' Scott added, 'I have bespoken one of the handsomest dinners he [Doyen] can give us, as I know it will give them pleasure to be treated smartly.'

Although Scott had more news to give to his wife, he deliberately kept his letter short to ensure that it would go in Lord Castlereagh's diplomatic bag. 'I suppose my poor epistle', he wrote about it, 'will travel with all the diplomatic secrets of Europe.' He was beginning to tire to get home, particularly to be reunited with his wife and children, to whom he had unfailingly referred with tender affection in all his letters from Brussels and Paris. He, therefore, assured Mrs Scott that he would not be staying in London longer than a day or two before proceeding to Abbotsford.[187] He expected to be meeting his friend, Daniel Terry, the actor, in London, whom he had apprised of his trip to Paris shortly before his departure from Abbotsford, to which he had also referred in the same letter. For Terry, having been trained as an architect before he had turned to the theatre, had given Scott valuable advice and assistance over the design and plantations at Abbotsford. 'I can assure you,' Scott had, therefore, written to Terry, 'that Abbotsford is now looking delightful and repaying with interest the many hours' labour that you and I bestowed upon plans and execution some three years since.'[188]

In following up these discussions and collaboration with Terry over additions to Abbotsford, spread over several years, after his return home from Paris, Scott was to show Terry the plan of a book gallery and con-cealed staircase for his [Scott's] study, which apparently he was to model, according to Lockhart, on 'a favourite cabinet of Napoleon's at the Élysée Bourbon Palace,[189] where, as has already been explained, Napoleon had lodged during 'the hundred days'. Although there is nothing to show that Scott obtained access to the interior of the Élysée Bourbon Palace, which, as has also been already explained, was occupied by the Emperor of Russia at the time of his [Scott's] visit, it is certain, on the evidence of Gala's journal, that Scott bought from Monsieur Debure, the royal bookseller, 'a description of Paris, in several volumes recommended by M. Chevalier'.[190] Herein, therefore, might have been his source for his future project of imitating Napoleon's favourite cabinet in adding an *escalier dérobé* to the book gallery in his own study at Abbotsford.

Besides expecting to be meeting Terry in passing through London from Paris, Scott was also counting on seeing Byron again at the latter's house or in the same drawing-room of their common publisher, John Murray, where they had first met the previous spring. Scott had not forgotten his promise to Murray to let him have 'a highland article on my return' from Paris for the *Quarterly Review*. He also intended to discuss with Murray the proposal he had lately received in Paris from Archibald Constable, his Edinburgh publisher, and to which he had assented, namely, to raise the impression of the forthcoming editions of *The Field of Waterloo* and *Paul's Letters to his Kinsfolk*.[191] Even if Constable had not informed him, as he might well have done, that notices of the impending publication of *Paul's Letters to his Kinsfolk* had appeared the previous week in the national newspapers,[192] the need to complete his travel book as soon as possible after his return to Abbotsford was another factor weighing with him for expediting his home journey. He was counting on his travel book's topical interest and variety of subjects rather than on any appeal of personality for 'a speedy dispersion' of the first edition.[193] Much of its enduring value, however, lay in the faithful and rounded mirror it held up of Scott's personality. As Lockhart was to put it so succinctly, 'the whole man, just as he was, breathes in every line'.[194] Scott himself was to have the satisfaction of seeing the first edition of 6,000 copies 'dispersed' within three months of publication, and the entire second edition of 2,000 copies ordered before it was to issue from the press—a 'far greater success than I dreamed of'.[195]

As for his expected meeting with Byron in London, Scott was bearing in mind 'the subject of *De Montfort*',[196] that is, his intention to discuss the possible production at Drury Lane Theatre of that play of Joanna Baillie's, which he had singled out, in a note to *Rokeby* (1813), in illustration of her ability to 'display such intimate acquaintance with the operations of human passion'.[197] Her plays, in fact, had been published under the general title of *Plays on the Passions* (1798–1812). They were all marked by lyrics and songs interspersed in their narrative and dialogue, which was a practice that Scott had also extensively adopted to notable effect in his verse romances and novels.

As Scott meant to call, while in London, at the house of Joanna Baillie's friend, Sir George Beaumont, mainly to hear of her movements,[198] he wrote her the letter to which reference has already been made, and in which he recapitulated his account of the battle of Waterloo and summarised his impressions of Paris, Wellington, the Russian review, and the French political scene, adding the fresh information that he had asked Wellington if he had actually seen Bonaparte during the battle of Waterloo. 'He [Wellington] said, "No, but at one time from the repeated shouts of "Vive l'Empereur" he thought he must be near', which Scott himself could bear out from his own personal calculation at Waterloo of the comparatively short distance separating the two generals.[199] Accordingly Scott not only bore this episode in mind for incorporation into *Paul's Letters to his Kinsfolk*[200] but transmuted it into a brilliantly imaginative piece of creative writing.

The continued hold of the battle of Waterloo on Scott's mind was reflected in 'the wild and imaginative poem' that he had begun to write shortly before his departure from Paris. He recited the first part of it to Gala while they were waiting for Lady Alvanley and her daughters to join them and other tourists for an excursion to the celebrated châteaux of Malmaison and St Cloud.[201] Scott completed the poem shortly after his return home and represented it as an off-shoot of *The Field of Waterloo*.[202] He gave it the title of 'The Dance of Death' (1815), because it consisted of a vision by a brave Highland soldier of 'strange phantoms', resembling the witches in *Macbeth*, who sing 'a ghastly roundelay' of the impending slaughter at Waterloo, including that of Gray Allen himself, as the Highland soldier was named. Scott echoed the very words of the witches in a later reference to the poem as 'a hurly-burly sort of performance'.[203] It was another exercise by him in 'the marvellous', which he followed up even at Malmaison, although in a very different way and entirely without the weird Gothic details of the poem. For Malmaison had been the favourite residence of the Empress Josephine, Napoleon's first wife, who had been born a creole at Martinique, one of the French West Indian colonies. Shortly after her birth a negro soothsayer had predicted that Josephine 'would rise to a dignity greater than that of a queen, yet fall from it before her death', and that 'she would die in a hospital'.[204] The prediction was another instance of the prophecy *motif* that Scott had made the fulcrum on which the plot of *Guy Mannering* turned. (He was to employ the same *motif* for the plots of *The Bride of Lammermoor* and *A Legend of Montrose*.) In Josephine's case, the soothsayer's prediction seemed to Scott to be 'one of those vague auguries delivered at birth by fools or impostors which the caprice of Fortune sometimes matches with a corresponding and conforming event'.[205] For Josephine, having risen to the dignity of empress as Napoleon's consort, had suffered the mortification of having been divorced by him after having failed to give him the son that his dynastic ambitions had required. Moreover, she had died at Malmaison only the year before Scott's excursion to it, that is, in 1814, shortly after Napoleon's first abdication; and 'her house, as the name *Mal-maison* implies, had once been a hospital'.[206]

Josephine herself had apparently related the soothsayer's prophecy many times and had added to its details as she had grown older, which explained its existence in several versions. Scott, for his part, claimed

The Empress Josephine at Malmaison by Pierre Paul Prud'hon. (Louvre)

that he could himself vouch for its existence before the events which the prophecy was supposed to predict, 'for it was told me many years ago, when Buonaparte was only general of the army of Italy, by a lady of rank who lived in the same convent with Josephine'.[207]

Scott held it to be in keeping with Napoleon's alleged proneness to superstition that he had originally been extremely reluctant to divorce Josephine, despite pressure to do so from his counsellors, because of his belief that there was attached to his union with her 'a spell' affecting his 'strange and visionary ideas about his own fated destiny'. At the same time Scott did not doubt that Josephine had 'deserved to be beloved' by Napoleon, however notoriously imprudent she might have been over expenditure on dress and jewellery.[208] In other words, Scott shared the general respect for her evinced by contemporary English travellers to Paris, which arose not only from 'the great taste' with which they found that Josephine had embellished the grounds and interior decoration of her charming château but from the high regard in which the memory of her amiable character was held by everyone in the neighbourhood of Malmaison.[209] The same excellent taste had first been on display to Scott and his fellow-travellers at Brussels, when they had visited the royal château of Lacken. Naturally it was even more to her credit in their eyes that she had laid out the grounds both at Lacken and Malmaison in 'the English fashion', and not in the long, straight lines favoured by the rival Dutch fashion.[210]

Bearing in mind Scott and Gala's recent visit to the excellent private collection of the hospitable Baron Denon as well as their esteem for Canova's statues, it was particularly fascinating to them to find on show at Malmaison, as specimens of Josephine's taste, a fine bust of Denon by Canova together with the celebrated statue of Hebe as a dancing nymph by the same artist.[211] Scott was so struck by this statue that he was to evoke it in *The Heart of Midlothian*[212] as the best means he could possibly think of to convey an idea of the sheer beauty of Effie Deans's countenance. His impulse, under the immediate impact of the statue, was to claim that it 'might have been placed beside any of the Grecian monuments in the Halls of Sculpture [at the Louvre], without suffering much disparagement'.[213]

The 'Grecian monuments' at the Louvre that Scott had particularly in mind were, besides the *Apollo Belvedere*, the invaluable antique sculptures that had been excavated in Italy in the eighteenth century only a few years before Scott's birth, following the discovery of Pompeii and Herculaneum. Many of these sculptures, representing some of the best surviving Greek statues, had been added to the great Borghese art collection, which had been bought by Napoleon for the Louvre from Prince Camillo Borghese, the second husband of Napoleon's sister, Pauline. This circumstance was the reason why Scott singled out 'the Borghese pictures' in *Paul's Letters to his Kinsfolk*[214] as having been 'honestly bought and paid for by Buonaparte'. In actual fact, Camillo Borghese had been induced, or obliged, by Napoleon to sell his great collection to him, and at the time of Scott's visit to Paris Borghese was endeavouring to recover it, which explains why part of it is nowadays in the splendid Borghese Gallery in Rome, while the unrecovered part is among the prized treasures of the Louvre.

Scott coupled 'the Borghese pictures' with the 'fine paintings' that he and Gala saw at Malmaison, which belonged predominantly to his favourite Italian school. Malmaison itself had an added historical association of interest to Scott, in that Napoleon, on fleeing to Paris from Waterloo, had spent much of his time in Josephine's former residence. In fact, he had passed his last night there[215] before leaving Paris for ever in the hope of escaping to America from Rochefort, instead of which he had been intercepted by the Royal Navy, taken prisoner, and exiled to St Helena under the charge of Admiral Sir George Cockburn, who was afterwards to make his own despatches and journal available to Scott[216] for the *Life of Buonaparte*.[217]

Scott was perfectly aware that, for all Malmaison's hold on Josephine's affections, it was St Cloud that had been Napoleon's favourite residence, commanding as it did 'unrivalled views' of Paris, including the magnificent park called Bois de Boulogne. Moreover, St Cloud's historical associations were such as to draw a great influx of visitors daily to its château. For the *coup d'état* that had first brought Napoleon to power by his overthrow of the Directory in 1799, had taken place at St Cloud,[218] which had also been chosen by him as the scene for the celebration of his marriage to Marie Louise of Austria, following his divorce from Josephine. Above all, the signing of the capitulation of Paris to the Allies, following Napoleon's defeat at Waterloo, had taken place at St Cloud only a few weeks before Scott's visit to its château.[219]

It was, therefore, with high expectations that Scott's party, including Lady Alvanley and her daughters, drove to St Cloud from Malmaison on a splendid summer afternoon. They were not disappointed, so much so that the beauty of the view from the terrace of the château, lighted up by a rich sunset, and followed by melodious singing by one of Lady Alvanley's daughters, in sight of a grand fountain pouring down numberless streams in cascades, drew out the romantic poet in Scott. Accordingly, on returning to his hotel with Gala at a late hour, he composed a fine lyric, called 'St Cloud',[220] infused with delicate sentiment and evocative imagery. Even the distant drums and bugles, that he loved to hear at close of day in picturesque or historic environs,[221] had not been wanting on this excursion, as Prussian and British troops were encamped in the Bois de Boulogne.[222] The excursion had evoked for Scott not so much the *fêtes champêtres* of Watteau as the garden scenes of Tasso and Ariosto, his earliest and best-loved masters of chivalry and romance. (Byron was to dub him 'the Ariosto of the North' in *Childe Harold's Pilgrimage*.[223]) Several years later, when Scott himself created a garden scene in *Kenilworth*,[224] he appears to have drawn for it partly on his own recollections of the atmosphere and fountain of St Cloud and partly on his reading about Italian art as interpreted by Tasso and Ariosto.

Scott sent a copy of his lyric to Lady Alvanley and her daughters, in token, as he acknowledged to Gala, of 'the gratification he had received from the society of these and other distinguished friends' on his various excusions.[225] Then he called with his fellow-traveller at the British Embassy for their passports the day before they left Paris. In the evening they attended their last assembly at the embassy, which Lord and Lady Castlereagh gave for the leading members of the diplomatic corps. The guests also included Canova, although Scott and Gala do not seem to have been presented to him.[226] There is nothing to show, therefore, if they heard that Castlereagh was arranging for Canova to go to England to give his opinion on the Elgin Marbles, following their removal to London by Lord Elgin from Athens. On the other hand, Scott and Gala could not but have read in the English newspapers of the heated public controversy that was going on over the artistic importance of the Elgin Marbles. Some of their detractors were representing them as junk, whereas the majority of art critics and connoisseurs were holding them to be priceless treasures. Canova, for his part, was to pronounce them 'the works of the ablest artists the world has seen'. Accordingly the British government was to purchase them from Lord Elgin for the nation and house them in the British Museum.

At Lady Castlereagh's assembly Scott saw Lady Shelley for the last time in Paris. She turned up late at the embassy from the Théâtre Français, where Mlle Mars 'acted superbly'. Lord Castlereagh, with his tall, handsome figure and animated conversation, seemed to Gala to stand out for 'elegance and dignity of deportment'. Scott too considered his appearance to have 'all the grace of the Seymours', from whom he was descended.[227] His private secretary, who had been forwarding Scott's letters home in Castlereagh's diplomatic bag, was called Joseph Planta. He was a young diplomat, whose father, of Swiss origin, was the principal librarian of the British Museum. Before the assembly Planta admitted Scott and Gala to the private apartments of the embassy, which had originally been sumptuously furnished by Princess Pauline Borghese as its former occupier. Thus they had an opportunity of forming an idea of the taste that had prevailed during the imperial reign of Napoleon, when he had attempted to revive the courtly splendours of the *ancien régime*, complete with a newly created nobility. Although Gala pronounced the taste to be 'on the whole, favourable', he could not deny that the green velvet, gold embroidery, pier glasses, enamalled clocks, and other glittering *objets d'arts* in the apartments 'displayed that love of shew and extravagance in which the grandees of the Emperor's court endeavoured to outshine each other'.[228]

Scott himself left no specific record of his own opinion of the taste represented by these apartments, but he had already expressed himself in much the same ambivalent terms as Gala regarding the worldly grandeur represented by Paris. The odd 'mixture of real taste and genius, with so much frippery and affectation', that had earlier been responsible for his forecast that 'I shall probably leave the capital of France without being able to determine which train of ideas it has most frequently excited in my mind', remained a dominant impression with him well after his departure from Paris. Thus, while the supreme happiness he had felt at seeing such spectacular scenes of Paris under Allied occupation, at meeting Wellington and the heroes of Waterloo, and at experiencing such a wealth of historical associations, remained as fresh and vivid in his memory as the most dearly cherished recollections of his early youth, the image of Paris as 'a Vanity-fair' on account of its 'worldly grandeur and display' seemed to take increasing hold of his mind. Accordingly, when he was to hear, a year later, from Joanna Baillie that she too intended to make the pilgrimage to Waterloo and go on from there to Paris, he was to write to her that 'Paris I am not anxious to see again but I trust you will see it once. There is more of good and bad in it than any where else in the world. I do not mean *moral* good of which there is rather a paucity but worldly grandeur and display. It is a Vanity-fair'.[229]

Both Scott and Joanna Baillie belonged, of course, to the generation for whom Bunyan's *Pilgrim's Progress* (1678–84), with which the idea and image of 'a Vanity-fair' were inextricably connected, had been a standard Sunday reading book in early life. Not surprisingly, therefore, he was specifically to evoke Bunyan's Christiana in *The Heart of Midlothian*[230] as analogous to his heroine, Jeanie Deans, who is morally the most heroic of all his female characters. His idea of 'the wasting effects of luxury and vanity' was to be best expressed in the *Life of Buonaparte*,[231] in his introductory analysis of French society on the eve of the outbreak of the French Revolution. In it he was to allege that 'luxury and vanity had totally ruined a great part of the French nobility', so that they had presented 'a melancholy contrast to their predecessors' of the age of chivalry, and even, much less remotely, of the age of 'the Great Condé', when 'the nobles of France, with their retainers, actually formed the army of the kingdom'.

The public place that seemed to qualify more than any other in Paris for the epithet of 'a Vanity-fair', on the score of its shops of jewellery and fashions, was the Palais Royal.[232] It was precisely to it that Scott, following the lead of most of the foreign visitors, resorted on his last day in Paris for the silk shawls, jewellery, and 'little trinkets' that he meant to take home with him for his mother, wife, daughters, and their governess. He was accompanied by Sophia Dumergue and Sarah Nicolson, who helped him to choose the silk presents, after Lady Alvanley had promised to smuggle a lace veil for Mrs Scott through customs in England.[233] Sophia also appears to have introduced him to the family of the famous French watchmaker, Abraham Louis Briquet,[234] before he called with her on the old French royalist general, Louis Armand, and his wife, to whom the

Dumergues had been 'uncommonly friendly' at their Piccadilly home in London during the Armands' exile from France. General Armand was a newly created peer of France with the title of Duc de Sérent. Scott found him and his wife comfortably installed in an elegant hotel, although he afterwards reported to Mrs Scott that the Duchess of Sérent had not fully reciprocated the hospitatility that she and her husband had received from the Dumergues in London.[235]

Scott urged 'our Piccadilly friends', as he and Mrs Scott familiarly called the Dumergues and Sarah Nicolson, not to remain in Paris after the French had begun to murder English and Prussian officers and soldiers, although only at night and in disreputable places such as the gambling dens and brothels of the Palais Royal. In view of these murders Scott considered that he and Gala left Paris in time, after they had employed part of their last day in farewell visits, notably 'to our friend M. Chevalier, of whom we took leave with much gratitude for the kindness he had shown during our stay'. Scott also made sure that he would not be returning without a present for his beloved forester, Tom Purdie, and other domestics. He had, therefore, bought Purdie 'the very thing for him', namely, a snuff-box, which Gala (who had accompanied Scott to a tobacconist's for it) described as 'then much in fashion—representing the cross-cut of a small tree, in which the veins and knots were carefully imitated'.[236] This snuff-box was to give rise to one of the most charming anecdotes in Washington Irving's description of his first visit to Scott at Abbotsford two years after Scott's departure from Paris. The anecdote was to be effectively condensed by Lockhart in the *Life of Scott*,[237] whence it is well worth extracting for insertion in this narrative not only for its own sake but in illustration of the point already made about the excellent rapport that Scott was to establish between himself and his dependants. Lockhart's version reads as follows:

> When the amiable American visited Scott, he walked with him to a quarry, where his people were at work. 'The face of the humblest dependant,' he says, 'brightened at his approach—all paused from their labour to have a pleasant "crack wi' the laird". Among the rest was a tall straight old fellow, with a healthful complexion and silver hairs, and a small round-crowned hat. He had been about to shoulder a hod, but paused and stood looking at Scott with a slight sparkling of his blue eyes as if waiting his turn; for the old fellow knew he was a favourite. Scott accosted him in an affable tone, and asked for a pinch of snuff. The old man drew forth a horn snuff-box. "Hoot man," said Scott, "not that old mull. Where's the bonnie French one that I brought you from Paris?"—"Troth, your honour," replied the old fellow, "sic a mull as that is nae for week-days." On leaving the quarry, Scott informed me that, when absent at Paris, he had purchased several trifling articles as presents for his dependants, and, among others, the gay snuff-box in question, which was so carefully reserved for Sundays by the veteran. "It was not so much the value of the gifts," said he, "that pleased them, as the idea that the laird should think of them when so far away."'

CHAPTER V

Return Journey to Abbotsford

Scott's departure from Paris with Gala took place on 9 September 1815, when they rose at daybreak for the purpose of reaching Rouen that night on the way to Dieppe. Although their hotel attendant first provoked their anger at failing to secure horses for them at the appointed hour, which made it necessary for them to stop at Louviers before Rouen, the fineness of the day and the beauty of their drive restored their equanimity.[1] They passed through Marly and St Germain, which, being situated on the summit of a hill overlooking the Seine and one of the most extensive forests of France, almost rivalled St Cloud for its views. More significantly for Scott as a newly established Jacobite novelist, following the publication of *Waverley*, St Germain was the place where King James II had sought refuge after his expulsion from England, and where the Stuarts had established their headquarters. Accordingly Gala, who had not been admitted into the secret of the authorship of *Waverley* (although his suspicions pointed strongly to Scott), was anxious to hear what Scott might say when they halted at St Germain to look at the famous château where James II had resided as guest of Louis XIV of France. Scott, for his part, did not entirely pass over the subject, and mentioned one or two well-known anecdotes about the Stuarts at St Germain. Gala, however, perceived that the topic was one to which Scott was unwilling to refer, 'and I, therefore, forebore to press it so much as I confess I felt *inclined* to do'.[2]

On walking up to the terrace of the château, Scott and Gala admired the extensive view. It included the site at which, as Scott explained in *Paul's Letters to his Kinsfolk*,[3] Blücher, in his and Wellington's march on Paris after the battle of Waterloo, had crossed the Seine in order to threaten the capital from its vulnerable southern side and force its surrender without bloodshed. Bearing in mind that St Germain had been a royal residence ever since the time of Louis VI in the eleventh century, in other words, long before Versailles, and that the situation of Versailles was inferior to that of St Germain, Scott and Gala could not help wondering at the preference given by Louis XIV to Versailles—'"the favourite without merit", as it was called by the wits of the court'.[4]

On the other hand, the heavy design of the château of St Germain, which Napoleon had converted into a military college, and the neglected condition in which Scott and Gala found it, seemed to make it look to them more like a state prison than a palace. It had, in fact, served as a sort of state prison for several of the many English detainees in France during the Napoleonic Wars, a number of whom were personally known to Scott.[5] One of them, Sir Alexander Don, was the member of parliament for Scott's own county of Roxburghshire. He had been imprisoned for some twelve years.[6] Scott probably afterwards had him particularly in mind in a forceful and moving passage in the *Life of Buonaparte*[7] outlining the incalculably harsh effects suffered by the detainees during and after their long imprisonment. At the same time Scott was to represent the detainees in the château of St Germain as having benefited from 'the acts of benevolence and charity' of the Empress Josephine in her last years, after her retirement to her villa at Malmaison, which lay near St Germain.[8]

It was dark before Scott and Gala reached Louviers, and, as they had anticipated, the inn, where they were obliged to stop, was poor and comfortless. As they were resolved to start as early as possible, in order to breakfast at Rouen, they ordered their bill before going to bed. It was grossly immoderate. Scott, not usually easily vexed, 'remonstrated more fluently, as he himself said, than he had ever done in the French language'.[9] But, as usual on such occasions, they had the worst of it, and were obliged to submit to their sulky landlady. Scott, who had observed on the way to Paris from Brussels that the Prussians frequently left the French inns without paying their bills,[10] attempted to revenge himself on their landlady by telling her that in a day or two she too would suffer the same mortifying treatment from her Prussian lodgers. But again, with imperturbable *sang-froid*, she won the argument by answering 'c'est possible', and at the same time politely hinting that it was perfectly proper for her English lodgers to pay a little extra and thereby make up for the defaulting Prussians.[11]

When the landlady left their rooms, Scott observed to Gala how hazardous it was to attempt anything in a foreign language beyond the usual routine of conversation. 'It continually happens,' he said, 'that you either fail to give the intended effect to what you wish to say, or not infrequently miss the mark entirely; in short, you say not what you *wish*, but what you *can*.'[12]

Their room was a garret opening by a corridor to the courtyard of the inn, where there was considerable noise and some quarrelling. They had not been long asleep when they were awakened by a noise of someone attempting to get into the room. Their pistols were as usual in readiness, and they started up, fully prepared to defend themselves against the suspected intruders. Their peremptory demand of 'Qu'est ce que c'est' was answered by a gentleman who apologised as being a stranger and an Englishman, and had mistaken the number of his apartment.[13]

This incident appears to be the one that Scott was to recall several years later in a significant letter, in the sense that he was to reveal in it to an intimate friend how highly he had come to regard Gala as a travelling companion not only for 'his taste and accomplishments' and 'his matchless good humour' but for 'his ready gallantry and spirit'. For Scott was to explain that 'one night we were apparently in the predicament of fighting for our lives—I was even then a horse in point of strength and fearless by constitution and yet with his [Gala's] delicate person and softer breeding he was the foremost of the two'.[14]

It was certainly to Gala's credit that in his own record of the bedroom incident at the inn he made no attempt to represent himself as the more gallant of the two. While acknowledging that they had *both* displayed 'so much good courage', he agreed with Scott in regretting that it 'should have been thrown away to so little purpose'.[15] The incident, which had seemed to open with all the hallmarks of those roadside adventures familiar to Scott and Gala from their reading in *Gil Blas* and the picaresque novel, and which indeed Scott had himself imitated in *Waverley*,[16] had flopped into the kind of anti-climax that Byron was to excel in contriving in his satiric narratives.

In any event, Scott and Gala had no sooner got away from the inn than they found themselves responding with delight to the picturesque scenery on their drive to Rouen at an early hour along the banks of the Seine, which broadened and deepened at the approach to its mouth. Rouen itself was full of British troops, with whom Scott, as usual, immediately entered into conversation. When they reached the old, large, Gothic cathedral, they found the space in front of it filled with people, the women in their finery, as it was a holiday. On entering the magnificent portal, they found a service going on in the presence of the cardinal archbishop,[17] one of whose most distinguished predecessors was Cardinal d'Amboise, the Chief Minister of Louis XII in the late Middle Ages. He was commemorated by a splendid tomb and by the celebrated Tour d'Amboise—better known by the name of 'the Butter Tower'—which Gala ascended for a spectacular view of the countryside, while Scott walked about the church, and was well rewarded by the grandeur of the nave and aisles and the brilliancy of the stained-glass windows, which rivalled those of Nôtre Dame in Paris.[18]

Eventually Scott found the inscription on the wall behind the high altar which recorded that the heart of Richard I of England was buried in the cathedral. Close to it another inscription recorded the burial place of the Duke of Bedford, Regent of France. On one side of the apse was a handsome effigy of Richard I representing him exactly as a knight of chivalry, in full armour, and with a couchant hound at his feet.[19]

Scott was to recreate him in *The Talisman* as a central figure in the Crusades, complete with an oriental setting of adventures, intrigues, rivalry, colour, and pageantry. He was also to incorporate Richard I into the plot of *Ivanhoe* and to round it off, significantly, with an extract from *The Vanity of Human Wishes* as a moral comment on the fate of 'the heroic Coeur-de-Lion'. For that 'generous, but rash and romantic monarch' had met his death near Limoges from a wound inflicted by an obscure archer while he had been laying siege to the castle of Châlus.

From the cathedral of Rouen Scott and Gala hastened to the Palais de Justice, one of the city's finest buildings, in a Gothic style of architecture after Scott's heart. The building had formerly been the seat of the parliament of Normandy from the time of the Hundred Years' War to the French Revolution. The most celebrated name connected with it was that of Corneille, who had practised law in it before making his mark as a dramatist. Scott and Gala inspected it as well as the monument to Joan of Arc, who had been burned at the stake in the market-place of Rouen by the English after her capture by their Burgundian allies. Gala, however, was unwilling to detain Scott, who had become impatient to get home, so that their sight-seeing was more brief than they could have wished.[20] They, therefore, resumed their drive to Dieppe, and passed through such diversified country that their last evening in France was particularly delightful. On arriving at the port, they found that the packet was due to sail to Brighton in the late evening, and they booked their passage in her. After a short walk through the town, they went on board, and sat on deck, while several parties of English passengers entered the vessel in a quiet and silent manner, which contrasted with the bustle of the foreigners, particularly of a young French passenger, accompanied by several friends, who had evidently just risen from the dinner table. The traveller, having received a series of rapid and vigorous farewells from his friends, who no doubt had heartily drunk success to his voyage, 'had altogether rather a bewildered expression of countenance'. Scott was much amused with the group, who drew the inevitable Shakespeare quotation from him, as he whispered to Gala: 'Our fellow passenger looks almost as if he could say with poor King John to Faulconbridge, when he comes to comfort him in his sickness, "Oh cousin! thou art come to *set mine eye*."'[21]

As for Scott's passage in the sailing boat, it proved tedious beyond measure: 48 hours, with nothing to eat but a few oysters, a crust of bread, and a little ordinary French wine. Scott and Gala eventually succeeded in reaching Brighton on the morning of 12 September 1815. As there was then no pier, they were carried ashore on the shoulders of a couple of sailors. When the customs-house official heard Scott's name, he would hardly look at his trunks, so that Scott wrote to his wife shortly afterwards that 'I might have had them [the trunks] stuffed with lace if I had known of his politeness'. Scott also assured her that, despite the fatiguing Channel crossing, he had felt no sickness, and was so much better after breakfast ashore that he confirmed to her his intention of setting his face northwards for Abbotsford after a day in London with Gala.[22]

One of the first persons they had met on the beach was a friend of Scott's, Sir Edmund Antrobus, a London bank director. He invited them to dinner, at which Scott was in excellent spirits, entertaining both Gala and their host with anecdotes of himself as a young advocate in Edinburgh and as an amateur actor in private theatricals with his friends.[23] He tended to look back upon those convivial years with nostalgia, and to conceive of himself and his fellow-advocates at that period of life as the Scottish and latter-day counterparts of 'the young Templars' of London in the age of the last Stuarts, who had appealed to his imagination in the course of his editing the works of Dryden and Swift. In fact, he was to employ two such 'Templars' to introduce the plot of *The Heart of Midlothian*[24] before creating, a few years later, the genial, rattling Templar called Reginald Lowestoffe in *The Fortunes of Nigel* (1822).

Scott was well aware that the 'Templars' of London derived their name from the site of the old district of that city which was—and still is—called the Temple, because the church and headquarters of the English Knight Templars had stood there in the Middle Ages. The Temple in London, therefore, corresponded to the Temple in Paris that Scott had lately visited with Gala.

Gala had originally intended to take leave of Scott on reaching London in order to visit some friends in the neighbouring country, but no sooner had they arrived at the capital by the night coach from Brighton, and established themselves at Long's Hotel in Bond Street, than he was easily persuaded by Scott to change his mind and accompany him to the north. Scott, for his part, was informed by Daniel Terry that Charles Mathews, the celebrated comedian, was about to leave London by coach for Leamington, where he had a theatrical engagement.[25] Scott had long enjoyed Mathews's brilliant mimicry and humour in Edinburgh on Mathews's regular provincial tours from London.[26] Eager to get across the border to Scotland, he expressed a wish to accompany Mathews, and as an additional inducement proposed that he and Gala should take Derbyshire on their way for its scenic beauties instead of following the dull and well-known stages of the Great North Road. They, therefore, called on Mathews in Lisle Street off Leicester Square, but were told by Mrs Mathews, who was herself an actress, that he was out on business for his journey into Warwickshire. Scott explained to her that, in addition to the pleasure of travelling in her husband's company, he wished to revisit Kenilworth near Leamington for its ruined castle.[27] He arranged with her without difficulty to postpone Mathews's departure from the afternoon to the evening in order that her husband would be able to have an early dinner with himself and Gala at Long's Hotel before all three of them boarded the coach for Warwickshire. He intended to get Byron and Daniel Terry to join them at the dinner.[28] Mathews had never met Byron before,

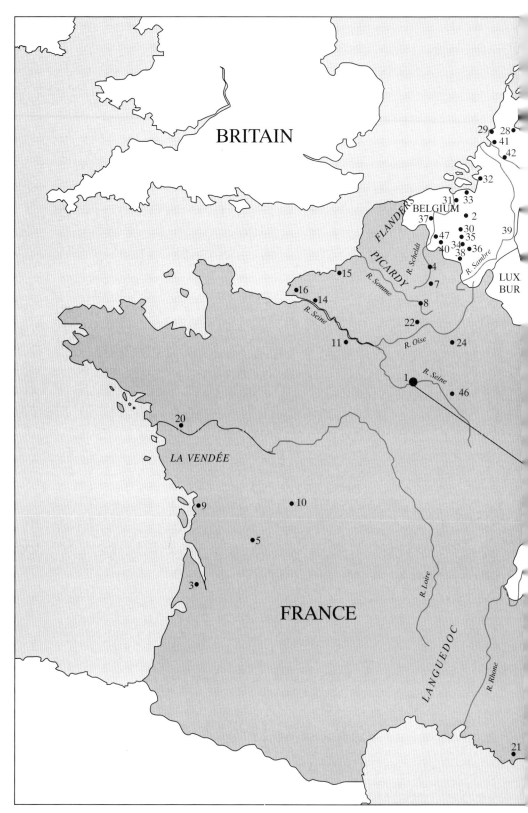

France and the Low Countries in 1815

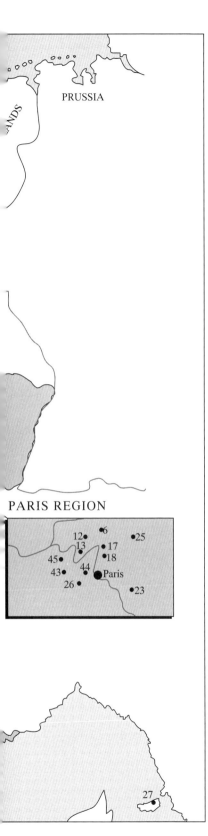

PRUSSIA

PARIS REGION

Key

but Byron, having seen Mathews perform in all the leading London theatres, fully shared Scott's view that Mathews's 'imitations'—as his mimicry was commonly called—were unique, in that Mathews had the genius to identify himself not only with the look, tones, and manners of the persons he personified but also with their *minds*. Accordingly Byron called him 'this modern Proteus'.[29]

Not being a reader of novels, Mathews had only lately taken up *Waverley*, but it had made him an enthusiast for Scott's fiction. He was then engaged in forming a collection of pictures connected with the theatre, which was to become celebrated, and which is nowadays perhaps the most prized treasure of the Garrick Club in London. Scott had heard of it, but had not yet seen it. Mrs Mathews showed it to him and Gala. It included portraits of famous actors by Zoffany and other artists, notably of David Garrick in several of his best-acclaimed Shakespearean rôles.[30] Scott had long envied the theatregoers of the generation before him who had seen Garrick in the flesh: 'that abridgment of all that was pleasant in man'. On the other hand, he consoled himself with the thought that his own generation had John Kemble and Mrs Siddons, who, though inferior in range, were in many ways not less excellent than Garrick.[31] Kemble's only fault, in Scott's view, was an occasional inability to conceal his studied acting manners. In that respect he stood out as 'a natural contrast' to the late George Cooke,[32] the other great actor who was also well represented in Mathews's collection. Scott recalled Cooke so vividly, especially in the name part of Shakespeare's *Richard III*, that he had already described, in a letter to Joanna Baillie, Cooke's 'terrible visage and savage utterance' in one of the scenes of the play; and many years later he was to claim to Lockhart that 'I recollect [Cooke] as well as if he now stood before me'.[33]

Having chatted with Mrs Mathews over her husband's collection, Scott took leave of her in expectation of seeing Mathews at the appointed dinner hour. It was pouring with rain, but he declined her offer of sending for a coach, even of making use of her umbrella: 'he declared he never considered any sort of weather an impediment to his moving about free from encumbrance of any kind'. He was wearing his usual country-house dress: dark-green jacket and black neckcloth, which Mrs Mathews thought 'odd enough for London'. As he walked leisurely away with Gala towards Leicester Square, he looked back at Mrs Mathews 'with one of his fascinating smiles, and with a playful nod of his head, as if to reassure me that he was doing what was agreeable to him'.[34] Contrary to her impression that he was going back to Long's Hotel in Bond Street, he called with Gala at Byron's house in Piccadilly Terrace, but failing to find him there, they were directed by Lady Byron to look for him in Albemerle Street at John Murray's. There they found the usual assembly of authors, critics, scholars, and travellers,[35] portraits of whom Murray had lately begun to hang on the walls of his rooms from the studios of the leading painters and engravers,[36] so that he was to form a collection as celebrated

Charles Mathews by George Harlow. (Garrick Club, London)

as that which Scott and Gala had just seen at Mrs Mathews's. (Scott's own portrait by Gilbert Stewart Newton was to represent him wearing precisely the country-house dress that Mrs Mathews had dubbed 'odd enough for London'.[37])

Although Byron was not in Murray's assembly, he was apparently expected later, his more usual hour of call at his previous meetings with Scott having been in early or mid-afternoon, so much so that Scott afterwards referred to him and other authors in Murray's circle as his 'four o'clock friends'.[38] Pending Byron's arrival, or another attempt at communicating with him, Scott remained to talk business with Murray, while Gala parted for a while from Scott to make preparations for their journey. Murray undertook to forward 'my [Scott's] great package from France with all its contents' to Abbotsford.[39] These included a newly published book about Napoleon's extra-marital affairs in separation from the Empress Josephine during his campaigns in Egypt and Eastern Europe. Its title was *Amours Secrètes de Napoléon Buonaparte* (1815), and it appears to have served Scott as his earliest source of information about the Polish beauty called Countess Marie Walewska, to whom he afterwards referred briefly and discreetly in the *Life of Buonaparte*[40] without mentioning her name or the circumstances of her original meeting with Napoleon. He merely recorded that during Napoleon's exile at Elba after his first abdication he had been visited by a lady 'with a boy about five or six years old', and that Napoleon had received her with great attention, 'but at the same time with an air of much secresy [sic]', which had led Elba's inhabitants to conclude her to be the Empress Marie Louise, Napoleon's second wife after his divorce from Josephine. In reality, she was 'known by those near Napoleon's person to be a Polish lady from Warsaw, and the boy was the offspring of an intrigue betwixt her and Napoleon several years before'.

Scott gathered from Murray that he was acting as agent for the French publishers of *Amours Secrètes de Napoléon Buonaparte*. Murray himself had 'a great many interesting works in the press',[41] including Jane Austen's *Emma* (1816), of which Scott shortly afterwards wrote, at Murray's suggestion, a well-known, highly favourable review for publication in the *Quarterly Review*.[42] He particularly admired Jane Austen's novels for 'their strong resemblance [to human nature] and correct drawing'.[43] He was afterwards to read chapters of *Emma* and *Northanger Abbey* (1818) to his 'evening circle', although the novel of Jane Austen's that appears to have given him most delight was *Pride and Prejudice* (1813).[44]

Jane Austen, for her part, was a warm admirer of Scott's poetry, and, on going up to London from her brother's house at Chawton for proof-reading of *Emma* a few weeks after Scott's departure for Scotland, she received a copy of *The Field of Waterloo* on loan from Murray. Having 'heard much of Scott's account of Paris', she also asked for the loan of a copy of *Paul's Letters to his Kinsfolk*,[45] in which Scott commended another newly published book called *Travels in France during the Years 1814–15*.

130

It contained one of the best accounts of the French theatre as he had lately seen it in Paris, with particular reference to Talma, Mlle George, and Mlle Mars. Although the book was published anonymously, Scott described it as 'the joint production of two young gentlemen, whose taste for literature is hereditary'.[46] They were named Archibald Alison and Alexander Fraser Tytler,[47] both of Edinburgh. Alison's father was the author of the influential *Essays on the Nature and Principles of Taste* (1790), while Tytler was the son of a judge with the title of Lord Woodhouselee, who was also a historian. Scott had attended his lectures on history at Edinburgh University. He had also seen a great deal of the Tytler family when he had lived as a neighbour of theirs at Lasswade Cottage outside Edinburgh after his marriage. He still felt grateful to the family, 'who were very kind to us as newly entered on the world'.[48]

Scott naturally compared notes about Paris under Allied occupation with Murray before he rejoined Gala at Long's Hotel, where he confirmed to him Byron's impending arrival as their guest for dinner with Daniel Terry and Charles Mathews. Like Mathews, Gala had never seen Byron before. The high expectations that had been raised in both of them by Byron's celebrity were not disappointed by his appearance. Mathews afterwards told his wife that Byron was 'the only man he ever contemplated, to whom he felt disposed to apply the word *beautiful*'.[49] Gala thought Byron, who was then in his twenty-eighth year, one of the handsomest men he had ever seen. Byron's dark hair, clustered elegantly over his fine forehead, contrasted with his pale countenance. His eyes, of a light colour, fringed with dark eye lashes, though keen and bright, did not seem to Gala to have a very pleasing expression; whereas those of Scott, shrouded by his large eye-brows, possessed fully as much power, and far more benevolence. Byron's dress, though plain, was 'very recherché'; and his behaviour was courteous and dignified. He had not yet written *Don Juan* and the other poems in which his satiric vein was to supersede the romanticism of *Childe Harold's Pilgrimage* and the so-called 'Turkish Tales'. But Gala was familiar enough with the occasional bitterness in Byron's early work to detect it at intervals in his talk during the dinner.[50]

Scott himself was the principal talker of the party, everyone being naturally keen to have his account of the remarkable scenes and persons he had so recently visited. Byron listened with sincere respect and pleasure, however unpalatable the restoration of the Bourbons was to him, and however ill he wished to the cause in which the victorious British army had been engaged at Waterloo. He took much interest in the individual instances of British valour and prowess mentioned by Scott, and asked many questions about friends of his who had taken part in the battle, or were then in Paris. He particularly impressed Gala with the feeling he displayed in alluding to the loss of the gallant relation of his called Major Howard, whose fate he was shortly to mourn so movingly in his own Waterloo stanzas in canto three of *Childe Harold's Pilgrimage*.[51]

In contrast to this spirit of sympathy was the remark Byron made when Scott related the story of a young officer of Byron's acquaintance who had been shot in the head while conveying an order from the Duke of Wellington, and yet had staggered on, and had delivered his message when at the point of death. 'Ha!' said Byron, 'I daresay he could do as well as most people without his head—it was never of much use to him.'[52]

In his recollection of this and other remarks, which Scott, after Byron's death, passed to his friend, Tom Moore, for the *Life of Byron*, Scott tended to represent Byron's cynical wit as nothing more than 'fun, frolic, and whim' marking 'a most brilliant party'. Byron's jocular vein contrasted with the melancholy, even gloomy, moods to which Scott, at his private meetings with him, had observed him to be prone.[53] In the course of the dinner party Gala mentioned to Byron the information that he and Scott had gathered in Paris about the religious differences that had again erupted in Languedoc between the Catholics and Huguenots, and that three persons had already been killed, following an exchange of blows. 'What, only three?' Byron replied, with a fixed look at him.[54]

Byron was then expecting a son and heir by his wife Annabella.[55] In the event, however, Lady Byron was to be delivered of a daughter, Ada, whom he was to address tenderly, but also as 'born in bitterness', in canto three of *Childe Harold's Pilgrimage*.[56] For shortly after her birth his marriage was to break up and he was to leave England for good. When he and Scott, therefore, parted at the end of the dinner in London, 'with much feeling of mutual regard', as witnessed by Gala, they were never to see each other again. Gala, for his part, was convinced, from the respect that Byron felt and demonstrated for Scott, that 'he [Scott] was of all persons the most likely to have had influence in soothing the irritated feelings of the wayward childe, and bringing his actions more under the control of his better judgment'.[57]

As Byron fully shared Scott's high opinion of Joanna Baillie's *Plays on the Passions*,[58] the best known of which were *The Family Legend* and *De Montfort*, Scott appears to have had no difficulty in securing a promise or undertaking from him to propose to his fellow-members on the Committee of Management of Drury Lane Theatre that they consider producing, or rather, reviving one of her plays, for *De Montfort* had already had a first performance at Drury Lane, with John Kemble and Mrs Siddons in the leading parts. *The Family Legend*, which was founded on a Scots tradition relating to a well-known feud between two Highland chieftains, had also been staged during Scott's previous visit to London in the spring of 1815, complete with the prologue that he had written for its earlier Edinburgh production.[59]

Scott himself was unable to call on Joanna Baillie at her home in Hampstead, contrary to the intention he had announced to her from Paris; but shortly after his return to Abbotsford from London he wrote to her that 'I do most devoutly hope that Lord Byron will succeed in his proposal of bringing out one of your dramas'. Scott also assured her that 'Byron is your sincere admirer',[60] to which Byron himself was to attest publicly and most handsomely in his preface to *Marino Faliero* (1821). In the event, however, Byron appears to have met with opposition to a revival of *De Montfort*,[61] as its first production, despite the prestige of its leading players and the splendour of its staging, had not been a success. Nevertheless Byron persisted and urged the rising star of the day, Edmund Kean, to take the principal rôle in *De Montfort* (for Kemble was about to retire from the stage), but Kean accepted it only several years later.[62]

As for Scott's transactions with Daniel Terry before or after the dinner party in London, the most significant project to emerge out of them appears to have been Terry's proposal to put on a dramatic version of *Guy Mannering* at Covent Garden, where he had long been securely established. (His eminently successful run at the Haymarket Theatre in *The Man of the World* was for the summer season of 1815 only.) For no sooner had Scott put *Paul's Letters to his Kinsfolk* behind him than be began not only to correspond with Terry from Abbotsford about the projected production[63] but to make contributions to it in various forms, in strict secrecy between them over his own share in it as well as over the authorship of the novel, which had not been disclosed even to Joanna Baillie.[64] It was to be the first of many adaptations by Terry of the Waverley Novels: hence Scott's word for them: 'Terrifications'.

Although Scott himself left no record of his journey from London to Abbotsford except for a few retrospective references to it scattered in his private letters, it was excellently covered by Gala with detailed descriptions mixed with quiet humour, and complete with Scott's own dialogue and ballad recitations as well as with vignettes of the comic entertainment and mimicry provided by their fellow-traveller, Charles Mathews, *en route* to Leamington. Gala proved, to some extent, a sort of Boswell to Scott, observing him carefully for anecdotes and reminiscences, and fully sharing Scott's warm response to the topography of the English midland and northern counties as well as of the Scottish border, with particular reference to the historical and literary associations drawn out in Scott by a wealth of mediaeval castles and stately homes on their route. Although much of the appeal of Gala's journal—next to its vivid descriptions—sprang from the immediacy and freshness of its impressions of Scott, Gala evidently worked up parts of it in later life, so that Scott's response to several places on their route was related to the later Waverley Novels, in which Scott, on branching out from Scottish into English history, was to draw on the topography of the midland and northern counties, as observed by himself and Gala, for such novels as *Ivanhoe*, *Kenilworth*, and *Peveril of the Peak*. Indeed even before the composition of *Ivanhoe* Scott was to draw on the topography of the same counties for the opening chapters of *Rob Roy*.

The journey to Abbotsford started on 14 September 1815, very early in the morning after the dinner with Byron, when Scott, Gala, and Mathews travelled by coach till a late hour to Dunstable. Mathews was very amusing, the more so, according to Gala, as Scott, 'with that tact and good manners which distinguished him, avoided anything that might have the appearance of an attempt to draw out his talents'. Their earlier exertions, however, in London at length began to tell upon them, and an occasional doze overtook most of the party some time before they reached their first destination. As they entered Dunstable, they were aroused by a low sound of a mail-coach horn, and, on being more fully awakened, they found that it was Mathews himself who was the performer: 'the imitation was certainly perfect'.[65]

They agreed to start again at an early hour in the morning, as Mathews wished to reach Leamington in sufficient time to prepare for his entertainment, and accordingly they were called before six o'clock. Although the carriage was at the door, and Scott and Gala were quite ready to set out, no Mathews appeared; and when Gala accompanied the waiter to his door, he had evidently just been aroused from slumber, and was annoyed at Scott and Gala being kept waiting, as it was on his account that they had risen so early. In reproaching the porter for not having followed his instructions to awaken him in good time, and on no account to forget to make plenty of noise, 'as I am the most sleepy headed fellow in the world', Mathews gave another brilliant performance in imitation of the alleged faulty conduct of porters. He did so as he appeared at the door of the inn, and as all the people who were up were standing round the chaise. 'They evidently thought they had a very singular and funny gentleman as their lodger, though I [Gala] do not believe they had the slightest idea who he was'. On observing a parrot in the courtyard of the inn where Mathews stopped to breakfast with Scott and Gala, he immediately addressed his brother mimic, 'and uttered so very strange a collection of sounds, that the bird was struck dumb with surprise at finding itself as it would seem so much exceeded in its own way by everything that he did'.[66]

They arrived at Leamington at an early hour, and lodged at the leading hotel with fine trees and green fields around it.[67] Mathews's entertainments on his provincial tours were called 'At Homes', and consisted of recitations, songs, imitations, and ventriloquy. At first he was somewhat nervous of performing in the presence of Scott, who had noticed that, for all his great humour, Mathews was 'often subject to fits of deep melancholy',[68] analogous to Byron's gloomy moods. His nervousness at Leamington sprang particularly from a comic character sketch he was due to perform of an old Scotswoman and a Presbyterian minister speaking broad Scots in the rain, which he feared might flop in Scott's judgement. Moreover, for all his celebrity in the provinces, he was not very well known at Leamington. Scott's good humour, however, restored him to his usual gaiety, and besides filling the house, he drew general applause. His sketch of the Scotswoman was very favourably received, and both Scott and Gala thought his other imitations capital.[69]

On joining them after the performance for supper, he was in high spirits, and gave them further good imitations. He also related anecdotes of the celebrated actors represented in the picture gallery that he was forming at his house in London. He particularly delighted them with tales of George Cooke, who was notorious for outrageous behaviour, on and off the stage, when drunk, as he so often was.[70]

On 15 September they went to see Warwick Castle, which Scott afterwards described in *Kenilworth*[71] as 'that fairest monument of ancient and chivalrous splendour which yet remains uninjured by time'. Several international artists, including Canaletto, had painted pictures of it. Mathews, who had first seen it only a few months previously,[72] contrived to give its well-known Scottish house-keeper, Mrs Hume, a private hint who her visitor was, and although there were several parties in the castle, 'the old lady declared she "must boo" to talent, and attend her great countryman in preference to them all'. Her civility was indeed great, for she showed Scott everything which she thought likely to interest him, including some apartments upstairs to which the public were never admitted. Scott, for his part, told her that he had seen Lord Brooke, the son and heir of the Earl of Warwick, at Paris, and her inquiries about him, and the interest she took in the family were so hearty and sincere, that Scott was quite charmed with her, and they soon became great friends.[73] Evidently he looked upon her as a classic example of what he afterwards called in *The Heart of Midlothian*[74] 'exported Scotswomen' of the lower orders in England, and of whom he created two excellent specimens, in the same novel, in the persons of Mrs Bickerton and Mrs Glass.

His delight in Mrs Hume was personally best expressed in the letter that he wrote about her, on returning home, to another 'exported Scotswoman', but of superior rank, intelligence, and culture, who had married into the English aristocracy, and now bore the title of Lady Compton (afterwards the Marchioness of Northampton). Her former name was Margaret Maclean Clephane, and as one of Scott's brightest and favourite correspondents, she had supplied him—as had her mother—with valuable information about Highland life, manners, and songs for *Waverley*. As she had lately taken up residence at her husband's mansion in Northamptonshire, which adjoined Warwickshire, Scott was aware at the time of his visit to Warwick Castle that he was 'within twenty miles of you'. He, therefore, confessed to her that, had he been alone, he would certainly have availed himself of the open invitation to her house that her husband had given him the previous spring. 'But having still with me my fellow traveller on the continent ..., I thought it would be too like the descent of a Scottish clan upon you'. Scott then went on to confirm the point already made in the previous chapter, namely, that this was his *first* visit to Warwick Castle, and, in revealing his enthusiasm for it, he also confirmed his great liking for Mrs Hume. 'By the bye,' he wrote to Lady Compton, 'I saw Warwick Castle, which is the finest thing of the kind I ever saw, thought of, or could conceive.

If you have not already seen it, pray dear Lady Compton, make a party there as soon as ever you conveniently can. I made great friends with the old housekeeper who is quite *unique* in her way too, and I advise your Ladyship to do so or you will only see half what is to be seen. As I hope the impression I made on the old lady's heart may be lasting (though not dangerous), I think you had better mention me to her, for I assure you she has two ways of showing the place—esoteric and exoteric (I hope I have spelled these cursed words right—I like to be learned upon occasions).'[75]

Needless to say, Scott knew perfectly well that the title of Earl of Warwick had been held by various families as premier earls of England, and that Warwick Castle had repeatedly changed hands in the Middle Ages and later periods since its erection in the eleventh century on the orders of William the Conqueror. The families included 'the mighty Beauchamps and Nevilles', as Scott called them several years later on recommending his daughter-in-law not to miss seeing the parish church of St Mary near Warwick Castle, where the tombs of the Earls of Warwick lay 'in the most magnificent stile [*sic*] of Gothic display and in high preservation'.[76] The names of several of them were already familiar to Gala and Scott from their prominence in Shakespeare's plays on the Wars of the Roses. The greatest of them was Richard Neville, commonly called 'the kingmaker', to whom Scott was to refer in one of the chapters set in the Isle of Man in *Peveril of the Peak*.[77] For the Nevilles and Beauchamps had extensive estates and castles in various parts of England as far north as the border with Scotland. Their portraits on display in Warwick Castle, together with splendid paintings in full and half-length of Tudor and Stuart kings and queens, were by several artists whose works Scott had lately seen in the Louvre, especially Rubens, van Dyck, and Holbein. Rubens's compatriot and collaborator, Frans Snyders, whom Scott invariably associated with, and highly admired for, paintings of the chase, was represented by a masterpiece in the State Dining-Room, which was dominated by the celebrated painting of Charles I on horseback from the studio of van Dyck. The painting was to draw a great scene from Scott in *Woodstock*[78] as well as a tribute to 'that Flemish painter—Antonio Vandyke—what a power he has!'.

Van Dyck's 'power', as Scott was to spell it out through Frank Osbaldistone in *Rob Roy*,[79] lay in the 'ease and dignity' stamped on his figures, in his 'richness of colouring', and in the 'breadth and depth of shade' of his compositions. Undoubtedly van Dyck was the artist *par excellence* whom Scott, as a Jacobite novelist, studied for authentic details of dress, accoutrements, genealogy, and touches of character. Van Dyck's most talented English protégé, William Dobson, was represented in one of the drawing-rooms of Warwick Castle by a portrait that again appealed to Scott's Jacobite sentiments and stirred his historical imagination. For it was that of his colourful hero, the Marquess of Montrose. Moreover, the very suit of armour that Montrose wore in Dobson's portrait was on show for Scott and other visitors in the Great Hall of the castle, together with the armour of the parliamentary general in the Civil War between the Royalists and Roundheads, whom Scott had dubbed 'fanatic Brooke' in *Marmion*, and who had been shot through the eye by a sniper after his troops had stormed Lichfield Cathedral.[80] Brooke's and Montrose's armoured figures, together with those of numerous equestrian and jousting knights in the Great Armoury, presented an irresistible temptation to Charles Mathews to enliven them with his singular powers of voice, so that, according to Gala,[81] 'sundry strange sounds were occasionally heard to issue from those ancient warriors', in ignorance, on the part of Mrs Hume, that the celebrated mimic was in the room, and in disapproval by her of 'the liberty taken with those grim and stately personages'.

The Great Hall of the castle was precisely the sort of mediaeval, chivalric structure on which Scott was to model, albeit on a much smaller scale, his own entrance hall at Abbotsford, complete with the French cuirass that he had brought over from the field of Waterloo. The Great Hall's most popular objects of curiosity were probably those associated with the legendary, superhuman feats of Guy, Earl of Warwick, to which Scott afterwards alluded in several of the Waverley Novels,[82] perhaps most facetiously of all in *The Fortunes of Nigel*.[83] For one of these objects purported to represent the ribs of a dun cow, 'certainly large enough for an elephant',[84] which Guy of Warwick was reputed to have slain with a sword more than 4 feet long, which was also on display in another room of the castle.[85] Accordingly, in *The Fortunes of Nigel*, Scott was to put this riposte in the mouth of Nigel's Scottish servant, Richie Moniplies, on being asked in London why he pretends to be of noble birth, when he is really a son of an old butcher in Edinburgh: 'I hear muckle of an Earl of Warwick in these southern parts —,' Richie replies, 'Guy, I think, his name was—and he has great reputation here for slaying dun cows and boars, and such like; and I am sure my father has killed more cows, and boars, not to mention bulls, calves, sheep, ewes, lambs, and pigs, than the haill Baronage of England.'

At the time of Scott's visit to Warwick Castle all its valuable possessions, particularly the paintings, were under grave threat of sale, because George Greville, the 2nd Earl of Warwick, who then owned them, and who had done a great deal to improve the castle by way of additions and acquisitions, had overreached himself financially. In consequence the outlying estates were being sold off, and strict economy was being practised to restore solvency.[86] Accordingly Scott noticed that as a result of 'the unfortunate circumstances' of the Earl of Warwick, there was 'an air of neglect about everything'.[87] But Scott reported the effects of these circumstances neither to Lady Compton nor to any of his other correspondents. He recorded them after his next visit to Warwick Castle, in 1828, accompanied by his younger daughter Anne. By then solvency had been restored to the castle, and Scott had been keeping his celebrated journal. In it he again declared that 'Warwick Castle is still the noblest sight in England'. He was particularly delighted to find 'my old friend Mrs Hume in the most perfect preservation, though, as she tells me, now eighty-eight'. She again went through her duty wonderfully, though she complained of her memory. He noticed that she had discarded 'a mass of black plumes which she wore on her head' on his earlier visit, and which had seemed to him to resemble the famous enchanted helmet in Horace Walpole's novel, *The Castle of Otranto* (1764). The insolvent 2nd Earl of Warwick had died the year after Scott's first visit, but his son and heir, Henry Greville, whom Scott had met at Paris as Baron Brooke, invited him and Anne to lunch in the castle with himself and Lady Warwick. Scott was 'pleased to see Lord Warwick show my old friend [Mrs Hume] kindness and attention'. It was common knowledge by then that, as Scott put it in his journal,[88] the castle's 'fine collection of pictures would have been sold by distress, if Mrs Hume, my friend, had not redeemed them at her own cost'. In fact, it was only on her death in 1834, aged ninety-three (two years after Scott's own death), that it was revealed that this servant of the Warwick family for seventy years had been able to pay off the castle's most pressing creditors and save the pictures from her own money, amounting to more than £30,000 in the form of gratuities from visitors whom she had taken around the castle![89]

At Warwick Castle, on his first visit of 15 September 1815, Scott was introduced by Mathews to one Mr Hall, who superintended the operations of workmen in Yorkshire. He too was travelling northwards, and on returning to Leamington in Scott's company from the castle, he agreed to take part of Scott and Gala's post-chaise as far as North Yorkshire.[90] But they first visited Kenilworth, which was historically linked with Warwick in several ways, as its castle had been the principal seat of Robert Dudley, the powerful Earl of Leicester and the favourite of Queen Elizabeth. His brother, Ambrose Dudley, was one of the Earls of Warwick, and as such had owned Warwick Castle when Queen Elizabeth had made her celebrated journey from London to Kenilworth via Warwick. Kenilworth Castle was as ancient, and had been as grand, as Warwick Castle, but whereas the latter was marvellously preserved, the former was largely a magnificent ruin. Nevertheless only the border castles of Scotland, and perhaps Carlisle Castle, seem to have exercised a more powerful stimulus upon Scott's imagination than the ruins of Kenilworth Castle. Both Gala and Mathews attested to the minuteness with which he examined its surviving fortifications and enclosures,[91] so that, when he wrote *Kenilworth* a few years later, he set a whole third of the action of that novel in Kenilworth Castle, peopling it with a range of historical and fictitious characters, and he revealed not only a mastery of its original structural features but, more significantly, exploited them skilfully as a framework for the intricate intrigues, conflicting interests, and drama of the plot. At the same time he recreated the celebrated revels, complete with masques and stag hunt, associated with Queen Elizabeth's visit to the Earl of Leicester's 'princely castle',[92] preceded by a stop at his brother Ambrose Dudley's Warwick Castle.

The ruins themselves, as Scott saw them on the spot with Gala and Mathews, later drew out in his novel[93] a variant of Dr Johnson's theme in *The Vanity of Human Wishes* on 'the transitory value of human possessions, and the happiness of those who enjoy a humble lot in contentment'. Scott noticed 'decent children begging' among the ruins, 'a thing uncommon in England',[94] unlike Scotland in his time; and he observed 'the same unseemly practice' when he revisited Kenilworth with his daughter Anne in 1828 before proceeding to Warwick Castle. But by then the ruins were being 'preserved and protected', thanks in no small measure to the publicity and visitors drawn to them by his novel, whereas on his first visit 'these trophies of time were quite neglected'.[95] His comments on them remained so indelibly impressed on Mathews's memory that, on publication of Scott's novel, Mathews declared that, even if Scott had not admitted him into the secret of the authorship of the Waverley Novels, it would not have been hard for him 'to prove who the *Great Unknown* was'.[96]

Mathews parted from Scott and Gala for Northampton after the visit to Kenilworth Castle, while Hall proceeded with them towards Derbyshire. Scott himself had earlier suggested to Gala that they might perhaps drive through Leicestershire for Ashby-de-la-Zouch,[97] which he had visited a few years previously during a halt at Coleorton on a similar journey from London to Scotland with his friend and fellow-poet Wordsworth.[98] There was a stately ruined castle at Ashby that he had thought Gala might have liked to see. It had been built, or rather, rebuilt by Lord Hastings,[99] of whom Gala already knew as a leading character in Shakespeare's *Richard III*. Mary Queen of Scots had been a prisoner in the castle for a time. Within a mile of it was a mediaeval tilting-ground on the edge of a picturesque wood; and in the neighbourhood of Ashby, which was famous for its mineral springs, lived a friend of Scott's called Mr Thomas Moore (not the poet Tom Moore), to whom Gala had been given to understand that Scott would have wished to have paid his respects.[100] In the event, however, the proposed diversion into Leicestershire was dropped for reasons that remained unexplained by Gala, possibly following objections by Mr Hall, or, more likely, on Scott's realising that a halt at Ashby-de-la-Zouch would have militated against his need to return home without undue delay, bearing in mind that Derbyshire was likely to detain them not only with its scenic beauties but with its celebrated geological phenomena, or 'wonders', as Scott afterwards called them in *Peveril of the Peak*.[101] Gala, for his part, never imagined that within three years Scott was to confer literary celebrity on Ashby-de-la-Zouch with *Ivanhoe*.[102] For Scott was to exploit its central position and its ruined castle and tilting-ground to recreate a series of dramatic tableaux of mediaeval chivalry and pageantry in the tradition of Froissart's *Chronicles* and Chaucer's *The Knight's Tale*, with particular reference to a spectacular tournament, attended by royalty and the rank and file of the midland and northern counties of England. Likewise Gala never imagined that he was destined to see Ashby-de-la-Zouch, in keeping with the Regency vogue for spas, become 'a place of fashionable resort', principally for the baths that were erected there as a development of its mineral springs shortly after the publication of *Ivanhoe*, and which were to be named 'the Ivanhoe Baths'.[103]

From Ashby-de-la-Zouch Scott's party made for Matlock. As they drove through a beautiful part of the country in the evening, at no great distance from Derby, they came to a fine park in which was a good example of the kind of old English manor house that Scott had long admired,[104] and that indeed he intended to emulate at Abbotsford with his projected plantations and liberal hospitality to rich and poor alike. For the old English manor house also represented for Scott the traditional social values and beliefs of a resident country gentry, the absence of which he had regretted in his remarks in *Paul's Letters to his Kinsfolk*[105] on the French *noblesse campagnarde* in the light of his observations on the road from Brussels to Paris. Accordingly he said to Gala: 'Now, there, is a fine specimen of an ancient hall,—quite an English scene, not much picturesque beauty about it, but so soft and rich, with that hospitable old mansion embosomed among old woods.'[106]

The house and the balmy summer evening reminded Scott of the opening stanza of a ballad called 'Cumnor Hall' by William Mickle, which had been a favourite of his ever since it had first appeared in print when he had been a schoolboy in Edinburgh. The opening stanza, which he recited to Gala, still fascinated him with its verbal melody and evocative imagery:[107]

> The dews of summer night did fall,
> The moon, sweet regent of the sky,
> Silver'd the walls of Cumnor Hall,
> And many an oak that grew thereby.

On the other hand, Cumnor Hall, however fine a specimen of an old English manor house in Berkshire, had also been the scene of the alleged imprisonment and murder of Amy Robsart, the first wife of Robert Dudley, Earl of Leicester. He was suspected of having plotted her murder in his ambitious aspirations as Queen Elizabeth's favourite, perhaps even as her lover. The ballad, which represented Amy Robsart lamenting her cruel fate as a prisoner in Cumnor Hall before going on to describe her gruesome murder, was to serve Scott as the principal theme of *Kenilworth*, as he was himself to acknowledge in the introduction to that novel, complete with a reprint of the whole text of the ballad. Indeed he was originally to wish to call the novel *Cumnor Hall*.[108] Moreover, he was purposely to open and end it with mottoes[109] from Mickle's poem to suggest his conception and presentation of Amy Robsart as the typical tragic figure of the old ballads. When he came to do so, however, Cumnor Hall, which he himself had never seen on his journeys to and from London, had only lately been pulled down completely by its owner, Lord Abingdon,[110] so that Scott's description of it in the novel[111] was to be very much like that of the Derbyshire mansion as observed by himself and Gala on their way to Matlock.

Their post-chaise reached Matlock on 18 September 1815 in time for supper at the Old Bath Hotel, close to the famous medicinal waters which had been used for over two centuries. Situated on the river Derwent, their hotel commanded a grand view of a line of precipices that had recently drawn from Edinburgh the landscape painter, Hugh Williams, whom Scott had described as 'a very good artist'. For Williams had caught the public eye with his views of the Highlands of Scotland, including Loch Katrine, where Scott had set *The Lady of the Lake*, on which account Williams had been commissioned by Edinburgh's Theatre Royal to paint the scenery for a dramatic version of that immensely popular poem.[112]

From Matlock Scott was anxious to visit Dovedale, which was inextricably associated in his mind with Charles Cotton, 'the native poet of Derbyshire', as Scott called him in *Peveril of the Peak*.[113] Cotton had celebrated the beauties of the river Dove in his continuation of Izaak Walton's *The Compleat Angler* (1676). Dovedale, moreover, was believed to be the 'happy valley' of Dr Johnson's *Rasselas* (1759). Before going to see it, however, Scott fulfilled another long-standing wish of visiting the old mansion of Haddon Hall, which was owned by the Duke of Rutland, of Belvoir Castle, but which had originally belonged to the old Norman family of the Peverils. As Scott was to explain at the opening of *Peveril of the Peak*, this family claimed descent from William the Conqueror.

Haddon Hall lay only a few miles from Matlock in picturesque surroundings on the river Wye, a tributary of the Derwent. On walking up to the gate of the old mansion with Gala, Scott immediately observed the arms and motto of the old family of the Vernons, who had become the proprietors of Haddon Hall after the Peverils in the early Middle Ages. The motto was in the old style of chivalric wit,[114] which Scott afterwards cleverly reproduced in dialogue form through Diana Vernon in *Rob Roy*.[115] Scott also recalled—in the same library scene between Diana and her lover, Frank Osbaldistone—what the old poets, including Shakespeare in *Henry IV*, had written about the more historic representatives of the Vernon family.

Scott and Gala found that Haddon Hall afforded an exact idea of the style of architecture and furniture of various mediaeval and later periods, thanks to its careful preservation by the Rutlands, even though they had not used it as a dwelling for more than a century. Scott examined every part of it very attentively,[116] and he afterwards drew on it for his own description of the interior apartments of Martindale Castle in *Peveril of the Peak*.[117] Although he deemed it to contain 'some of the most interesting remains of antiquity I have seen any where', he acknowledged that it gave him 'a most singular and rather uncomfortable view of our ancestors' accomodations [sic]', everything in it being 'clumsy and gigantic, from the salting trough, which resembles a clumsy canoe, to the stairs which consist of solid blocks of huge beams, not sawn into planks but formed of square beams'. Even the special glory of Haddon Hall, which was the Long Gallery or ballroom, was reached by an ascent of 'a most primitive character'. Despite all these defects, however, Scott was to urge his elder son, Walter, many years later, to go and see the 'magnificent show' of Haddon Hall, when Walter was to be stationed in the vicinity of it at Sheffield as an army officer. 'I would give a little money to visit [it] again,' Scott was to write to him.[118]

From Haddon Hall Scott and Gala travelled over the wild district of the northern part of Derbyshire as far as Castleton in order to visit the wonders of the Peak. As Scott afterwards explained in *Peveril of the Peak*,[119] Castleton derived its name from the great Gothic fortress (once considered impregnable, but then in ruins), which had been erected by William Peveril, a natural son of William the Conqueror. It lay on the summit of a steep hill, and on hearing it referred to as 'Peveril's Place in the Peak', Gala had no idea that that name 'would afterwards become celebrated in romance'.[120] Below the hill was a huge cave called 'the Devil's Cavern', and at its entrance was a large pool of water appropriately called the Styx. Scott and Gala had obtained the guides, rockets, blue lights, and all that was necessary for crossing the Styx and viewing the cavern and other immense cavities nearby, several of them with stalactites. Gala afterwards recollected Scott laughing heartily at being laid flat in the boat by which it was necessary to enter on account of the lowness of the archway. Having turned on their lights inside the cavern, they heard the thunder of an echo among the rocks produced by a blast of gunpowder by miners speculating for veins of metallic ore. Scott, for his part, was resolved to surprise the guardian of these subterranean regions by an echo he was not prepared to expect. Therefore he fired, for the first time, the pistols that he and Gala had always carried with them on the continent, being determined, as he said, that they should not be loaded for nothing.[121]

Perhaps the cavern that impressed Scott most was one called 'the Speedwell Mine', which he was also to urge his son Walter not to miss seeing from Sheffield together with Haddon Hall and the Devil's Cavern. Although the Speedwell Mine had, in point of fact, 'sped extremely ill' as a mine, because the speculators for veins of lead ore had been forced to abandon the attempt after an outlay of thousands of pounds, Scott was to declare to Walter that it could 'scarce[ly] be matched' as a great natural curiosity. For the miners, after sinking a shaft for two or three hundred yards, had 'burst into an immense cavity where a subterranean river came from God knows where and fell into a bottomless abyss'.[122] Scott was astonished at the enterprise of the daring miners who, having discovered this great pool of water, over which Scott and Gala were rowed for some time in darkness, had flooded their own drift, 'and thus obtained the service of boats instead of horses for their subterranean carriage'. The cavity was so immense that its top could not be reached even by a rocket.[123]

Scott's interest in these caverns had been stimulated, the year before, by his voyage to the Western Isles of Scotland, where he had seen 'the three grandest caverns' in that country—Smoo, Macallister's Cave, and Staffa—which were also to inspire Mendelssohn, before long, to compose the *Hebrides Overture* and *Scottish Symphony*. The caverns had drawn memorable comment from Scott in the context of the prevailing wide interest, among poets, artists, travellers, and philosophers, in those forms of Nature that were held to induce terror or beauty or sublimity.[124] Moreover, these caverns, whether natural or artificial, formed part of the fashionable 'machinery' of Gothic literature and art, with particular reference to the hiding places of *banditti*, under the impact of Salvator Rosa and his imitators. Scott had expressly explained this circumstance in *Rokeby*,[125] in which he had incorporated several buccaneers, marauders, and highwaymen into the story, and had placed them in caves on the English side of the border with Scotland to complement their Scottish counterparts in *Waverley* and *Guy Mannering*. The highways on either side of the border at the time of Scott's journey still displayed gibbets with convicted *banditti* and other criminals hanging from them.[126]

When Scott and Gala visited Dovedale, they feasted themselves on more geological wonders, but this time in the context of 'the picturesque', for Dovedale derived its peculiar and romantic character largely from the huge masses of rock scattered along the wooded valley of the Derwent, many of them of very singular forms, beautifully fringed with ivy, and completely detached from the precipitous banks of the streams.[127] The rocks were locally known by the Celtic name of *tor*, which Scott was to retain in his allusions to the topography of Derbyshire in *Peveril of the Peak*,[128] in which he was to create a typical genre scene representing Derbyshire miners, complete with dialogue drawn from the information that he and Gala had gathered about the abortive fate of the Speedwell Mine as a speculative venture. Even the name of the mine was to reappear in the transmuted form of 'the Bonadventure Mine'.[129]

Although Scott was to recall in the same novel that the rough roads, or rather paths, of the Peak, which made hasty travelling impossible, had drawn much satire from Charles Cotton,[130] he himself did not in the least suffer the terrain to daunt his spirit despite his lameness. On the contrary, Gala, on observing him while he scrambled among the rude parts of Dovedale, noticed that, if Scott took a fancy to reach any particular spot, 'it was no ordinary difficulty that would prevent him from attaining his object.'[131] Accordingly he traversed many glens before they reached the most striking dale of all at Beresford, where Charles Cotton had erected the celebrated fishing house as a memento of his angling days with Izaak Walton. Scott's affection for *The Compleat Angler* was to shine through a review article that he was to contribute, many years later, to the *Quarterly*

Review on a delightful little book on salmon fishing by his illustrious friend, Sir Humphry Davy.[132]

From the Peak Scott and Gala proceeded with Mr Hall to Sheffield, apparently without having time for a visit to Chatsworth from Matlock. Later, however, Scott incorporated a hint of the social pre-eminence of Chatsworth's owners into the miners' scene in *Peveril of the Peak*.[133] His only object at Sheffield, through which he had passed on previous journeys to and from London,[134] and where they slept on 15 September 1815, was to provide himself with a tree planter's knife for Abbotsford from a celebrated warehouse of cutlery owned by a Mr Rogers. Accordingly, on calling in early morning at the warehouse and buying a knife of 'the most complex contrivance and finished workmanship', he handed Mr Rogers his card to have his name engraved on it. When he mentioned his acquisition to Gala at breakfast, the latter expressed a wish to equip himself with this ingenious tool, and on being directed to Rogers's shop, he produced a card with his name for the engraver. The master cutler eyed the signature for a moment, and exclaimed: 'John Scott of Gala! Well, I hope your card may serve me in as good stead as another Mr Scott's has just done. Upon my word, one of my best men, an honest fellow from the North, went out of his senses when he saw it—he offered me a week's work if I would let him keep it to himself—and I took him at his word.' This anecdote was often related by Scott with pleasure.[135]

There were few scenes in England more striking to Scott than that presented to his and Gala's view when they drove from Sheffield along the banks of the river Don in the West Riding of Yorkshire. For the river swept through a kind of richly cultivated amphitheatre blended with woodland, and then led to a mount on which rose the ancient castle of Conisborough. Once renowned as a royal Saxon residence before the Norman Conquest, the castle, particularly its noble round tower and massive flying buttresses, had first caught Scott's eye on an earlier drive in the mail coach at dawn,[136] exactly in 'the most romantic' setting in which he was to incorporate the castle and revive its former splendour in *Ivanhoe*.[137] For he was to set that novel partly in Leicestershire and partly in Yorkshire, complete with a Saxon nobleman as a leading character called 'Athelstane of Coningsburgh'. He was also to recommend Conisborough to his son Walter as another 'great curiosity' that was well worth visiting from his army barracks at Sheffield.[138]

Scott's only regret was that he could not have more time than 'a transient view' of the castle of Conisborough from the post-chaise that he shared with Gala and Mr Hall, for the antiquary in him would have wished to follow up certain striking resemblances between the oldest features of the castle and the singular buildings called 'Duns' that he had observed in the Shetland and Orkney Islands the previous year on his tour of the Northern and Western Isles of Scotland.[139] But he was obliged to proceed with his companions through Wakefield and Leeds towards Ripon along the Great North Road, which Scott was to exploit brilliantly for the epic journey of Jeanie Deans in *The Heart of Midlothian*.[140] He was to do so, however, not for aesthetic effects but dramatically and imaginatively, for he firmly believed that the Great North Road was 'the dullest in the world, as well as the most convenient for the traveller'.[141] His own more casual observations on this and other roads, as well as on the inns, publicans, ostlers, porters, and suchlike characters that he encountered on his journey with Gala and on later ones with other companions, were perhaps best reflected in numerous little sketches of minor roadside figures and incidents scattered in his novels, most of which were constructed round a framework of a journey, usually from England to Scotland or vice versa. This structure constituted perhaps Scott's most obvious link with the novelists of the eighteenth century, particularly Fielding and Smollett.

At Ripon Scott and Gala's principal interest—besides the venerable Minster—was the picturesque ruins of Fountains Abbey in the beautiful park of Studley Royal, the seat of the Marquess of Ripon.[142] The abbey presented a fine specimen of the style of Gothic architecture of the reign of King Henry III in the thirteenth century. As it had suffered no unusual acts of violence at the time of the dissolution of the monasteries, its extensive remains afforded a more exact picture of monastic establishments than perhaps anywhere in Britain. Scott afterwards associated Friar Tuck, 'the buxom confessor of Robin Hood's gang' in *Ivanhoe*, with Fountains Abbey.[143]

From Ripon Scott and Gala crossed through an extremely rugged tract of country to Middleham in the North Riding of Yorkshire, near which their fellow-traveller, Mr Hall, occasionally resided when superintending the operations of the workmen. After examining, under his guidance, the process of smelting the lead ore, with which the district abounded, but which Gala afterwards dubbed 'one of the most unwelcome occupations it is possible to conceive', Scott and Gala parted from Hall, and proceeded to Rokeby near Greta Bridge, where Rokeby Park, the beautiful mansion of Scott's friend, John Morritt, lay.[144] Situated on extensive grounds, and with plantations after Scott's heart, the mansion was where Scott had partly written the verse romance of *Rokeby*,[145] which he had dedicated to Morritt. Gala was perfectly familiar with the poem, the action of which alternated between Rokeby and the nearby Barnard Castle at the time of the battle of Marston Moor in the Civil War between the Royalists and Roundheads. Scott had been looking forward to seeing Rokeby Park and Morritt again ever since his departure from Paris, especially as Morritt had himself been to Paris the year before among the earliest travellers to the continent immediately after Napoleon's first abdication and the entry of the Allied army of occupation.[146] Scott had also wanted to tell Morritt of his happy meetings and excursions in Paris with their common friends, Lady Alvanley and her daughters, one of whom had presented him, before his continental trip, with two picturesque views of Rokeby Park and its environs.[147] Above all, Scott had been looking forward to showing Rokeby Park and its treasures to Gala, for Morritt, as a man of wealth and taste, had embellished his mansion with masterpieces from Europe, including the celebrated painting of Venus and Cupid by Velasquez, which is nowadays known as 'the Rokeby Venus', and is in the National Gallery in London. Unfortunately, however, Scott and Gala learned, on arriving at Rokeby Park, that Mrs Morritt was gravely ill, so that they curtailed their stay, and Gala was also forced by unfavourable weather to give up his projected survey of the mansion's grounds. Nevertheless he appears to have seen enough of its interior riches and antiquities to prompt Scott to write afterwards to Morritt that 'he was delighted with Rokeby and its lord'.[148] The antiquities included many of the monuments that had been found in a well-preserved Roman encampment near Rokeby.[149] For Scott and Gala's journey had now brought them close to the chain of communications and defences that the Romans had established between York and Carlisle, culminating in Hadrian's Wall on the border with Scotland.

Gala made sure that he did not pass so near the Barnard Castle that Scott had celebrated in his poem[150] without visiting its picturesque ruins. Scott, for his part, wanted to see again the magnificent view of the wooded valley of the river Tees from the massive Baliol's Tower of the castle, which was named after its founder, Barnard Baliol, the ancestor of a dynasty of mediaeval kings of Scotland.[151] Near one of the windows of Baliol's Tower Scott pointed out to Gala the device of the hated hunch-back, Richard III of the House of York, engraved on the wall of the castle, which he had often made his residence during the Wars of the Roses in order to terrorise the party of the House of Lancaster in the North of England.[152] The castle itself lay just inside the county of Durham, whence Scott and Gala crossed into Westmorland along the Great North-West Road to Carlisle via Brough and Appleby. They stopped at Appleby, mainly for memorials of the family and barony of Clifford, one of the oldest and most powerful in the north of England. Accordingly they first visited Appleby Castle, followed by the mediaeval church of St Lawrence, where the tomb of the famous Lady Ann Clifford lay, together with that of her mother, the Countess of Cumberland.[153] Lady Ann's celebrated diary, parts of which Scott retained vividly enough in his memory to recall them to Gala, was among the many relics of the Clifford family in the castle of Appleby, which commanded a fine view of the river Eden. The relics included richly inlaid armour, ornaments, and portraits of Lady Ann, one of whose distinguished ancestors, Henry, Lord Clifford, had been slain in the battle of Bannockburn. Scott, however, had represented him in *The Lord of the Isles*[154] as having been killed earlier in an ambush, which exemplified the liberties he regularly took with chronology as a historical novelist and poet.

After Appleby Scott and Gala halted at Penrith in Cumberland, driving past the ruined Brougham Castle, which also had belonged to the Clifford family, one of whose less martial members had drawn a notable lyric from

Wordsworth, which Scott highly admired.[155] It was called 'Song at the Feast of Brougham Castle'. Scott took Gala outside Penrith to examine the ancient sites traditionally associated with King Arthur and his Knights of the Round Table,[156] on which he had drawn for the verse romance that he had written the year before *Waverley* called *The Bridal of Triermain* (1813). He also showed Gala the Roman camp of Petreia, as Old Penrith used to be called before it became the scene of constant border warfare between the English and the Scots. It was from Petreia, in fact, that Scott afterwards ornamented a trellised walk around the courtyard walls of Abbotsford with Roman deities dug up at the ancient station.[157]

Scott left Gala in no doubt about his personal interest in the country through which they travelled, for it reminded him of the happy days he had spent at Grasmere on a visit with Mrs Scott to Wordsworth as well as to Southey at Keswick,[158] shortly after Scott had found himself famous as a poet with the publication of *The Lay of the Last Minstrel*. On that visit he had climbed, despite his lameness, to the summit of Helvellyn, one of the highest peaks in the Lake District, for a spectacular panorama of encircling mountains, lakes, rivers, and distant sea.[159] Although Wordsworth, as Scott and Gala correctly assumed, was then living in his new home at Rydal Mount near Grasmere, Southey had not yet returned to Keswick from his tour of the field of Waterloo and the Low Countries; while Coleridge, who had shared Greta Hall at Keswick with Southey, had left the Lake District for good, and was at Calne in Wiltshire, writing the work that was to make him best known as a critic, namely, *Biographia Literaria* (1817).

Gala attested to Scott's esteem for the three Lake Poets,[160] several of whose compositions he occasionally recited, besides regularly quoting from them in his novels either directly in the narrative or in the chapter headings. Thanks to his earlier visit to Wordsworth and Southey, which he had followed up with another stay at Keswick[161] shortly before Southey had been appointed poet laureate on Scott's recommendation, Scott had come to know the topography of the Lake District closely. Accordingly he made it the setting not only of *The Bridal of Triermain* but also of several chapters in *Guy Mannering*[162] as well as towards the end of *Waverley*,[163] in the narrative of the retreat of the Jacobite Highland army on Carlisle from Derby. In all these works Scott had also drawn on his recollections of his earliest and important visit to the Lake District in 1797, when, as a young advocate on a summer holiday from Edinburgh, he had first met a vivacious, dark-eyed, young lady named Charlotte Carpenter, who was then a ward of Lord Downshire, and had fallen in love with her at Gilsland near Carlisle, fully resolved to make her, after a short interval, his wife. Indeed Charlotte Carpenter was shadowed as 'my Lucy' in the tender courtship scenes marking the introductions to the cantos of *The Bridal of Triermain*.

These circumstances explained why Scott, on arriving at Carlisle from Penrith in the stage coach, said to Gala, as they were walking about the town: 'I am always glad to visit Carlisle. I was married here, and never spent happier days than when I used to take excursions in this neighbourhood.' Scott then proceeded with Gala on his usual visit to St Mary's Cathedral, where he had married Charlotte, and which he was to revisit unfailingly for the same purpose on his numerous stops at Carlisle on later journeys between Abbotsford and London.[164]

On walking out of the cathedral, Scott and Gala lingered for some time in the historic castle and on the esplanade in front of its Gothic gate, which Scott had incorporated into the remarkable scene of the execution of Fergus Mac-Ivor, the Jacobite Highland chieftain, in *Waverley*.[165] The scene had already begun to attract general attention, which was to lead to amusing legends in Scott's remaining lifetime, such as the story that was to be related by his daughter Anne, after she and her father, on revisiting Carlisle, had found a guide pointing out 'Fergus Mac-Ivor's *very* dungeon' to visitors to the castle.[166] At the time of Scott's visit with Gala, however, Scott himself was reluctant, as at St Germain in Normandy, to refer too particularly to the castle's connection with the Jacobite rebellion of 1745 in order to protect his anonymous authorship of *Waverley*. Instead, as he sauntered with Gala about the ramparts, he repeated to him the story in the celebrated ballad of 'Kinmont Willie',[167] describing the storming of Carlisle Castle by a band of Lowland Scots, led by their chief, the Duke of Buccleuch, in order to rescue a marauder imprisoned in the castle's dungeon. Scott had first published the ballad in *Minstrelsy of the Scottish Border*.[168]

In their saunter about the ramparts of the castle Scott and Gala walked past the spikes on which the heads of executed or slain Scotsmen used to stand—exactly as Scott had represented the head of Fergus Mac-Ivor after his execution outside Carlisle.[169] 'The poor *plaids* who were strap'd up' at Carlisle were also the subject of a couple of verses that Scott read on a pane of glass in an inn at Carlisle. He afterwards represented them to John Morritt as 'the only rhimes [*sic*]' that the philosopher David Hume 'was ever known to be guilty of'.[170] Their immediate appeal to Scott sprang not only from their witty and pithy satire on Carlisle but from their celebration of the beautiful walks of the nearby Corby Castle, which Scott revisited with Gala on driving out of Carlisle:

> Here chicks in eggs for breakfast sprawl,
> Here Godless boys God's glories squall,
> Here Scotchmen's heads do guard the wall,
> But Corby's walks atone for all.

At Corby Scott enjoyed the hospitality of an old acquaintance called Mr Howard, although the antiquary in Scott felt that Howard's handsome modern house did not 'assimilate so well with the scenery as the old, irregular, monastic hall with its weather beaten and antique appearance which I remember there some years ago'.[171] Scott's attention, on leaving

Corby, was drawn by Gala to an advertisement of the impending publication of *The Field of Waterloo* in a copy of the latest issue of the *Edinburgh Review* that Gala had bought at Carlisle. 'Oh! have they got that in already?' Scott exclaimed, 'Then it's time I were at home.'[172] Accordingly they crossed the border into Scotland after an evening's halt at Longtown, in the course of which Scott referred to what Gala afterwards described in his journal[173] as 'a period of his [Scott's] youthful days, which, from his tone and manner, I have no doubt had a powerful influence over his feelings'. Indeed that 'powerful influence' *still* operated on his feelings, and was to continue to do so practically to the end of his life.[174] For the period in question represented the great passion that Scott had cherished, a couple of years before his marriage to Charlotte Carpenter, for another young lady called Williamina Belsches, whom he had kept loving and desiring over two years in the hope that she would eventually commit herself to him, but who had, in fact, engaged herself to, and married, a rival suitor called William Forbes. Although Williamina Belsches was dead when Scott referred to this 'period of his youthful days' in his conversation with Gala at Longtown without undoubtedly mentioning her name at all, or spelling out the circumstances of this great but blighted passion, which had caused him deep distress and bitterness,[175] Scott had partly shadowed his feelings for Williamina in *Rokeby*, three years after her death, in the persons of Wilfrid Wycliffe, who represented Scott, and Matilda Rokeby, who represented Williamina Belsches.[176] But, as Scott had done so in a very general way, and as Gala, being much younger than Scott, had never been admitted into Scott's feelings at the actual 'period of his youthful days', Gala, although familiar with *Rokeby*, had seen nothing personally significant in Wilfrid's passion for Matilda. When, however, several years after Scott's conversation with him at Longtown, Gala read *Kenilworth*, in which Scott shadowed his former obsessive passion for Williamina Belsches in the persons of Edmund Tressilian and Amy Robsart respectively, and he did so much more explicitly, and in a much more cautionary context, than he had done in *Rokeby*, Gala's memory recurred to 'our conversation at Longtown'. He then recorded in his journal[177] that one passage in *Kenilworth* in particular,[178] which Scott had put in Tressilian's mouth, suggested 'a train of feeling very similar to those to which he [Scott] gave utterance' at Longtown.

Gala also recorded that, on entering Scotland from Longtown, they drove through much the same route that Scott had made Harry Bertram, the hero of *Guy Mannering*, take for his own journey from the Lake District to Liddesdale in Roxburghshire on the Cheviot Hills.[179] They travelled, in other words, in a region not only renowned for its picturesque beauty but 'in the vicinity of places which were among the first to arouse the powers of Scott's imagination, and had been his favourite haunts from the days of his early youth'. In particular, he had made them his 'haunts' for his collection of border ballads, which he had published in *Minstrelsy of the Scottish Border*, including the ballad of Johnny Armstrong, the renowned freebooter, whose place of execution Scott pointed out to Gala before he promised to show him some day the circle of stones where a cruel Liddesdale tyrant called Lord Soulis (also commemorated in another border ballad) had been burned for his crimes. In fact, Scott told Gala: 'I should well like another raid into Liddesdale some day; I have not seen it for these many years.'[180] 'Raid' was his metaphor for his earlier excursions in search of ballads and antiquities in 'this wild, solitary, and pleasingly rural' country, as he had described it in *Guy Mannering*,[181] complete with dismantled and ruined towers of old border castles. These included his favourite Hermitage Castle, which, Scott explained to Gala, was 'at no great distance' from the road they were travelling on, and which, as its old, grey, massive outwork loomed into sight in its secluded valley, 'inspires a feeling somewhat akin to awe'.[182]

Gala, for his part, had observed that, throughout their journey to Flanders and Paris, Scott had worn a silver ring on his finger, which, as Scott himself had already explained in a note on Hermitage Castle in *Minstrelsy of the Scottish Border*,[183] had been found in the ruins of that castle, and had been presented to him by his printer's brother. The ring was of great antiquity, and was embossed in high relief with the device of the renowned Douglas family, whose deeds, notably those of Sir James Douglas, had been recently celebrated by Scott in *The Lord of the Isles*. Scott was to continue to wear the ring nearly to his dying day, shortly before which he was to write *Castle Dangerous* (1831) with Sir James Douglas as a protagonist.

The road near Hermitage wound through groups of green hills and led Scott and Gala to the beautiful banks of the river Teviot, on which stood Branxholm Castle, one of the old seats of the Scott clan. Scott had made it the scene of *The Lay of the Last Minstrel*. They passed it towards sunset, and arrived at Abbotsford on 24 September 1815. Scott found a happy group ready to welcome him and Gala: his wife and children, their governess, and his beloved forester, Tom Purdie—nearly all the household, not forgetting Scott's dumb friends, were assembled at the door of the country house. Tom Purdie's simple mind had entertained no small apprehensions for the consequences of Scott's journey to foreign countries, particularly France; hence almost his very first remark to Scott was: 'sae ye hae gotten awa' free them after a''.[184] Meanwhile the family group were joined by James Ballantyne, Scott's printer, and James Skene, Scott's close friend and himself a former traveller to France and other parts of the continent. Both of them, like most of Scott's family, had been expecting him and Gala to come home much sooner, so much so that Ballantyne had arrived from Edinburgh with proof-sheets of *The Field of Waterloo*, booksellers' letters, and other business papers. Accordingly Gala 'felt it incumbent on me to take a considerable portion of the blame for the wandering life we had been leading to myself, many of the objects of our tour having, as I insisted, been visited almost entirely on *my* account'.[185]

Very little time was allowed to pass before Scott was called upon by his children to unlock his luggage in order to show the souvenirs, and distribute the presents, from the boulevards and the Palais Royal, and specimens of silk and other ware from Derbyshire. The collection of caricatures that both Scott and Gala brought back with them excited particular mirth, enlivened as they were with descriptions and anecdotes from Scott,[186] who also astonished Tom Purdie with the ingenuity of the shape of the snuff-box that he had selected for him in Paris as well as with the sophisticated workmanship of the tree planter's knife that he had bought for himself at Sheffield. In the grip of his happy feelings, however, at his return to his family circle, Scott disappointed his wife and daughters slightly. For in his absence she and the girls had fitted up the drawing-room of the cottage with new chintz furniture, and had been looking forward to the pleasure which they had supposed the surprise of the new arrangements would give him. But Scott had betrayed no consciousness that any change had taken place, so that Mrs Scott's patience could hold out no longer, and she drew his attention to the spruce, fresh room they had prepared for him. Vexed with himself for his blindness, he threw out some word of admiration every now and then before bedtime 'to reconsole *mamma*', whom he also mollified with the presents of lace and jewellery from Paris.[187]

The contrast between 'this quiet bird's nest of a place', as Scott put it in his first letter to John Morritt after his return to Abbotsford, 'and the late scene of confusion and military splendour which I have witnessed' in Flanders and Paris, was so stunning that for four or five days Scott was content 'to saunter up and down in a sort of indolent and stupefied tranquillity'.[188] His only attempt at occupation was to entertain his guests and superintend his plantations on foot or mounted on a new cob instead of his old charger, 'Daisy', who had surprised Scott by 'looking askant at me like a devil', on being brought to the door of Scott's house in expectation that he ['Daisy'] would signify, by the usual tokens, his pleasure at seeing his master. On the contrary, 'Daisy' had resisted every attempt of Scott's to mount him, so that in parting with him, after repeated rebuffs over several days, Scott had concluded that 'Daisy' had 'certainly taken some part of my conduct in high dudgeon and disgust'. On somebody's suggesting that 'Daisy might have considered himself as ill used by being left at home when the *laird* went on his journey', Scott agreed, and remarked, with laughter, that 'maybe some bird had whispered Daisy that I had been to see the grand reviews at Paris on a little scrag of a Cossack, while my own gallant charger was left behind'.[189]

As soon as Gala, Ballantyne, and Skene left Abbotsford, Scott set about, with characteristic industriousness, despatching his literary commitments. They were so numerous and varied that he was perfectly justified in claiming to another favourite correspondent, Lady Louisa Stuart, that 'it would have required Briareus ... to get handsomely through all I have been doing since I came home'.[190] For, besides correcting the proofs of

151

The Field of Waterloo, completing *Paul's Letters to his Kinsfolk* and seeing it through the press, writing the review of *Emma* for Murray, and joining in the contributions to Daniel Terry's dramatisation of *Guy Mannering* for Covent Garden Theatre, Scott started another novel—his third—*The Antiquary*, and projected another verse romance—the last he was to write—*Harold the Dauntless*. All this mass of composition was executed while Scott was resuming his legal duties in Edinburgh as a Principal Clerk to the Court of Session. Moreover, he honoured in the most handsome manner his promise to Murray to send him 'a highland article on my return' from Paris, for he filled more than a third of a whole issue of the *Quarterly Review* with it.[191]

Although the article itself was ostensibly a review of the newly published correspondence of the eminent Scottish judge and politician called Duncan Forbes of Culloden, in effect Scott turned it into a kind of sociological study of the Highland clans, with particular reference to their 'patriarchal system'. But whereas, in this context, he had previously equated the Highland clans with the Vendeans and the Cossacks, in his article for the *Quarterly Review* Scott extended his range of parallels to the patriarchal tribes of India and Afghanistan, who were not unlike the Tartar tribes whom he had seen in Paris. This extension of his interest in primitive communities sprang from his reading, with absorbing interest, shortly after his return from Paris, Sir John Malcolm's *History of Persia*, followed by another newly published pioneering work on the Afghan tribes by a former Governor of Bombay, Mountstuart Elphinstone.[192] Accordingly Scott first emphasised how forcibly he had been 'struck with the curious points of parallelism between the manners of the Afghan tribes and those of the ancient Highland clans'. Then he proceeded to claim that the books of Malcolm and Elphinstone served 'strikingly to show how the same state of society and civilisation produced similar manners, laws, and customs, even at the most remote periods of time, and in the most distant quarters of the world'.[193] Scott's observation smacked strongly of the kind of reasoning adopted in the seminal *Essay on the History of Civil Society* (1767) by Adam Ferguson,[194] one of the leading figures of the Scottish Enlightenment and a founding father of modern sociology.

The Duke of Wellington's 'Waterloo Despatch'

as first published in an extraordinary issue of the London Gazette

Downing Street, July 22, 1815

Major the Honourable H Percy arrived late last night with a despatch from Field Marshal the Duke of Wellington, K.G., to Earl Bathurst, his Majesty's Principal Secretary for the War Department, of which the following is a copy:-

Waterloo, June 19, 1815

My Lord,—Buonaparte, having collected the 1st, 2nd, 3rd, 4th and 6th corps of the French army and the Imperial Guards, and nearly all the cavalry on the Sambre and between that river and the Meuse, between the 10th and the 14th of the month, advanced on the 15th and attacked the Prussian posts at Thuin and Lobez, on the Sambre, at daylight in the morning.

I did not hear of these events till the evening of the 15th, and I immediately ordered the troops to prepare to march; and afterwards to march to the left, as soon as I had intelligence from other quarters to prove that the enemy's movement upon Charleroi was the real attack.

The enemy drove the Prussian posts from the Sambre on that day; and General Ziethen, who commanded the corps which had been at Charleroi, retired upon Fleurus; and Marshal Prince Blucher concentrated the Prussian army upon Sombreffe, holding the villages in front of his position of St Amand and Ligny.

The enemy continued his march along the road from Charleroi towards Brussels, and on the same evening, the 15th, attacked a brigade of the army of the Netherlands, under Prince de Weimar, posted at Frasne, and forced it back to the farm-house on the same road, called Les Quatre Bras.

The Prince of Orange immediately reinforced this brigade with another of the same division under General Perponcher, and in the morning early regained part of the ground which had been lost, so as to have the command of the communication leading from Nivelles and Brussels, with Marshal Blucher's position.

In the mean time I had directed the whole army to march upon Les Quatre Bras, and the 5th division, under Lieutenant-General Sir Thomas Picton, arrived at about half-past two in the day, followed by the corps of troops under the Duke of Brunswick, and afterwards by the contingent of Nassau.

At this time the enemy commenced an attack upon Prince Blucher with his whole force, excepting the 1st and 2nd corps, and a corps of cavalry under General Kellerman, with which he attacked our post at Les Quatre Bras.

The Prussian army maintained their position with their usual gallantry and perseverance against a great disparity of numbers, as the 4th corps of their army, under General Bulow, had not joined, and I was not able to assist them as I wished, as I was attacked myself, and the troops, the cavalry in particular, which had a long distance to march, had not arrived.

We maintained our position also, and completely defeated and repulsed all the enemy's attempts to get possession of it. The enemy repeatedly attacked us with a large body of infantry and cavalry, supported by a numerous and powerful artillery, but all were repulsed in the steadiest manner. In this affair, his Royal Highness the Prince of Orange, the Duke of Brunswick, and Lieutenant-General Sir Thomas Picton, and Major-General Sir James Kempt, and Sir Denis Pack, who were engaged from the commencement of the enemy's attack, highly distinguished themselves, as well as Lieutenant-General Charles Baron Alten, Major-General Sir C Halket, Lieutenant-General Cooke, and Major-Generals Maitland and Byng, as they successively arrived. The troops of the 5th division, and those of the Brunswick corps, were long and severely engaged, and conducted themselves with the utmost gallantry. I must particularly mention the 28th, 42nd, 78th, and 92nd regiments, and the battalion of Hanoverians.

Our loss was great, as your Lordship will perceive by the enclosed return; and I have particularly to regret his Serene Highness the Duke of Brunswick, who fell fighting gallantly, at the head of his troops.

Although Marshal Blucher had maintained his position at Sombreffe, he still found himself much weakened by the severity of the contest in which he had been engaged, and as the fourth corps had not arrived, he determined to fall back, and concentrated his army upon Wavre; and he marched in the night after the action was over.

This movement of the Marshal's rendered necessary a corresponding one on my part; and I retired from the farm of Quatre-Bras upon Genappe, and thence upon Waterloo the next morning, the 17th, at ten o'clock.

The enemy made no effort to pursue Marshal Blucher. On the contrary, a patrol which I sent to Sombreffe in the morning, found all quiet, and the enemy's vedettes fell back as the patrol advanced. Neither did he attempt to molest our march to the rear, although made in the middle of the day, excepting by following with a large body of cavalry (brought from his right) the cavalry under the Earl of Uxbridge.

This gave Lord Uxbridge an opportunity of charging them with the 1st Life Guards, upon their debouche from the village of Genappe, upon which occasion

APPENDIX I

his Lordship has declared himself to be well satisfied with that regiment.

The position which I took up, in front of Waterloo, crossed the high-roads from Charleroi and Nivelles, and had its right thrown back to a ravine near Merbe Braine, which was occupied, and its left extended to a height above the hamlet Ter la Haye, which was likewise occupied. In front of the right centre, and near the Nivelles road, we occupied the house and garden of Hougomont, which covered the return of that flank; and in front of the left centre, we occupied the farm of La Haye Sainte. By our left we communicated with Marshal Prince Blucher at Wavre, through Ohain; and the Marshal had promised me that, in case we should be attacked, he would support me with one or more corps, as might be necessary.

The enemy collected his army, with the exception of the third corps, which had been sent to observe Marshal Blucher, on a range of heights in our front, in the course of the night of the 17th and yesterday morning; and at about ten o'clock he commenced a furious attack upon our post at Hougomont. I had occupied that post with a detachment from General Byng's brigade of guards, which was in position in its rear; and it was for some time under the command of Lieutenant-Colonel Macdonald, and afterwards of Colonel Home; and I am happy to add, that it was maintained throughout the day with the utmost gallantry by these brave troops, notwithstanding the repeated efforts of large bodies of the enemy to obtain possession of it.

This attack upon the right of our centre was accompanied by a very heavy cannonade upon our whole line, which was destined to support the repeated attacks of cavalry and infantry, occasionally mixed, but sometimes separate, which were made upon it. In one of these, the enemy carried the farm-house of La Haye Sainte, as the detachment of the light battalion of the legion which occupied it had expended all its ammunition, and the enemy occupied the only communication there was with them.

The enemy repeatedly charged our infantry with his cavalry; but these attacks were uniformly unsuccessful; and they afforded opportunities to our cavalry to charge, in one of which Lord E Somerset's brigade, Royal Horse Guards and 1st Dragoon Guards, highly distinguished themselves; as did that of Major-General Sir W Ponsonby, having taken many prisoners and an eagle.

These attacks were repeated till about seven in the evening, when the enemy made a desperate effort with the cavalry and infantry to force our left centre, near the farm of La Haye Sainte, which, after a severe contest, was defeated; and having observed that the troops retired from the attack in great confusion, and that the march of General Bulow's corps by Frichermont upon Planchenoit and La Belle Alliance had begun to take effect, and as I could perceive the fire of his cannon, and as Marshal Blucher had joined in person, with a corps of his army to the left of our line by Ohain, I determined to attack the enemy, and immediately advanced the whole line of infantry, supported by the cavalry and artillery. The attack succeeded in every point; the enemy was forced from his position on the heights, and fled in the utmost confusion, leaving behind him, as far as I could judge, ONE HUNDRED AND FIFTY PIECES OF CANNON, with their ammunition, which fell into our hands.

I continued the pursuit till after dark, and then discontinued it, only on account of the fatigue of our troops, who had been engaged during twelve hours, and because I found myself on the same road with Marshal Blucher, who assured me of his intention to follow the enemy throughout the night. He has sent me word this morning, that he had taken sixty pieces of cannon belonging to the Imperial Guard, and several carriages, baggage, etc., belonging to Buonaparte in Genappe.

I propose to move this morning upon Nivelles, and not to discontinue my operations.

Your Lordship will observe that such a desperate action could not be fought, and such advantages could not be gained, without great loss; and I am sorry to add that ours has been immense. In Lieutenant-General Sir Thomas Picton, His Majesty has sustained the loss of an officer who has frequently distinguished himself in his service; and he fell, gloriously leading his division to a charge with bayonets, by which one of the most serious attacks made by the enemy on our position was defeated.

The Earl of Uxbridge, after having successfully got through the arduous day, received a wound, by almost the last shot fired, which will, I am afraid, deprive his Majesty for some time of his services.

His Royal Highness, the Prince of Orange, distinguished himself by his gallantry and conduct till he received a wound from a musquet-ball through the shoulder, which obliged him to quit the field.

It gives me great satisfaction to assure your Lordship that the army never, upon any occasion, conducted itself better. The division of Guards under Lieutenant-General Cooke, who is severely wounded, Major-General Maitland, and Major Byng, set an example, which was followed by all; and there is no officer, nor description of troops, that did not behave well.

I must, however, particularly mention, for His Royal Highness's approbation, Lieutenant-General Sir H Clinton, Major-General Adam, Lieutenant-General Charles Baron Alten, severely wounded; Major-General Sir Colin Halket, severely wounded; Colonel Ompteda, Colonel Mitchell, commanding a brigade of the 4th division; Major-Generals Sir James Kempt and Sir Denis Pack, Major-General Lambert, Major-General Lord E Somerset, Major-General Sir W Ponsonby, Major-General Sir C Grant, and Major-General Sir H Vivian; Major-General Sir O Vandeleur, Major-General Count Dornberg. I am also particularly indebted to General Lord Hill for his assistance and conduct upon this as upon all occasions.

The artillery and engineer departments were conducted much to my satisfaction by Colonel Sir G Wood and Colonel Smyth; and I had every reason to be satisfied with the conduct of the Adjutant-General, Major-General Barnes, who was wounded, and of the Quarter-Master-General, Colonel Delancey, who was killed by a cannon-shot in the middle of the action. This officer is a serious loss to His Majesty's service, and to me at this moment. I was likewise much indebted to the assistance of Lieutenant-Colonel Lord Fitzroy-Somerset, who was severely wounded, and of the officers composing my personal staff, who have suffered severely in this action. Lieutenant-Colonel the Honourable Sir Alexander Gordon, who has died of his wounds, was a most promising officer, and is a serious loss to His Majesty's service.

General Kruse, of the Nassau service, likewise conducted himself much to my satisfaction, as did General Tripp, commanding the heavy brigade of cavalry, and General Vanhope, commanding a brigade of infantry of the King of the Netherlands.

General Pozzo di Borgo, General Baron Vincent, General Muffling, and General Alava were in the field during the action, and rendered me every assistance in their power. Baron Vincent is wounded, but I hope not severely; and General Pozzo di Borgo received a contusion.

I should not do justice to my feelings, or to Marshal Blucher and the Prussian army, if I did not attribute the successful result of this arduous day to the cordial and timely assistance received from them.

The operation of Baron Bulow upon the enemy's flank was a most decisive one; and, even if I had not found myself in a situation to make the attack which produced the final result, it would have forced the enemy to retire if his attacks should have failed, and would have prevented him from taking advantage of them if they should unfortunately have succeeded.

I send with this despatch two eagles, taken by the troops in this action, which Major Percy will have the honour of laying at the feet of his Royal Highness. I beg leave to recommend him to your Lordship's protection. I have the honour, etc.

(signed) WELLINGTON

Ney's Letter to Fouché

The Prince of Moskwa (Marshal Ney) to His Excellency the Duke of Otranto (Joseph Fouché)

M. Le Duc,—The most false and defamatory reports have been spreading for some days over the public mind, upon the conduct which I have pursued during this short and unfortunate campaign. The journals have reported those odious calumnies, and appear to lend them credit. After having fought for twenty-five years for my country, after having shed my blood for its glory and independence, an attempt is made to accuse me of treason; an attempt is made to mark me out to the people, and the army itself, as the author of the disaster it has just experienced.

Forced to break silence, while it is always painful to speak of one's self, and, above all, to answer calumnies, I address myself to you, Sir, as the President of the Provisional Government, for the purpose of laying before you a faithful statement of the events I have witnessed. On the 11th of June I received an order from the minister of war to repair to the imperial presence. I had no command, and no information upon the composition and strength of the army. Neither the Emperor nor his minister had given me any previous hint, from which I could anticipate that I should be employed in the present campaign. I was consequently taken by surprise—without horses, without accoutrements, and without money, and I was obliged to borrow the necessary expenses of my journey. Having arrived on the 12th at Laon, on the 13th at Avesnes, and on the 14th at Beaumont, I purchased, in this last city, two horses from the Duke of Treviso [Marshal Mortier], with which I repaired, on the 15th, to Charleroi, accompanied by my first aide-de-camp, the only officer who attended me.

The Emperor ordered me immediately to put myself at the head of the 1st and 2nd corps of infantry, commanded by Lieutenant-Generals d'Erlon and Reille, of the division of light cavalry of the guard under the command of Lieutenant-Generals Lefebvre Desnouettes and Colbert, and of two divisions of cavalry of the Count Valmy—forming, in all, eight divisions of infantry, and four of cavalry. With these troops, a part of which only I had as yet under my immediate command, I pursued the enemy, and forced him to evacuate Gosselies, Frasne, Millet, Heppegnies. There they took up a position for the night, with the exception of the 1st corps, which was still at Marchiennes, and which did not join me till the following day.

On the 16th I received orders to attack the English in their position at Quatre-Bras. We advanced towards the enemy with an enthusiasm difficult to be described. Nothing resisted our impetuosity. The battle became general, and victory was no longer doubtful, when, at the moment that I intended to order up the first corps of infantry, which had been left by me in reserve at Frasnes, I learned that the Emperor had disposed of it without advising me of the circumstances, as well as of the division of Girard of the second corps, on purpose to direct them upon St Amand, and to strengthen his left wing, which was vigorously engaged with the Prussians. The shock which this intelligence gave me, confounded me. Having no longer under me more than three divisions, instead of the eight upon which I calculated, I was obliged to renounce the hopes of victory; and in spite of all my efforts, in spite of the intrepidity and devotion of my troops, my utmost efforts after that could only maintain me in my position till the close of the day. About nine o'clock, the first corps was sent me by the Emperor, to whom it had been of no service. Thus twenty-five or thirty thousand men were, I may say, paralysed, and were idly paraded during the whole of the battle from the right to the left, and the left to the right, without firing a shot.

It is impossible for me, Sir, not to arrest your attention for a moment upon these details, in order to bring before your view all the consequences of this false movement, and, in general, of the bad arrangements during the whole of the day. By what fatality, for example, did the Emperor, instead of leading all his forces against Lord Wellington, who would have been attacked unawares, and could not have resisted, consider this attack as secondary? How did the Emperor, after the passage of the Sambre, conceive it possible to fight two battles on the same day? It was to oppose forces double ours, and to do what military men, who were witnesses of it, can scarcely yet comprehend. Instead of this, had he left a corps of observation to watch the Prussians, and marched with his most powerful masses to support me, the English army had undoubtedly been destroyed between Quatre-Bras and Genappe; and this position, which separated the two allied armies, being once in our power, would have opened for the Emperor an opportunity of advancing to the right of the Prussians, and of crushing them in their turn. The general opinion in France, and especially in the army, was, that the Emperor would have bent his whole efforts to annihilate first the English army—and circumstances were favourable for the accomplishment of such a project; but fate ordered otherwise.

On the 17th, the army marched in the direction of Mont St Jean. On the 18th, the battle began at one o'clock; and though the bulletin which details it makes no mention of me, it is not necessary for me to mention that I was engaged in it. Lieutenant-General Count Drouet has already spoken of that battle, in the House of Peers. His narration is accurate, with the exception of some important facts which he has passed over in silence, or of which he was ignorant, and which it is now my duty to declare. About seven o'clock in the evening, after the most frightful carnage which I have ever witnessed, General La Bédoyère came to me with a message from the Emperor, that Marshal Grouchy had arrived on our right, and attacked the left of the English and Prussians united. This general officer, in riding along the lines, spread this intelligence among the soldiers, whose courage and devotion remained unshaken, and who gave new proofs of them at that moment, in spite of the fatigue which they experienced. Immediately after, what was my astonishment, I should rather say indignation, when I learned, that so far from Marshal Grouchy having arrived to support me, as the whole army had been assured, between forty and fifty thousand Prussians attacked our extreme right, and forced it to retire!

Whether the Emperor was deceived with regard to the time when the marshal could support him, or whether the march of the marshal was retarded by the efforts of the enemy, longer than was calculated upon, the fact is, that at the moment when his arrival was announced to us, he was only at Wavre upon the Dyle, which to us was the same as if he had been a hundred leagues from the field of battle.

A short time afterwards, I saw four regiments of the Middle Guard, conducted by the Emperor, arriving. With these troops he wished to renew the attack, and to penetrate the centre of the enemy. He ordered me to lead them on: generals, officers and soldiers all displayed the greatest intrepidity; but this body of troops was too weak to resist for a long time the forces opposed to it by the enemy, and it was soon necessary to renounce the hope which this attack had for a few moments inspired. General Friant had been struck with a ball by my side, and I myself had my horse killed, and fell under it. The brave men who will return from this terrible battle will, I hope, do me the justice to say, that they saw me on foot with sword in hand during the whole of the evening, and that I only quitted the scene of carnage among the last, and at the moment when retreat could no longer be prevented. At the same time, the Prussians continued their offensive movements, and our right sensibly retired; the English advanced in their turn. There remained to us still four squares of the Old Guard to protect the retreat. These brave grenadiers, the choice of the army, forced successively to retire, yielded ground foot by foot, till, overwhelmed by numbers, they were almost entirely annihilated. From that moment, a retrograde movement was declared, and the army formed nothing but a confused mass. There was not, however, a total rout, nor the cry of *'Sauve qui peut'*, as has been calumniously stated in the bulletin. As for myself, constantly in the rear-guard, which I followed on foot, having all my horses killed, worn out by fatigue, covered with contusions, and having no longer strength to march, I owe my life to a corporal who supported me on the road, and did not abandon me during the retreat. At eleven at night I found Lieutenant-General Lefebvre Desnouettes; and one of his officers, Major Schmidt, had the generosity to give me the only horse that remained to him. In this manner I arrived at Marchienne-au-Pont at four o'clock in the morning, alone, without any officers of my staff, ignorant of what had become of the Emperor, who, before the end of the battle, had entirely disappeared, and who, I was allowed to believe, might be either killed or taken prisoner. General Pamphele Lacroix, chief of the staff of the second corps, whom I found in this city, having told me that the Emperor was at Charleroi, I was led to suppose that his Majesty was going to put himself at the head of Marshal Grouchy's corps, to cover the Sambre, and to facilitate to the troops the means of rallying towards Avesnes; and, with this persuasion, I went to Beaumont. But parties of cavalry following on too near, and having already intercepted the roads of Maubeuge and Philippeville, I became sensible of the total impossibility of arresting a single soldier on that point, to oppose the progress of the victorious enemy. I continued my march upon Avesnes, where I could obtain no intelligence of what had become of the Emperor.

In this state of matters, having no knowledge of his Majesty nor of the major-general, confusion increasing every moment, and, with the exception of some fragments of regiments of the guard and of the line, every one following his own inclination, I determined immediately to go to Paris by St Quentin, to disclose as quickly as possible the true state of affairs to the minister of war, that he might send the army some fresh troops, and take the measures which circumstances rendered necessary. At my arrival at Bourget, three leagues from Paris, I learned that the Emperor had passed there at nine o'clock in the morning.

Such, M. le Duc, is a history of the calamitous campaign.

Now, I ask those who have survived this fine and numerous army, how I can be accused of the disasters of which it has been the victim, and of which your military annals furnish no example. I have, it is said, betrayed my country—I who, to serve it, have shown a zeal which I perhaps have carried to an extravagant height: but this calumny is supported by no fact, by no circumstance. But how can these odious reports, which spread with frightful rapidity, be arrested? If, in the researches which I could make on this subject, I did not fear almost as much to discover as to be ignorant of the truth, I would say, that all has a tendency to convince that I have been unworthily deceived, and that it is attempted to cover, with the pretence of treason, the faults and extravagances of this campaign—faults which have not been avowed in the bulletins that have appeared, and against which I in vain raised that voice of truth which I will yet cause to resound in the House of Peers. I expect, from the candour of your Excellency, and from your indulgence to me, that you will cause this letter to be inserted in the Journal, and give it the greatest possible publicity.

MARSHAL PRINCE OF MOSKWA

Paris, June 26, 1815

Ode to the Duchess of Angoulême

published anonymously by
Aubrey de Vere
London 1815

I

Faint wanderer of an exiled race,
  Sad Orphan of a martyred Sire!
Come to thy first, last resting place,
  From worldly pomp and woe retire.
Come in thy tearless agony,
With marble cheek and frozen eye;
    Oh come, all hopeless as thou art,
And lay thee down in peace, and still thy bursting heart.

II

Victim of too severe a fate,
  Wert thou too lightly tried before,
Snatched from the ruins of a State,
  And sprinkled with paternal gore?
Were all thy trials deemed too few,
That still thy wounds must bleed anew—
    Still must it be thy mournful doom,
To pine o'er sorrows past, and brood o'er woes to come?

III

Oh! nursed in pomp and born to power,
  To wisdom's influence, beauty's spell!
What lot was thine—the Orphan's dower—

Where was thy home—the Felon's cell!
Thy woes at length by time beguiled,
Once more deceitful fortune smiled;
    And woke thee with so grand a strain,
The rush of sudden joy was almost felt like pain.

IV

Then was thy hour of triumphing;
    If aught of mortal frailty
Around that chastened heart could cling,
    Or stain thine angel purity.
But thine was joy so softened down
By sorrow's unforgotten frown,
    That still through smiles and tear-drop stole,
As new born Hope and Memory blended in thy soul.

V

Sad was thy pensive countenance,
    In silent prayer upraised to Heaven;
In prayer for thy repentant France,
    Guilty so late, so soon forgiven.
Such wert thou, when th'acclaiming throng,
Bore thee triumphantly along:
    So calm, so holy seemed thy joy,
Even hearts unused to melt were touched to sympathy.

VI

But oh, how deep emotion swept,
    When first that solemn mass was sung,   [see note a]
When kneeling thousands bowed and wept,
    And joined in prayer thy trembling tongue.
For then, as paused the organ's roll,
Thy moan came sadly on the soul;
    Thy shrouded form, pale, bent in prayer,
Appeared as if long-lost Religion's self was there!

VII

Lo! where with pomp and pageantry,
    Yon dark, funereal train of woe,   [see note b]
March in their mute solemnity,
    To wailing dirges, soft and slow!
Once more thy tortured moan is heard,

163

FROM ABBOTSFORD TO PARIS AND BACK

Responsive to each sacred word,
    Blent with the organ's plaintive tones
Pouring sad requiem o'er the consecrated bones.

VIII

Aye! thousands wept, and thousands blest,
   And thousands round thy footsteps hung;
As new-born reverence swelled the breast,
   As pity probed, repentance stung.
Yet these the men—oh mortal stain!
When shall we trust Mankind again?
    The same-same breath that fauned thy way,
Welcomes th'usurper back, and ratifies his sway!

IX

Yes, all Mankind shall feel the shock,
   That rends time-hallowed sympathies,
And learn from guilty France to mock
   All human laws, all human ties.
Mercy shall lift her wings, and hence
Depart with frank-eyed confidence;
    And Fear shall call on Murder's arm,
To strike resistance down, and quell each vain alarm.

X

Frenchmen! we curse your very name,
   Unblushing in your worthlessness,
Stampt with each varied brand of shame,
   By word of utter faithlessness.
At once so cringing and so proud,
Base in distress, in triumph loud,
    So fierce, yet abject—mean, though vain;
Ne'er may degraded Man bend to such yoke again!

XI

Today Napoleon forced to fly,
   With taunt and threat, and curse and scorn;
God save King Louis! is the cry,
   Home on triumphant shoulders borne.
To peace ye pour the suppliant vow,
To meek Religion's shrine ye bow,
    Abjure stern Conquest's red career,
And bend to Science voice with no unwilling ear.

XII

Yet now, poor hirelings of a day!
  Weak changelings of a shallow hour!
Ye spurn a Monarch's righteous sway,
  Invoke a Despot back to power,
The sacred bonds of Peace disclaim,
And scoff Religion's holy name,
    And kneeling at Bellona's car,
Bid weeping Science seek some happier shore afar.

XIII

Awake, awake! we do but dream!
  We dream of troubles past from Earth—
Awake! 'tis Fancy's feverish gleam,
  Shadowing terrific visions forth;
The bloody Spectre of the past
Hath risen o'er our rest at last;
    Sweeps in unreal terrors by,
With terror-stricken mien, and woe-denouncing cry!

XIV

Awake? alas, this is not sleep—
  No dream—we feel—we hear—we see—
In vain o'er wasted hours we weep,
  And trembling scan Futurity!
We thought, oh fools, his light was quenched,
His fires decayed, his lustre blenched:
    Nor dreamt a Sun so darkly set,
Might o'er the World arise in storm and terror yet.

XV

Lo! Discord claps her raven wings,
  And lurking Havoc inly smiles;
The sultry Siroc blows, and brings
  The Daemon of ten thousand ills:
For now the Spoiler of the Earth
Comes, like the Eastern Idol, forth;
    Around his mad'ning victims reel,
And cast their limbs beneath his pitiless chariot-wheel.

165

XVI

Or haply, like th'Arch-fiend, when first
   The confines of the world he trod;
Fierce from his bonds so lately burst,
   Scathed by the Thunderbolts of God:
When every Angel-guard at last
With guileful tongue and swift wing past,
    He bent malignant o'er his prey,
With flattering smiles to curse, and tempting to betray.

XVII

And yet, by Heaven, 'twas nobly bold,
   (Howe'er the day be lost or won)
Thus like the Roman chief of old,
   To dare another Rubicon.
Yet was not then, that Roman heart
So fiercely tried as now Thou art:
    One final strife was his to fight,
But thou must turn to stem the World's united might.

XVIII

Foul Rebel! did no tongue defy,
   No arm thy desperate march oppose?
And Louis, wert thou doomed to fly,
   'Mid coward friends and pitying foes?
Oh! better to have braved the strife,
The Tyrant's frown, th'assassin's knife,
    Mournfully in royal state enthroned,
Thy lost, devoted Race, and faithful Peers around.

XIX

So erst, still in misfortune great,
   Sternly composed, calm in despair,
So erst Rome's awful Senate sat,
   Nor raised an arm, nor breathed a prayer;
Dauntless they sat, though wild at hand
Barbarians stormed, with fire and brand;
    Immoveable, to Fate resigned,
Rome was triumphant still in her unconquered mind.

APPENDIX III

XX

Yet when from modern man expect
  The vigour of an earlier day?
Dimly at best do we reflect
  The worth of Ages past away.
The virtues of the days gone by
Shine like the blessed Stars on high,
    Pouring through Time's long, troubled night,
A guiding ray serene, inimitably bright!

XXI

We're fallen upon portentous times,
  A stormy yet degenerate age;
Our world a Theatre of crimes,
  A tragic scene, a bloody stage.
In after-days we little guess
How poorly in our nakedness,
    How base of heart, how mean of mind,
Our deeds shall stand amid the annals of mankind.

XXII

And after-ages, when thy doom
  Is but a tale of History,
Shall mourn around thine exiled tomb,
  Sad daughter of Adversity!
Aye, they shall weep, when tears are vain,
Their tears shall deepen every stain,
    When thou art gone beyond the sky,
Throned in immortal Peace, with Him that dwells on high!

Note a: 'When first that solemn mass'. St.VI,1.2—soon after the restoration of the Bourbons, this mournful service was performed, in honour of the memory of Louis XVI and Marie Antoinette.

Note b: 'Yon dark, funereal train'. St.VII,1.2—Alluding to the funeral procession that accompanied the late-discovered relics of the royal martyrs to the tombs of their ancestors.

Saint Cloud

(Paris, September 5, 1815)

Soft spread the southern summer night
  Her veil of darkness blue;
Ten thousand stars combined to light
  The terrace of Saint Cloud.

The evening breezes gently sigh'd,
  Like breath of lover true,
Bewailing the deserted pride
  And wreck of sweet Saint Cloud.

The drum's deep roll was heard afar,
  The bugle wildly blew
Good-night to Hulan and Hussar,
  That garrison Saint Cloud.

The startled Naiads from the shade
  With broken urns withdrew,
And silenced was that proud cascade,
  The glory of Saint Cloud.

We sate upon its steps of stone,
  Nor could its silence rue,
When waked, to music of our own,
  The echoes of Saint Cloud.

Slow Seine might hear each lovely note
  Fall light as summer dew,
While through the moonless air they float,
  Prolong'd from fair Saint Cloud.

And sure a melody more sweet
   His waters never knew,
Though music's self was wont to meet
   With Princes at Saint Cloud.

Nor then, with more delighted ear,
   The circle round her drew,
Than ours, when gather'd round to hear
   Our songstress at Saint Cloud.

Few happy hours poor mortals pass,—
   Then give those hours their due,
And rank among the foremost class
   Our evenings at Saint Cloud.

Notes and References

(Place of publication is London unless otherwise stated. All references to the Waverley Novels are to the Oxford edition, 1912–1925, unless otherwise stated.)

CHAPTER I pp.1 to 32

1. *Letters* IV, 76.
2. *PL*, p.467.
3. *Letters* IV, 75.
4. For Grierson's error (*Letters* IV, 75n.2) in identifying the 'new Gaudeamus poem' with 'The Dance of Death' instead of *The Field of Waterloo*, see *Notes & Index*, p.112, col.1.
5. See Scott's note to the text of the *The Field of Waterloo* in *P.W.*, p.519.
6. *Letters* IV, 91.
7. Cf. *PL*, p.194.
8. Cf. *Letters* IV, 212 & n.1.
9. Ibid. 74, 75.
10. Ibid. 76.
11. Johnson I, 144–8; J C Corson, 'Scott Studies I–II', rpt from *University of Edinburgh Journal*, Autumn 1955, pp.109–1.
12. Johnson I, 147; Lockhart II, 119–20.
13. Cf. *Letters* I, 183–4, 275; XII, 96; Lockhart II, 119–20.
14. Lockhart V, 38–45.
15. Ch. XI: Anne Elliot's talk with Captain Benwick about contemporary poets.
16. Cf. Lockhart IV, 56–8; V, 26–30.
17. Cf. 'In truth I am not sure it would be considered quite decorous for me as a Clerk of Session to write novels. Judges being monks, Clerks are a sort of lay-brethren from whom some solemnity of walk and conduct may be expected.' (Scott to J B Morritt [28 July 1814], *Letters* III, 479).
18. *Letters* X, 166n.1, 172–5, 260; *Journal*, p.396.
19. Smiles I, 272–3; *Letters* IV, 75 & n.1.
20. Lockhart V, 38–52.
21. *Letters* III, 334, 335–6, 338–9, 341, 342–6, 365, 373.
22. Ibid. IV, 66–7; Lockhart V, 46–7.
23. XIII, April 1815, pp.215–75.
24. *Letters* IV, 75.
25. Cf. F Jeffrey, 'Walter Scott' in *Essays from the Quarterly Review*, n.d., p.271n.
26. Cf. *Caledonian Mercury*, 3 July 1815; Simpson I, 54–5.

27. Introduction to Canto II, *P.W.*, p.102, col.1. There were *two* Alexander Pringles of Whytbank & Yair: father and son. Scott was very friendly with both, and indeed with the entire Pringle family. But his fellow-traveller was Alexander Pringle *junior*. The distinction between father and son is not made by Professor E Johnson in *Sir Walter Scott The Great Unknown*, either in the text or in the index (see II, p.1383, col.2); in consequence the misleading impression is conveyed (see I, 495) that it was Alexander Pringle *senior* who was Scott's fellow-traveller. For correct distinction see *Notes & Index*, p.598, col.2.
28. Cf. *Letters* I, 479; IV, 74.
29. *Journal of a Tour to the Continent in Autumn 1815 with Sir Walter Scott, etc.* MS 991, National Library of Scotland.
30. Cf. Lockhart IV, Chs. XXVIII–XXXII.
31. Cf. canto III, sts. XIII–XVII, XXVIII & nn. XXXII & XXXIV; canto IV, st. X & n.XXXIX.
32. 'Extracts from a Journal kept during a Coasting Voyage through the Scottish Islands' in *Edinburgh Annual Register* for 1812 (publ. 1814), vol. V, pt.II, 431–46; *Letters* IV, 22.
33. Lockhart III, 157, 126.
34. *Letters* IV, 78; XII, 135; *PL*, pp.6–7.
35. *PL*, p.220; *Letters* IV, 78; XII, 136; Gala p.33.
36. Cf. *PL*, p.222.
37. Ibid. pp.8–9, 13–14; *Letters* IV, 214.
38. Cf. Lockhart I, 51; *Letters* IV, 214; *PL*, pp.195, 228.
39. *Letters* IV, 214.
40. Cf. *Waverley*, Ch. III, p.19.
41. *Letters* IV, 214.
42. Cf. *Journal*, pp.546–7.
43. *PL*, p.18.
44. Ch. XXII, p.183.
45. *PL*, pp.17–18.
46. Cf. Chs. XXXVIII–XXXIX.
47. Chs. III, p.24; IV, p.30; XL, pp.363–4; XLI, pp.368–9.
48. Cf. Lockhart X, 260.
49. Canto III, sts. XIII–XVII & n.XX
50. *PL*, pp.26–7.
51. Ch. XLVI, p.348.
52. *Letters* III, 398.
53. Ibid. XII, 136; *PL*, pp.223–5; Gala p.29. Cf. also *Life of Buonaparte* VIII, 338–9.
54. *Letters* IV, 78; *PL*, pp.230–32; Gala p.26; Gordon II, 337.
55. *PL*, pp.223; Gala pp.29, 31. Cf. also *Life of Buonaparte* VIII, 394.
56. *PL*, 389.
57. Cf. *Letters* III, 151, 240; IV, 97, XII, 153.
58. *PL*, p.231; Gordon II, 337. Rubens's tomb is not in Antwerp's cathedral, as stated by Scott, but in the church of St James's, as stated by Gala pp.27–8.
59. *PL*, p.230; *Letters* XII, 136.
60. Cf. *PL*, p.324.
61. IV, line 11.
62. Ch. I, p.7. Cf. also Ch. XXVI, p.324 & *Journal*, p.102.
63. *PL*, pp.239–40.
64. Cf. Ibid. pp.340–41; Lockhart V, 94.

65. Gordon II, 326.
66. *PL*, p.340.
67. Oxford edn (publ. 1906), p.72.
68. *PL*, p.225.
69. Cf. D E Sultana, *The Journey of Sir Walter Scott to Malta* (Gloucester & New York, 1986), p.33.
70. *PL*, pp.225–8. Cf. *Life of Buonaparte* V, 264–5, 351–2.
71. *PL*, p.228.
72. *Letters* XII, 135. Prof C Woodring ('Three Poets on Waterloo' in *The Wordsworth Circle, XVIII, No. 2, Spring 1987, p.84*) misdates Scott's arrival at Brussels as 'early September'.
73. For Scott's correction, in later edns of *PL*, of 'a very gross error' on his part in the 1st and 2nd edns of *PL*, (p.229), 'stigmatizing the Archbishop of Liège [*sic*]', instead of the Archbishop of Ghent, as the leader of the Flemish clergy's opposition to religious toleration, see *Misc. Pr. W.* I, 481n.1.
74. *PL*, pp.229–30, 233, 406.
75. Ibid. pp.229, 389.
76. Ibid. pp.232-3, 390.
77. Cf. *The Abbot*, Ch. X, pp.93–4; *The Betrothed*, Ch. X, pp.91–2; *Letters* V, 211; D E Sultana, *op.cit.*, p.85.
78. Cf. Lockhart X, 244; H R Sefton, 'Scott as Churchman' in *Scott & his Influence* (University of Aberdeen, 1983), pp.240–41.
79. Ch. XXXIX, pp.348–51.
80. Chs. XXXV–XXXVI.
81. *PL*, pp.161–2; *Letters* IV, 81, 93.
82. Gordon II, 337; *Letters* IV, 83; Gala pp.38–9; *PL*, p.232.
83. Line 6.
84. Gala p.35; Bruce, 7 August 1815.
85. Cf. Simpson pp.15–16; Longford *Wellington* I, 495.
86. Cf. *Peveril of the Peak*, Ch. XXVII, p.349.
87. *PL*, pp.9–10.
88. Cf. Simpson pp.23–4.
89. *PL*, p.233–4.
90. Ibid. p.14. Cf. *The Heart of Midlothian*, Ch. XIV, p.173.
91. E.g., the dress of Jeanie Deans in her celebrated interviews with the Duke of Argyle and Queen Caroline in *The Heart of Midlothian*, Chs. XXXV, pp.91, 425; XXXVI, p.430. See also Ch. XXVIII, p.322, and *The Fair Maid of Perth*, Ch. II, p.8: '... the beauty of Catherine [Glover], though concealed beneath her screen—which resembled the mantilla still worn in Flanders ...'.
92. E.g. the Regent Moray in *The Abbot*, Ch. XVIII, p.200, and Henry Smith, the armourer in *The Fair Maid of Perth*, Ch. IV, p.36.
93. *PL*, p.14.
94. Cf. Gala p.34; Bruce, 8 August 1815.
95. Cf. Lady Shelley I, 177.
96. Cf. Ch. XXI, p.213.
97. *PL*, pp.235, 99–100; Gala pp.40–41.
98. *PL*, pp.235–6.
99. Ibid. p.221.
100. *Letters* IV, 83; Gala pp.42–3.
101. Ibid.; *Letters* XII, 138; *PL*, pp.236–7.
102. St. IX.

103. *PL*, pp.97–9, 157.
104. Ibid.; *Letters* IV, 83; Gala p.43.
105. Lockhart V, 54–8.
106. E.g., p.13, last paragraph echoes Charles Bell's letter in Lockhart V, 55–6.
107. *PL*, pp.95–7.
108. St. XXI.
109. Cf. *PL*, pp.97, 103; Appendix I, p.156.
110. Canto VI, Sts. XIX–XXXVIII.
111. Cf. Scott's review of J W Croker's *The Battles of Talavera* in *QR*, Nov. 1809, p.428: '... *The Battle [sic] of Talavera* is written in that irregular Pindaric measure first applied to serious composition by Mr Walter Scott, and it is doing no injustice to the serious author to say, that in many passages, we were, from the similarity of the stanza and of the subject, involuntarily reminded of the battle of Flodden, in the sixth book of *Marmion* ...'.
112. Cf. *Letters* V, 24, 143.
113. *The Field of Waterloo*, St. XXI; *PL*, p.169.
114. St. XXI
115. XVII–XXXII.
116. St. XXIX, line 1.
117. St. XVII, line 20.
118. Sts. XVII, line 9; XVIII, line 2.
119. Vol. XVI, Oct. 1816, No. XXI, pp.172–208.
120. *PL*, pp.70–193. The information in Johnson I, 494, that 'Britain, Russia, Prussia, Austria, each pledged 180,000 men and put the Duke of Wellington in command of this host' is incorrect. It is a misreading of Johnson's source: Sir A Bryant, *The Age of Elegance 1812–22* (1950), pp.215–16, 218. Wellington was not a sort of generalissimo over all the Allied armies. The Russian, Austrian, and Prussian armies (including Blücher's troops) were not under Wellington's command. The Russian and Austrian armies did not, of course, take part in the battles of Ligny and Waterloo. Wellington commanded only the army of the Low Countries (British, Dutch, Belgians, etc.). Blücher commanded the Prussian army of the Lower Rhine. See Longford *Wellington* I, p.465. Even Oman (p.196) seems to have been under the misapprehension that Wellington was Commander-in-Chief of all the Allied forces.
121. Cf. Chs .XLIV–XLVII.
122. Cf. *PL*, pp.155, 159.
123. *Letters* IV, 138; Gala p.37; Bruce, 7 August 1815.
124. Cf. *PL*, pp.167–72; *Letters* IV, 81, 82, 93, 212.
125. X.
126. St. XIII.
127. *PL*, p.171.
128. Sts. XII–XIV.
129. *PL*, pp.178–85; *Letters* IV, 81. 82.
130. St. XIII.
131. P.193.
132. Ibid. pp.180–82.
133. Cf. *Letters* XII, 137–8.
134. Lockhart V, 46.
135. Gordon II, 334; *Letters* XII, 138.
136. *PL*, p.144.
137. *Letters* IV, 92–3.

138. Ibid. 81, 93; *PL*, p.154.
139. *Letters* IV, 80.
140. Sts.XI–XII.
141. *PL*, pp.142–3.
142. Ibid. pp.176–7. 181–3, 185–6.
143. No. XIII.
144. *Letters* XII, 137 & n.1, 138; Gordon II, 334.
145. Pp.142, 145.
146. Ibid. pp.76, 380; Gala p.40; *Life of Buonaparte* VIII, 497.
147. P.187.
148. St. XIV.
149. Bruce, 8 August 1815; *Life of Buonaparte* VIII, 497; Longford *Wellington* I, 565.
150. *PL*, pp.98–9; Frazer pp.567, 572.
151. M M Maxwell-Scott, *The Personal Relics and Antiquarian Treasures of Sir Walter Scott*, 1893, pp.28–9.
152. Gordon II, 333–4; Lockhart IX, 195.
153. Gordon II, 333–8, 319–33. Gordon met Byron at Brussels shortly *after* meeting Scott, but in his memoirs he referred to Byron's visit *before* that of Scott. He also misdated Scott's visit (p.333): '1816' instead of 1815. For Scott's comment on Gordon's memoirs, of which he was sent a volume in manuscript in August 1827, see *Journal*, p.336.
154. Gordon I, 440–54; II, 276; Lockhart V, 46–7.
155. Commonly known then by its regimental number: 'the 92nd'.
156. Pp.103, 105. The information in Johnson I, 494, suggesting that the battle of Quatre Bras was a defeat for the Anglo-Dutch-Belgian army simply because *initially* the Dutch-Belgian troops under the Prince of Orange retreated before a fierce French onslaught, is not quite correct. The Dutch-Belgian retreat was reversed by the British troops under Generals Maitland and Picton who went to their rescue, resisted the French advance, and at the end of the day 'enjoyed'—as Scott put it (*PL*, pp.102, 106)—'the most decided proof of victory, for the British army bivouacked upon the ground which had been occupied by the French during the battle'. Wellington retained possession of Quatre Bras which commanded the road to Brussels. See Appendix I, p.154 and Longford *Wellington* I, 509. Johnson appears to have misread his source: Sir A Bryant, *The Age of Elegance 1812–22* (1950), p.220, which refers to 'Napoleon's victory', but at Ligny, not Quatre Bras.
157. St. XXI; *PL*, p.105.
158. See entry 'John Cameron' in *DNB*.
159. *Letters* XII, 138; IV, 212n.1.
160. Ibid. IV, 214; Gordon II, 271; *PL*, p.97; Gala p.42.
161. Chs. XXIX, XXXII.
162. Cf. Gordon II, 268–9; *New Letters of Rob. Southey*, ed K Curry (New York & London, 1965), II, 125–6.
163. P.91. For Scott's *later* apparent retraction of this admission, see his defence of Wellington in *Life of Buonaparte* VIII, 501–3 & nn.
164. Ibid. pp.92–3.
165. Longford *Wellington* I, 495.
166. Gordon II, 334; Gala p.44; Bruce, 9 August 1815.
167. Cf. *PL*, p.136.
168. Byron, note to *Childe Harold's Pilgrimage* III, St. XXVII, line 1.

169. *PL*, pp.195–6.
170. Ibid. pp.125, 194–5; Gala p.44; Bruce, 9 August 1815.
171. The date of De Lancey's marriage is erroneously given as '1813' in *Letters* IX, 247n.2 instead of 4 April 1815. See entry on De Lancey in *DNB*, and Lady De Lancey, *A Week at Waterloo in June 1815* (1906), p.118n.41.
172. Lady De Lancey, *op.cit.*, pp.13–15, 50–101; *PL*, 169. Simpson's version (p.46) of De Lancey's death is inaccurate.
173. *PL*, pp.124–5.
174. St. XXI.
175. *Letters* IX, 247–8.
176. Cf. *A Constable's Letter Book 1823–6*, MS 792 in National Library of Scotland, ff.556–7; *Letters* IX, 247n.2.
177. For Charles Dickens's response to it see his letter to Captain Basil Hall printed on pp.124–8 of Lady De Lancey's book.
178. *PL*, p.200; *Letters* IV, 79; *The Field of Waterloo*, St. VI.
179. Gordon II, 334; *Letters* XII, 139; Gala p.45.
180. *Letters* IV, 82; *PL*, pp.143–4; Simpson I, 54.
181. *PL*, pp.187–8.
182. Ibid. pp.142, 145, 180.
183. Ibid. pp.144–5; *Letters* IV, 93.
184. *PL*, p.205; *Letters* IV, 91. According to Elizabeth Longford (*Wellington* I, 547n.19), Wellington's original estimate of the slain was also 30,000, but this figure was afterwards found to be too high, and was reduced to 22,000 or 23,000.
185. *PL*, pp.81,93.
186. Ibid. p.198; *Letters* IV, 79, 91.
187. *Letters* IV, 91; *PL*, pp.200, 205–6, 208; Gala pp.46–7.
188. *Letters* XII, 139.
189. *PL*, pp.201–2; *Letters* IV, 91.
190. *PL*, pp.202–3.
191. Ibid. pp.204, 139–40; *Letters* IV, 80.
192. *The Field of Waterloo*, st. IV. Cf. R Southey, *The Poet's Pilgrimage to Waterloo*, Prt I, Section III 'The Field of Battle', st. 39.
193. P.201.
194. *Op.cit.*, st. 36.
195. *Childe Harold's Pilgrimage* III, st. 30.
196. Cf. *PL*, pp.136–41, 198; *Letters* IV, 81, 212n.1.
197. Gordon II, 334; *PL*, pp.139–40, 145–8.
198. *PL*, pp.203–4; *Letters* IV, 79–80.
199. *PL*, p.204.
200. *Letters* VII, 64.
201. *PL*, p.209; Gala p.46.
202. G Crabbe, *The Complete Poetical Works*, eds N Dalrymple-Champneys and A Pollard (Oxford, 1988), III, 359–61, 420–21. For two of Scott's quotations from Crabbe shortly before his trip to Flanders and Paris, see epigraphs in *Guy Mannering*, Chs. XXI, XXXVII.
203. See Appendix I, pp.153–7.
204. Pp.139–40, 275.
205. See Appendix I, p.155.
206. Pp.386–7.
207. Simpson pp.54–5.

208. *Letters* IV, 79; *PL*, pp.199–200, 206–8; Gordon II, 336.
209. *Letters* IV, 79; XII, 140; *PL*, pp.207–8; Lockhart I, 355–8.
210. *PL*, p.155; *Letters* IV, 80–81.
211. *Letters* X, 132.
212. Cf. *Notes & Index*, p.273, col. 1.
213. Longford *Wellington* I, 566.
214. *Letters* XII, 139.
215. Gala pp.49–50.
216. P.197.
217. Cf. Lockhart I, 51.
218. Cf. *PL*, pp.433–8.
219. Lockhart III, 269.
220. Ch. L, p.466.
221. Gordon II, 336; *Letters* IV, 79.
222. *PL*, pp.209, 213–14; Gordon II, 336.
223. *PL*, pp.210–13.
224. Ibid. pp.214–15.
225. Cf. *Letters* IV, 115; I, 489.
226. *PL*, pp.29–69.
227. Ibid. p.32.
228. Cf. Ibid. pp.41, 49.
229. Cf. *Life of Buonaparte* I, 278–9.
230. Cf. Lockhart V, 163, 212, 233.
231. Cf. vols I, i–ii; Chs. XIII–XIV, XVIII-XIX.

CHAPTER II pp.33 to 42

1. *Letters* XII, 138, 140; Bruce, 10 August 1815; *PL*, p.269. Both Johnson (I, 496) and Oman (p.197) erroneously represent Scott and his party as having hired and travelled in the low carriage not from Brussels to Paris, but practically on landing in Holland from Harwich for Bergen-op-Zoom and Antwerp.
2. Bruce, 10 August 1815. See entry about Sass in *Bryan's Dictionary of Painters and Engravers*, or in *DNB*.
3. *Letters* I, 489; III, 179.
4. Cf. *Journal*, p.230.
5. Gordon II, 325–7, 336–7; R Southey, *The Poet's Pilgrimage to Waterloo*, Part I, Section III, Sts. 11–12; Simpson, p.242.
6. Cf. *Letters* IV, 455.
7. Lockhart IX, 195–200; *Letters* IV 361n.1; *Journal*, pp.52 & n.3, 72 & n.2, 110.
8. Gala p.58; Bruce, 10 August 1815; *Letters* XII, 140.
9. Ch. XXVIII, p.303n.1.
10. *Letters* XII, 140; *PL*, pp.242–3.
11. Gala p.65; Simpson p.228.
12. *Letters* IV, 84; XII, 141; *PL*, pp.244–8; Gala pp.58–9.
13. Lockhart IV, 176.
14. *Letters* XII, 140–41; Gala pp.69–70.
15. *PL*, p.242.
16. Chs. LIX–LX.
17. *Letters* IV, 108.
18. Ibid. X, 140–41; Gala pp.69, 73, 99.

NOTES AND REFERENCES

19. St. XIII.
20. Pp.264, 273–4, 369–70.
21. Ibid. pp.263–4.
22. Ibid. pp.242–59.
23. Ch. LXIII, pp.460–63.
24. *Letters* XII, 140.
25. *PL*, pp.265–6.
26. Ibid. 267–8.
27. *Letters* XII, 140; Gala pp.63–4.
28. *PL*, p.269.
29. Ch. III, p.19.
30. *Letters* III, 240.
31. Ibid.; XII, 329.
32. *PL*, pp.250–51.
33. Ibid. p.251.
34. Ibid. pp.251–8.
35. Ibid. p.252; *Letters* IV, 108.
36. Ibid. pp.252–3, 256–7.
37. Cf. *Journal*, p.445.
38. Ch. XIV, pp.173–4.
39. Cf. *PL*, p.252.
40. Ibid. p.253.
41. I, 30–32.
42. *PL*, p.286.
43. Ibid. pp.276–7; *Letters* XII, 141; Gala pp.71–2.
44. *PL*, p.277.
45. Ibid.; 'On Landscape Gardening' in *Misc. Pr.W.* I, 778.
46. Cf. Gala p.74n.
47. Cf. *Letters* II, 11.
48. See Appendix I, p.153.
49. *Letters* IV, 83; XIII, 140; Gala p.31.
50. Cf. *PL*, pp.278, 369.
51. VII, 455, 477.
52. P.186.
53. *Letters* VII, 90.
54. Cf. ibid. IV, 84.
55. Bruce, 11 August 1815.
56. *PL*, p.271.
57. Ch. XXV, p.308n.1.
58. Chs. XXV–XXXIV.
59. Ch. XXV.
60. Introduction 1813 edn, p.xiii.
61. *PL*, p.272.
62. Ibid. pp.243–4; Gala p.58; Bruce, 19 August 1815.
63. *PL*, pp.244–5.
64. Cf. *Letters* I, 28; *Life of Buonaparte* II, 217.
65. *PL*, p.283.
66. Ibid. pp.282, 285–6.
67. Ibid. pp.278–80; *Letters* XII, 141.
68. *PL*, p.280.
69. Ibid. pp.282, 285; Gala pp.72–3.

70. A Young, *Travels in France during the Years 1787, 1788, 1789*, ed M Betham-Edwards (1913), pp.10, 82.
71. Bruce, 13 August 1815.
72. *Letters* IV, 70–71.
73. V, 109–24.
74. P.380.
75. *Letters* IV, 40.

CHAPTER III pp.43 to 80

1. *Letters* IV, 85, 86; XII, 142; *PL*, pp.288, 292, 293.
2. *PL*, pp.293–4.
3. Ibid. pp.289, 291–2; *Letters* IV, 85, 87, 89; X, 142.
4. *Letters* IV, 88, 96; XII, 142, 143; *PL*, pp.386, 464.
5. *PL*, pp.291–2.
6. Cf. *Letters* IV, 87, 88, 91, 100.
7. Cf. ibid., 88, 108; XII, 143, 145, 146–7; *PL*, p.465; Gala pp.122–4.
8. *Letters* IV, 117, 110.
9. Ibid. XII, 384.
10. Lines 65–74.
11. *Letters* IV, 120.
12. Cf. *Letters* IV, 91, 116; I, 484. For correct date of IV, 91, see *Notes & Index*, p.112, col. 2.
13. *PL*, p.18.
14. Cf. *Letters* V, 188.
15. Simpson p.129.
16. Gala pp.78–9; *Letters* XII, 142.
17. P.327.
18. *Letters* IV, 108–9; *PL*, pp.330–31.
19. *Letters* IV, 88; XII, 147; Gala pp.82–5, 216; *PL*, pp.327–8; Simpson p.124.
20. *Letters* IV, 88; *PL*, pp.293, 296; Gala p.81; Frazer p.598.
21. *PL*, pp.292, 293, 322–3.
22. Ibid. pp.298–301.
23. Ibid. pp.298–9.
24. Canto III, st. 40, lines 3–4.
25. Vol. XVI, No. XXI, October 1816, p.196.
26. *PL*, p.329; *Letters* IV, 109.
27. *PL*, pp.325–6.
28. *Letters* IV, 88; Longford *Wellington* II, pp.26–7.
29. *PL*, pp.326–7.
30. Gala p.159.
31. Ch. XXXV, p.377.
32. Cf. *Waverley*, Ch. XVII, p.122; *Guy Mannering*, Ch. XVII, p.144; Ch. XXX, p.253.
33. Gala p.159.
34. Pp.381–2.
35. Ibid. p.314; *Letters* IV, 108.
36. Cf. Gala p.159; Simpson p.188.
37. Cf. Simpson pp.201–2.
38. *PL*, pp.333–4.

39. Cf. John Scott, *A Visit to Paris in 1814* (1815), p.307.
40. *PL*, p.336; Gala pp.86–7; Simpson pp.222, 252; John Scott, *op.cit.*, p.315.
41. Gala p.6.
42. Pp.462–3.
43. P O'Leary, *Regency Editor: Life of John Scott* (Aberdeen, 1983), pp.76–7; *Letters* IV, 193.
44. P.463.
45. Ibid. pp.322–4, 341; Simpson p.121; Gala pp.79, 215–16.
46. *PL*, pp.338.
47. Ibid. pp.338–9.
48. Gala pp.160–61; John Scott, *op.cit.*, p.331.
49. *PL*, p.341.
50. Gala p.202.
51. Ch. XXXI, p.370.
52. *PL*, pp.337–8; Gala pp.158, 161.
53. Gala p.161; *Letters* II, 45–6.
54. Cf. *Bryan's Dictionary of Painters and Engravers* (1901–2), III, 74; *Diary of Joseph Farington*, ed J Greig, , VI, 4–5; *Lord Byron: Selected Letters and Journals*, ed L A Marchand (1982), p.372. Oman (p.200) seems to have misidentified 'Mr Hoppner'.
55. Gala p.158–9; *PL*, p.338.
56. Cf. *Journal*, p.476 & n.2; *Letters* X, 450–51.
57. P.330.
58. Ibid. p.334.
59. Cf. *Journal*, p.88; *PL*, pp.332, 335.
60. Cf. Gala pp.28, 85; Simpson pp.151, 201.
61. *PL*, p.335.
62. Ibid. p.338.
63. II, 281.
64. V, 87.
65. Cf. *Sir Walter Scott's Journal*, ed D Douglas (Edinburgh, 1891), p.290n.1; Oman p.202.
66. Gala pp.200–204.
67. Cf. IV, 63; *Letters* X, 72 & n.
68. Gala pp.163–4.
69. Ibid. p.195. Cf. *Catalogue of the Library at Abbotsford* by J B Cochrane (Edinburgh, 1838), p.35.
70. Scott's friend, the late George Ellis, had made the same point to Scott himself as far back as 1805: 'I have never been able to look at a volume of the Benedictine edition of the early French histories without envy.' (*Letters* I, 251n.1)
71. Ch. III, p.19.
72. Cf. VII, 217n.
73. *QR*, vol. V, January 1805, p.347.
74. *PL*, pp.288, 312, 314.
75. Ibid. p.312.
76. Ibid. pp.314–18; Gala p.119.
77. Gala pp.152–4; *PL*, p.312.
78. Simpson pp.162, 215.
79. *Letters* XI, 468n.2.
80. Pp.162–5, 215, 263.

81. Lockhart I, 55–9.
82. *Letters* XI, 468n.2; Gala p.113n.
83. P.120.
84. I, 164n.
85. Ibid. II, 101–2; *PL*, pp.318–19.
86. *PL*, p.320; *Life of Buonaparte* II, 101–2.
87. Bruce, 14 August 1815; Simpson pp.176–7; Gala pp.157–8.
88. Lady Shelley I, 123–4, 95; *Letters* XII, 142; *PL*, p.301.
89. P.318.
90. Simpson p.154, 162–5; Gala pp.115–16; *Journal*, p.227.
91. *PL*, pp.308, 305; Simpson p.164; Gala p.116.
92. Pp.308–9.
93. Gala pp.113–15; Simpson pp.162–3.
94. Cf. Gala p.75; *PL*, pp.308, 350, 379.
95. *PL*, pp.350–54; Gala pp.114–15.
96. Pp.350–54.
97. IX, 31.
98. Cf. John Murray to Scott, 8 November 1815: 'Southey arrived [in London] from his travels [to Waterloo and the Low Countries] ... He would not go near Paris. He says that if Paris is not burnt to the ground, then the two cities that we read of in Scripture have been very ill used.'
99. *PL*, p.355.
100. Ibid. p.293.
101. Ibid. p.356.
102. Ibid. p.370; Longford *Wellington* II, 16.
103. Lady Shelley I, 102.
104. P.170.
105. St. XXI.
106. *PL*, p.427.
107. *Letters* IV, 86; *PL*, p.433.
108. Pp.424–33. Contrary to Oman (p.201), Scott nowhere stated in his apologia for Fouché that the latter 'seemed to have come back to stay'. 'It is not to be supposed that Fouché will keep his ground in the ministry' was what Scott predicted (*PL*, p.430).
109. Ibid. p.426. Cf. *Life of Buonaparte* VIII, 415.
110. *Letters* IV, 103. Cf. Simpson pp.127, 191.
111. *Letters* III, 170.
112. Ibid. IV, 149, 378.
113. *QR*, vol. XVI, October 1816, No. XXI, p.192.
114. *Letters* IV, 103.
115. IX, 239–41; *Letters* VIII, 264.
116. *Letters* III, 271, 264, 266, 310.
117. Ibid. 391.
118. Cf. ibid., 170.
119. Ibid. IV, 133.
120. Ibid. III, 170.
121. Cf. ibid. IV, 87; Gordon II, 334.
122. *Letters* III, 150n. For Scott's later gratification at receiving 'many compliments from literary people' for his account of the battle of Waterloo see ibid. IV, 180.
123. Ibid. IV, 78–83, 85.

124. Ibid. 85 & n.1; XII, 144; *PL*, pp.52, 357, 431.
125. Cf. *Letters* IV, 87.
126. Longford *Wellington* II, 27.
127. This was a disputed point. For a contrary view, namely, that the Allies were in breach of article XII of the capitulation, see *History of Europe* by Sir A Alison (3rd edn, 1839–42), X, 970, 982–3.
128. *Letters* IV, 86–7.
129. Pp.357–8.
130. Ibid. p.431.
131. Gala p.108.
132. See Appendix II, pp.158–61.
133. Cf. pp.94–5, 99, 105, 108, 191.
134. Ibid. pp.115–16, 130, 131, 133, 177.
135. Ibid. pp.133–4.
136. *Letters* XII, 144; IV, 86; Simpson p.153.
137. *Letters* XII, 143–4.
138. Ibid., 144n.1.
139. Both Johnson (I, 503) and H Pearson (*Walter Scott*, 1954, p.126) misread this passage by identifying 'the persevering querist' with Scott.
140. *PL*, p.345.
141. Cf. *Letters* IV, 85, 87; Simpson p.156.
142. Cf. *PL*, pp.342, 378; Frazer p.596.
143. VIII, 515.
144. Ibid. IX, Appendix VIII, xcvii.
145. Ibid. VIII, 487n. 515.
146. *Letters* IV, 87–8; *PL*, p.358.
147. *PL*, pp.238–59, 362; *Letters* XII, 147.
148. *PL*, pp.362–4.
149. Lockhart IV, 310ff.
150. *PL*, p.364; *Letters* XII, 147.
151. Cf. *Letters* IX, 150, 172.
152. September 16, 1815.
153. Cf. Malcolm II, 109.
154. *PL*, p.304.
155. Ibid.
156. Ibid. pp.10–12; *Letters* I, 84, 86.
157. Chs. XLIIff.
158. Cf. Lady Shelley I, 107.
159. *PL*, p.465. Cf. Gala p.127 & n.; Simpson p.192.
160. See entry in *DNB* & *Notes & Index*, p.187, col. I, which corrects Grierson's footnote in *Letters* VI, 370.
161. Lockhart II, 225–6.
162. *Letters* VI, 370, 435, 504; VII, 4; VIII, 75, 106, 336, 431.
163. Ibid. IX, 25; *Journal*, p.228. The identity of James Hamilton Stanhope in the index of the *Journal* is inaccurate.
164. *Letters* IV, 87–8.
165. M M Maxwell Scott, *The Personal Relics and Antiquarian Treasures of Sir Walter Scott* (1893), plate V, footnote.
166. Lady Shelley I, 103; *Letters* IV, 93.
167. Pp.201–2; *Letters* IV, 91.
168. I, 142–3.

169. P.467.
170. *Letters* II, 101.
171. Gala p.111.
172. *Letters* XII, 142–3.
173. Cf. ibid. IV, 108.
174. Ibid. II, 326, 386, 417.
175. Ibid. XII, 110, 113.
176. Ch. XXXVII.
177. *Letters* XII, 143.
178. Ibid. IV, 93.
179. Ibid. 94–5.
180. Cf. Gala pp.96–7; Bruce, 18 August 1815; Frazer p.606.
181. Lockhart V, 90–91. Oman (p.202) confuses James Ballantyne with 'John Ballantyne' as Lockhart's source for the account of Scott's impression of Wellington.
182. Cf. *Letters* IV, 203–5; *Journal*, pp.6, 51; Lockhart III, 110.
183. Ch. XVIII, p.200.
184. *Letters* XII, 143; Gala pp.122–4; Simpson p.195.
185. *Letters* XII, 143; Gala p.124; Simpson p.193.
186. Simpson pp.191–2, 182.
187. Gala pp.122–4; Lady Shelley I, 109, 123; Simpson p.194.
188. Cf. Lady Shelley I, 106–7, 112, 116; II, 309.
189. Simpson p.195.
190. Ibid. pp.193–4, 230.
191. Pp.465–6.
192. Simpson p.195.
193. P.146.
194. Cf. Simpson pp.294–300.
195. *Letters* IX, 23–4. See also *Life of Buonaparte* VIII, 498.
196. *Letters* III, 378.
197. St. VI.
198. Cf. VII, 305–6, 319, 320, 332–3, 336. Scott's principal source for Napoleon's Russian campaign was the distinguished French historian, General Count Philip de Ségur (cf. VII, 217n).
199. Pp.367–8. See also *Life of Buonaparte* VII, 211, 319.
200. II, 238.
201. Cf. Scott's Introduction to *The Fortunes of Nigel*: '... the most picturesque period of history is that when the ancient rough and wild manners of a barbarous age are just becoming innovated upon, and contrasted by, the illumination of increased or revived learning, and the instructions of renewed or reformed religion. The strong contrast produced by the opposition of ancient manners to those which are gradually subduing them, affords the lights and shadows necessary to give effect to a fictitious narrative; ...'.
202. *Letters* III, 231, 271.
203. Cf. ibid., 398. Contrary to Johnson I, 500, Lord Cathcart was still the British ambassador to Russia. Before his appointment to St Petersburgh he was Commander-in-Chief of the forces in Scotland, where Scott appears to have come to know him.
204. Cf. *Letters* XII, 137.
205. Cf. Simpson p.193.

206. Cf. *Life of Buonaparte* VII, 206 and *Caledonian Mercury*, 28 August 1815; 'The marshal ... is descended from the family of Barclay of Tolly, or Towie, in Aberdeenshire.
207. Cf. [A Alison], *Travels in France during 1814–15* (1816) I, 32.
208. Cf. Scott's own statement (Ch. XX, p.186) that 'Scotland furnished soldiers of fortune for the service of almost every nation'.
209. *Letters* XII, 145.
210. Lady Shelley I, 116; *PL*, p.349; *Life of Buonaparte* VIII, 428; IX, 22.
211. *PL*, pp.307–8; Gala p.185.
212. P.466.
213. Gala p.124. After Scott's return from Paris to Abbotsford he wrote to R Southey that 'I saw Humboldt when I was at Paris but was not made known to him' (*Letters* V, 116). The reference is to *Friedrich* Humboldt, the celebrated naturalist and traveller, not to his brother Karl, the diplomatist and philologist. Their identity is confused in *Notes & Index*, p.502. See also Malcolm II, p.115: 'Aug. 14, 1815—Among others [at a dinner party in Paris], we had Baron Humboldt, the celebrated traveller in America.'
214. Gala pp.127–9.
215. Simpson pp.195–6.
216. *Letters* XII, 143.
217. Gala p.128.
218. Ibid.
219. P.466.
220. Simpson pp.196–7.
221. *Letters* XII, 143. Professor Johnson (I, 500) represents Wellington as telling Scott that 'there was nothing very rare about Napoleon as a General', that Napoleon was 'no better than his marshals', and that 'his own [Wellington's] victory he owed entirely to the British regiments who had served under him in Spain, the best infantry in the world'. But this information was not given to Scott by Wellington at the latter's headquarters in the Hôtel de la Reynière in August 1815. It was given by Wellington to General Allan, his private secretary, in July 1815 during a walk in the street outside the British Embassy. It was published 119 years later in *The Times* on 18 June 1934 (the 119th anniversary of the battle of Waterloo) as part of 'some extracts from the unpublished diary and letters of General Allan, who was private secretary to the Duke of Wellington in 1815'. The extracts were read by Hesketh Pearson, who in 1954 published selected pieces from them (as quoted above) in his biography of Scott (*Walter Scott His Life and Personality*, p.125), but he did so in such a manner as to suggest that the information he cited was given to Scott by Wellington at their meetings (including the dinner party) in the Hôtel de la Reynière in August 1815. It was a blatant case of *interpolated* information. Moreover, Pearson interpolated another passage, also purporting to be 'extracts from the unpublished diary and letters of General Allan', but, in fact, this passage is not to be found at all in the extracts published in *The Times*. This second passage represented Scott as enjoying 'his [Wellington's] humour, as when, on being asked by someone who intended calling at St Helena, whether he had any message for its chief resident, he laughingly replied: "Only tell Boney that I hope he finds my old lodgings at Longwood as comfortable as I find his in the Champs Élysées"'. These two interpolated passages were conflated by Pearson into one long extract on the same page of his book,

which was afterwards read by Professor Johnson, who seems to have been completely misled by Pearson, for Professor Johnson, apparently without checking *The Times* of 18 June 1934 (where Scott, of course, does not figure at all in the extracts from General Allan's diary), lifted the two interpolated passages from Pearson's book, and published them verbatim and *specifically as information gathered by Scott from Wellington*, with a reference reading 'London *Times* 6/18/1934 [*sic*: American form of dating], quoted by Pearson, *Life and Personality*, 125'.

222. *Letters* X, 156–7; *Journal*, pp.239, 242; *Life of Buonaparte* IX, Appendix No. VII; *Notes of Conversations with the Duke of Wellington 1831–51* by Philip Henry, 5th Earl of Stanhope (1886), p.132.
223. Longford *Wellington* I, 544, 566; II, 23. Frederick Ponsonby's own account of his awful mauling and miraculous survival at Waterloo is reprinted in Simpson, Appendix I, pp.279–81, but his identity is confused with that of his cousin, Sir William Ponsonby, who died in the battle.
224. A Ponsonby, *Henry Ponsonby* (1942), p.7; Lord D Cecil, *Melbourne* (1955), p.103.
225. St.XXI, line 9. For confusion of identity of William and Frederick Ponsonby, see note 223.
226. P.191. Sir William Ponsonby was originally represented by Wellington in the 'Waterloo Despatch' as having survived. See Appendix I, p.156.
227. *Letters* III, 304 & n.
228. *Byron's Letters* III, 136–8; *Lord Byron: Selected Letters & Journals*, ed L A Marchand (1982), pp.113n.2, 376.
229. Longford *Wellington* I, 433, 484, 490, 493; Marchand, *op.cit.*, p.113n.2.
230. Marchand, *op.cit.*, p.113n.2; *Byron's Letters* IV, 310 & n.1.
231. Cf. Longford *Wellington* I, 115, 442.
232. Cf. ibid., 141–4, 442, Lady Shelley II, 311–12.
233. Longford *Wellington* I, 441; *Letters* V, 188.
234. Simpson p.228; Lady Shelley I, 112.
235. P.382.
236. Cf. Lady Shelley I, 113–14, 146–7, 152–3.
237. *Letters* V, 437.
238. Longford *Wellington* II, 21; Lady Shelley I, 150.
239. Lady Shelley I, 135, 150.
240. Longford *Wellington* II, 22–3.
241. *Letters* IV, 230.
242. Cf. ibid. VII, 286–7; IX, 246.

CHAPTER IV pp.81 to 120

1. Lady Shelley I, 139.
2. Cf. ibid. II, 48 & n.1.
3. *Letters* V, 437.
4. Cf. ibid. II, 72 & n.1; VII, 60; Lockhart IV, 2; *Journal*, p.654.
5. Lady Shelley II, 48; *Letters* X, 307n.1.
6. Cf. Lady Shelley I, 139; *PL*, p.370; *Letters* V, 430.
7. Cf. Gala p.114.
8. VIII, 134–69.
9. P.351. See also *Journal*, pp.47, 233.
10. *Letters* IV, 94.

11. Pp.370–71.
12. *Letters* XII, 146.
13. Ibid. 144–5.
14. Ibid. 147, 148; VIII, 261; IV, 263.
15. Cf. Simpson p.263.
16. Cf. *Letters* XII, 146; *PL*, p.364. For heavy indemnity incurred by France under Treaty of Paris cf. *Caledonian Mercury*, 24 August 1815.
17. *Letters* IV, 96.
18. Introduction, p.xix.
19. P.289. Cf. Simpson p.152.
20. Gala pp.87, 99; Bruce, 14, 22 August 1815; Simpson p.182.
21. Cf. Gala pp.120–21.
22. Simpson pp.215, 153; *PL*, p.340; Lady Shelley I, 117.
23. II, 241n.
24. Ch. LXIX.
25. Simpson pp.261–3.
26. II, 275–97.
27. Simpson p.106.
28. *Journal*, p.224.
29. Bruce, 8, 16, 18 August 1815.
30. Cf. Simpson pp.153, 172; Gala pp.178, 150–51.
31. *PL*, pp.302–3.
32. Gala pp.100–108; Simpson p.198.
33. *PL*, p.376.
34. Simpson pp.113–15.
35. Ibid. p.114.
36. Gala pp.89–90.
37. *PL*, p.414.
38. Ibid. pp.287–8.
39. *Letters* XII, 148.
40. Pp.413–17.
41. Cf. ibid., p.59; G Lewis, *Life in Revolutionary France* (1972), p.87.
42. *PL*, pp.414–15.
43. Gala p.87.
44. *Letters* II, 464; VII, 42; 'Life of Kemble' in *Misc. Pr.W.* I, 821.
45. Gala pp.132–7; Bruce 19, 22 August 1815; Simpson p.156.
46. Cf. Lady Shelley I, 135; Simpson p.158.
47. Cf. Gala p.195; *Journal*, pp.410, 414.
48. Cf. *Letters* III, 240–41, 242, 244, 249.
49. Ibid. II, 290–94; 295–6, 300, 303, 307.
50. Cf. ibid. IV, 96, 120 & n.
51. Cf. *Caledonian Mercury*, 7 September 1815.
52. *Letters* II, 291, 296, 464.
53. Gala pp.132–7.
54. *Letters* III, 171–2.
55. Vol. 34, No. 67, September 1826, art. 10.
56. *Misc. Pr.W.* I, p.599.
57. III, 49–50.
58. Gala pp.137–41.
59. V, 85–6.
60. Gala p.153.

61. Ch. XXI, pp.318–19.
62. *Letters* IV, 88; XII, 146; Gala pp.174–8.
63. *Letters* XII, 146; Gala p.174n.
64. Ch. XXX, p.386.
65. Cf. *Journal*, p.493.
66. Cf. Gala p.257.
67. Ch. XIII, p.178.
68. *Letters* XII, 145.
69. Gala pp.151–2.
70. Cf. Appendix I, p.157.
71. *Letters* XII, 145.
72. Lockhart V, 82–4.
73. Cf. *Letters* IV, 87; XII, 144.
74. Ch. XV, p.166n.1.
75. P.466. Scott's acknowledgement, in this passage, of Lord Cathcart's hospitality is preceded (p.465) by an expression of gratitude for 'the extended hospitality of the Duke of Wellington, and of Lord and Lady Castlereagh'. But, contrary to what Lockhart (V, 82) stated about this passage, there is no mention in it of Lord Aberdeen as the third of the 'Noble Lords above mentioned [who] welcomed him [Scott] with cordial satisfaction', and were responsible for his seeing 'half the crowned heads of Europe'. In no part of *Paul's Letters to his Kinsfolk* is Lord Aberdeen mentioned, nor does he figure at all in Scott's letters from Paris or in the journals of Gala and Bruce, or in any of the other sources connected with Scott in Paris.
76. V, 83.
77. Gala pp.166–9; *Letters* XII, 146.
78. Cf. *PL*, pp.49–50.
79. Gala pp.169–73.
80. *Letters* XII, 146; IV, 88; *PL*, p.443.
81. Cf. *Letters* III. 456.
82. Gala p.93; *PL*, p.359.
83. Ch. V, pp.46–7.
84. P.359.
85. Gala pp.169–71.
86. *Letters* VIII, 376; I, 392; *Journal*, p.231.
87. Pp.438, 439.
88. P.440.
89. Cf. *Life of Buonaparte* II, 170–71; VIII,392–3.
90. Cf. *PL*, pp.51–2; Simpson pp.130–31.
91. Cf. *PL*, pp.37, 40, 400–402.
92. P.440.
93. Ibid. See also Lady Shelley I, 120.
94. *PL*, pp.443, 440.
95. IX, 37–46.
96. *PL*, pp.440–42.
97. *Letters* VIII, 375.
98. *PL*, pp.389, 393, 397.
99. Ibid. pp.397–400.
100. Ibid. pp.401, 404–5.
101. Ibid. pp.406–7.
102. Ibid. pp.401–3.

103. Pp.401–2, 406.
104. Ibid. p.403.
105. Ibid.
106. See Scott's Introduction to *Old Mortality*.
107. W S Crockett, *The Scott Originals* (Edinburgh, 1932), pp.169–80. Lockhart (I, 293) erroneously gives Paterson's Christian name as 'Peter'.
108. P.416.
109. *Letters* IV, 88–9.
110. Ibid. 87, XII, 146, 144.
111. Grierson's note (*Letters* XII, 146n.1) is confusing. He appears to have been unaware that there were *two* Russian reviews, one in Paris, the other at Vertus, for which reason Scott had originally thought of 'returning home by Laon' (ibid. XII, 144). See Lady Shelley I, 141, 149ff.
112. Pp.367–8
113. Ch. XVI, note III.
114. Chs. XV–XVII, XX, XXXIV
115. Malcolm II, 117, 115.
116. Lady Shelley I, 117.
117. Malcolm II, 117; *Journal*, p.226.
118. *PL*, p.365; Gala pp.149–50.
119. Lady Shelley I, 146; J B Priestley, *The Prince of Pleasure and his Regency 1811–20* (1971), pp.123–4.
120. Cf. D Daiches, *Edinburgh* (1980), p.136.
121. *Journal*, p.21. Cf. also p.403.
122. P.465. The district around the British Embassy at Rue de Faubourg St Honoré was afterwards described by Disraeli in *Coningsby* (Bk. V, Ch. VII) as the 'modish quarter' of Paris.
123. *Letters* XII, 146, 151; Lockhart IV, 2.
124. *Letters* XII, 146; VIII, 482.
125. Cf. ibid. III, 253; IV, 90; VIII, 24, 353.
126. Cf. Gala p.252.
127. Canto VI, st. XXXVI, line 8.
128. V, 88.
129. *Letters* XII, 100. See *Notes & Index*, p.319, col. 1, for correction of Grierson's note, which represents Lord Brooke as already (in 1807) 'Earl Brooke of Warwick Castle'. He was Baron Brooke. He became 3rd Earl of Warwick in 1816 on his father's death.
130. Cf. *Letters* IV, 107–8.
131. Cf. ibid. I, 138; XII, 198, 201, 202, 214, 216n.
132. 'Tale of Sir Thopas', *The Works of Geoffrey Chaucer*, ed F N Robinson (Oxford, 2nd edn, 1970), p.166, line 2089.
133. Cf. *Journal*, p.228. Oman (p.203) misrepresents Castlereagh as 'the ambassador' instead of Foreign Minister.
134. P.465.
135. Lockhart VII, 76–8. Scott's notion of phantoms as the creation of 'a disordered imagination' in environments of superstition was to recur in *The Betrothed*: cf. Ch. XV, pp.150–51.
136. *Letters* IX, 25 & n.; *Journal*, p.228. The biographical information about James Stanhope in the index of the *Journal*, (p.805) representing him as 'Charles, 3rd Earl Stanhope (1753–1816)' is inaccurate. He was *a son* of the 3rd Earl Stanhope, and committed suicide in 1825.

137. *PL*, p.418.
138. Ch. LIX, pp.426–7; 432; LXIX, p.504.
139. *PL*, p.419.
140. Canto III, st. VII, line 20.
141. Ch. XVIII, p.234.
142. Gala p.159.
143. *PL*, pp.417, 420; *Life of Buonaparte* VII, 9. According to Lady Shelley (II, 208), Napoleon, like Robespierre and Danton, 'often consulted' the celebrated fortune-teller, Madame Le Normand, who 'is clever enough to impose upon half the continent of Europe, and is consulted by crowned heads, and all the *beau monde* of Paris'.
144. E.g., IV, 129; VII, 9, 10, 161, 164.
145. Vol. XVI, No. XXXI, October 1816, p.196.
146. Ch. III, p.27; Ch. IV, chapter heading.
147. Pp.420–21.
148. Gala pp.187–90.
149. Cf. Longford *Wellington* I, plate 30 & pp.159, 257, 527, 550, 562, 566, 567; Lady Shelley I, 133.
150. Cf. Lockhart V, 94.
151. Pp.117–18.
152. *Letters* IV, 95–6; *PL*, p.366; Simpson pp.262–3.
153. II, 165.
154. Cf. *Letters* III, 465; *Waverley*, Ch. LXXII, p.527.
155. *Letters* IV, 95–6.
156. Ibid.
157. Pp.365–6, 385–6.
158. Gala p.192.
159. P Mansel, *Louis XVIII* (1981), p.107.
160. Cf. II, 135n, 147–8. For Scott's copy of Cléry's *Journal*, see *Catalogue of the Library at Abbotsford* by J B Cochrane (Edinburgh, 1838), p.323.
161. Ibid. pp.138, 147n.
162. Gala p.193; Simpson pp.236–7.
163. See Appendix III (a), pp.162–7.
164. *Letters* IV, 77 & n.1.
165. Cf. *Life of Buonaparte* VIII, 392–3; 'Ode to the Duchess of Angoulême', Appendix III (a), st. XVII, p.166.
166. Cf. Simpson pp.234–6.
167. Ibid. p.234; Gala p.193.
168. IV, 99–101.
169. J Barrow, *Life and Correspondence of Admiral Sir William Sidney Smith* (1848), I, 218–25; P Shankland, *Beware of Heroes: Admiral Sir Sidney Smith's War against Napoleon* (1975), 12ff.; Simpson p.237.
170. Cf. Barrow, *op.cit.*, II, 394–6, 403; Shankland, *op.cit.*, pp.200–201; Frazer p.604.
171. Introduction to Canto III, lines 80–88. For an interesting, later (1824) reference by Scott to Sir Sidney Smith's defence of Acre, see *St Ronan's Well*, Ch. XVII, p.194.
172. *Letters* II, 229.
173. Cf. *Life of Buonaparte* II, 32.
174. Simpson (p.236) refers to the Tower as 'the original dwelling of the *Grand Prieur de Malthe*', because after the suppression of the Order of the Knight

Templars in 1312, their property was made over to the Order of Knight Hospitallers, commonly known as 'Knights of Malta'.

175. Gala pp.194–5; *PL*, pp.299–300.
176. *PL*, p.300.
177. Lady Shelley I, 125, 133, 194; Simpson p.239; J B Cochrane, *op.cit.*, p.50. There is no copy of Charlotte Lennox's translation of Sully's *Mémoires* in the Abbotsford Library Catalogue.
178. Ch. I, pp.2–3.
179. *PL*, pp.249–50.
180. Introduction p.xxx. See also Ch. XXVII, p.338n. for Scott's interest in Sully's account of the so-called 'Le Grand Veneur' or hunting apparition.
181. Ch. XXI, p.319.
182. Gala pp.137–41.
183. *Letters* XII, 148–9.
184. Ibid. 149; IV, 89; Malcolm II, 123; Lady Shelley I, 149ff.
185. *Letters* XII, 148. Oman (p.204) misrepresents Sophia Dumergue as 'the royal dentist's sister' instead of his daughter.
186. Cf. ibid. I, 83–4, 87, 88.
187. Ibid. XII, 149, 146, 148.
188. Ibid. IV, 7–8.
189. Ibid. VIII, 18 & n.
190. Gala pp.195–6.
191. *Letters* IV, 89.
192. Cf. *Caledonian Mercury*, 28 August 1815.
193. *Letters* IV, 89, 180, 215, 225.
194. Lockhart V, 62–3.
195. *Letters* IV, 225–6.
196. Ibid. 96.
197. Canto I, note B.
198. *Letters* IV, 96.
199. Ibid. 93.
200. P.179. Scott represented 'the prodigious shouts of *"Vive l'Empereur"'* of Napoleon's guard in Wellington's full hearing as a signal of 'an instant [French] attack', with Napoleon himself as leader of his guard. At the same time 'the mist, as well as the clouds of smoke, rendered it impossible to see any object distinctly'. Scott, therefore, visualised Wellington as 'eagerly *hoping*', without actually *seeing*, that Napoleon was near him. In this situation Wellington, according to Scott, 'probably thought, like the Avenger in Shakespeare', that is, like Macduff, the avenger of Macbeth's murder of Lady Macduff and her children, that

> There thou shouldst be:
> By this great clatter one of greatest note
> Seems bruited [indicated].—

201. Gala pp.205–7.
202. *Letters* IV, 101–2.
203. Ibid. 114.
204. *Life of Buonaparte* III, 82; *PL*, pp.419–20.
205. *Life of Buonaparte* III, 82.
206. *PL*, p.420.
207. Ibid.; P W Sergeant, *The Empress Josephine*, n.d., p.20.

208. Cf. *Life of Buonaparte* VII, 8–9.
209. Gala p.207; *PL*, p.341; Lady Shelley I, 122–3.
210. Gala p.34; Bruce 8 August 1815. For Scott's later criticism of the Dutch fashion in landscape gardening, see 'On Landscape Gardening' in *Misc. Pr.W.*, I, 53.
211. Gala pp.207–8; *PL*, p.341.
212. Ch. X, p.110.
213. *PL*, p.341.
214. P.340.
215. Cf. ibid., p.349; Lady Shelley I, 122.
216. *Journal*, pp.217, 220.
217. IX, Chs. III–IV.
218. Cf. *Journal*, p.230.
219. Gala p.208.
220. See Appendix III (b), pp.168–9.
221. Cf. *PL*, p.273; *Waverley*, Ch. XLVI, p.348; & Scott's Prologue to Joanna Baillie's *The Family Legend* (1809), lines 3–4: 'Tis sweet and sad the latest notes to hear/Of distant music dying on the ear'.
222. Cf. st. III of 'St Cloud'; Gala pp.209–10; Simpson p.139.
223. Canto IV, st. 40, line 8.
224. Ch. XXVII, p.366.
225. *Letters* IV, 90; Gala p.209. Grierson's dating of *Letters* IV, 90, namely, '5th September 1815' is very nearly correct, even though J Corson (*Notes & Queries, p.112, col. 2*) redated it '13th Aug. 1815'. Scott was not even in Paris on 13th August 1815. He was at Chantilly on that date (*Letters* XII, 139). He arrived in Paris from Chantilly on 14 August 1815 (ibid., 142). Corson was misled by an interpolated and misdated note (which could not have been by Scott) written above Scott's letter to Lady Alvanley enclosing a copy of his poem 'St Cloud' to her. The note reads: 'Sent with lines written on a beautiful summer evening spent at St Cloud, 12th Aug. 1815'. And as Scott stated, in his letter to Lady Alvanley, that 'the enclosed [poem] came into my head last night during two or three hours that I happened to lie awake ...', Corson naturally concluded that Scott's letter should be dated '13th Aug. 1815'. But there is Gala's evidence (p.205) that he and Scott left Paris on 9 September 1815 (not '8th September', as stated by Grierson, *Letters* IV, 90n.2). Lockhart (V, 86–7) also misdated ('16th August') Scott's letter to Lady Alvanley enclosing 'St Cloud'. Finding that 'St Cloud' was dated 'September 5, 1815' in Scott's *PW*, Grierson accepted that date for Scott's letter to Lady Alvanley, but since Scott stated in it that he wrote 'St Cloud' *'last night'*, his letter should be dated '6 September 1815'.
226. Gala pp.211, 215–16. Gala does not seem to support Oman's statement (p.202), for which no reference is given, that Scott had been 'in company with Canova, the great sculptor'.
227. Lady Shelley I, 148; Gala p.215; *Journal*, p.228.
228. *Letters* XII, 145; Gala pp.211–12.
229. *Letters* IV, 263.
230. Ch. XXX, p.358.
231. I, 26–7.
232. Cf. *PL*, p.416.
233. *Letters* XII, 148 & n.2, 152.
234. Cf. ibid., 426; *Notes & Index*, p.334, col. 1.

235. *Letters* XII, 151–2.
236. Ibid. 150; Gala pp.217–19.
237. V. 93–4.

CHAPTER V pp.121 to 152

1. Gala pp.221–2.
2. Ibid. p.223.
3. P.352.
4. Gala p.223.
5. Cf. *Journal*, pp.249–50 & n.4.
6. Cf. ibid., p.129.
7. V, 78–9.
8. Ibid. VII, 18.
9. Gala p.224; *Letters* XII, 150.
10. Cf. *Letters* X, 141; IV, 84–5.
11. Gala pp.224–5.
12. Ibid. p.225.
13. Ibid. pp.225–6. See *Letters* XII, 150 for Scott's slightly different version of this incident.
14. *Letters* IX, 499.
15. Gala p.226.
16. E.g., Chs. XXIX–XXX.
17. Gala pp.228–9.
18. Ibid. p.229; cf. Simpson pp.270–71.
19. Gala p.230; Simpson p.271.
20. Gala pp.230–31.
21. Ibid. pp.232–3.
22. Ibid. pp.233–6; *Letters* XII, 149–50.
23. Gala pp.236–7; *Letters* XII, 150.
24. Ch. I, pp.7–8.
25. Gala pp.237–9.
26. Cf. *Journal*, pp.35, 44, 57.
27. Gala p.239; Mathews *Memoirs* II, 376. Mrs Mathews stated that Scott 'had long wished to visit Kenilworth'; but both Gala (p.256) and Lockhart (V, 88) wrote that Scott had seen Kenilworth before.
28. Mathews *Memoirs* II, 376–7.
29. Ibid. III, 156.
30. Ibid. II, 358–61; Gala pp.239–40.
31. Cf. *Letters* I, 354; III, 236.
32. Ibid. III, 236; X, 19; *Misc. Pr.W.*, I, 89.
33. *Letters* III, 236; X, 19.
34. Mathews *Memoirs* II, 377.
35. Gala p.240.
36. Cf. Smiles I, 271–2.
37. Ibid.; Lockhart X, 262.
38. Cf. *Letters* IV, 129; Smiles I, 267.
39. Gala p.240; *Letters* IV, 128; I, 488.
40. VIII, 271–2.
41. Cf. Smiles I, 287.

42. *Letters* IV, 167 & n.1., 168.
43. Ibid. VII, 4.
44. Lockhart VII, 4 & n.; *Journal*, p.114.
45. Jane Austen, *Letters*, ed R W Chapman (Oxford, 1959), pp.431–2.
46. *PL*, p.463.
47. See Sir Arch. Alison, *Some Account of my Life and Writings*, ed Lady Alison (Edinburgh & London, 1883), pp.111–12 & nn.
48. *Journal*, p.182.
49. Gala p.240; Mathews *Memoirs* II, 379–80.
50. Gala pp.240–42. Lockhart's version (V, 88) of what Gala actually wrote about his and Scott's meeting with Byron is edited to a degree approximating to distortion.
51. Sts. XXIX–XXX; Gala pp.242–3.
52. Gala p.244.
53. *Journal*, p.44; Lockhart V, 40, 42.
54. Gala p.244.
55. *Byron's Letters* IV, 327; Smiles I, 286.
56. St. 118, line 1094.
57. Gala p.244; Lockhart V, 40–41. Neither Gala nor Lockhart nor Mathews nor Scott himself provided any evidence of any truth in the story apparently believed and reprinted by Grierson (*Sir Walter Scott, Bart.*, 1938, p.127n.1) from Capt. Gronow's *Reminiscences and Recollections* (1889), I, 149–51. This represented Scott and Byron at another dinner party in London on Scott's return from Paris as guests of Sir James Bland Burges in Lower Brook Street, and in company with Gronow himself and J W Croker.
58. Cf. *Byron's Letters* III, 109, 180; IV, 86, 290; V, 203.
59. Cf. M S Carhart, *The Life and Work of Joanna Baillie* (New Haven, USA, 1923), pp.17, 152.
60. *Letters* IV, 120.
61. Cf. *Byron's Letters* IV, 336; M S Carhart, *op.cit.*, p.17; *Letters* IV, 120n.1.
62. Carhart, *op.cit.*, pp.122–3; *Byron's Letters* VIII, 208, 210.
63. *Letters* IV, 169, 180, 217–18 & n.2, 238.
64. Cf. Carhart, *op.cit.*, p.35.
65. Mathews *Memoirs* II, 376–7; Gala pp.245–6.
66. Gala pp.246–9.
67. Ibid. p.249.
68. Cf. *Letters* IX, 37.
69. Gala pp.249–50; Mathews *Memoirs* II, 380–81.
70. Gala pp.250–51.
71. Ch. XXV, p.342.
72. Cf. Mathews *Memoirs* II, 323.
73. Ibid. 381; Gala p.252.
74. Ch. XXVIII, p.330.
75. *Letters* IV, 107.
76. Ibid. IX, 37.
77. Ch. XV, p.180. Cf. also *Woodstock*, Ch. XXI, p.322.
78. Ch. VIII, pp.130–31.
79. Ch. X, p.110.
80. Cf. *Warwick Castle* by P Barker (York, 1986), pp.6–7.
81. P.253.
82. E.g., *Woodstock*, Ch. X, p.143.

83. Ch. II, p.23.
84. Mathews *Memoirs* II, 323. See allusion to dun cow and Guy of Warwick in *The Bride of Lammermoor*, Ch. XXIII, p.276.
85. P Barker, *op.cit.*, p.26.
86. Ibid. pp.45–6.
87. *Journal*, p.453.
88. Ibid.
89. P Barker, *op.cit.*, p.46.
90. Mathews *Memoirs* II, 381; Gala pp.255–6, 266.
91. Mathews *Memoirs* II, 382; Gala p.256.
92. Cf. Ch. XXV, p.345.
93. Ch. XXV, p.346.
94. *Journal*, p.453.
95. Ibid.
96. Mathews *Memoirs* II, 382.
97. Ibid. 381; Gala p.256.
98. *Letters* IX, 128–9; 216; XII, 115–16 & n.1; *Letters of William & Dorothy Wordsworth: The Middle Years Part I 1806–11*, ed E de Selincourt, revd M Moorman (Oxford, 1969), p.114n.2.
99. Cf. *Letters* II, 233; *Ivanhoe*, Ch. XIV, pp.145–6.
100. Gala pp.256–7.
101. Ch. III, p.24n.
102. Chs. VII–X.
103. Cf. Gala p.256n.
104. Gala p.257; cf. *PL*, pp.256–7.
105. Pp.252–3, 256–7.
106. Gala p.257.
107. Ibid. pp.257–8; Lockhart I, 181–2.
108. Lockhart VI, 266.
109. Chs. IV, XLI.
110. Cf. *Letters* XI, 5n.2.
111. Ch. III, pp.28–9.
112. Gala p.258; *Letters* II, 410–11.
113. Ch. XXIII, p.285.
114. Gala pp.258–9.
115. Ch. X, pp.109–10.
116. Gala pp.258–9.
117. Ch. VI, p.68 & n.1.
118. *Letters* XI, 350–51; Gala pp.259–60.
119. Ch. 1, para. 1.
120. Gala pp.261–2.
121. Ibid. p.261.
122. *Letters* XI, 349; Gala p.263.
123. *Letters* XI, 349; Gala p.262.
124. Lockhart IV, 280–90, 315–18, 330–33; *Lord of the Isles*, Canto III, notes C.& E.
125. Canto III, st. 14 & note G.; Canto VI, sts. 3–6. Cf. also Lockhart IV, 20.
126. Cf. *Journal*, p.486.
127. Gala p.263.
128. E.g., Ch. VI, p.69.
129. Ch. XXV, pp.320–21.
130. Ch. XXIII, p.285. Cf. also Ch. XXI, p.265; Ch. XXIII, p.287.

131. Gala pp.263–4.
132. 'Salmonia' in *Misc. Pr.W.* I, 792–804.
133. Ch. XXV, p.322.
134. Cf. *Letters* I, 361.
135. Lockhart V, 88–9; Gala p.264.
136. Cf. Lockhart III, 371, 379.
137. Ch. XLI.
138. *Letters* XI, 349–50.
139. Ibid.; *Ivanhoe*, ch. XLI, note L.
140. Chs. XXVIII–XXXIV.
141. Cf. *Journal*, p.486 & *Rob Roy*, Ch. III, p.24.
142. Gala pp.264–5.
143. Ch. XVI, p.175 & n.1.
144. Gala p.266.
145. Johnson I, 401; Lockhart IV, 16, 19–21.
146. Cf. *Letters* III, 456; W Partington, *Sir Walter Scott's Post-Bag* (1932), pp.105–6.
147. *Letters* III, 253.
148. Gala p.266; *Letters* IV, 100–101.
149. Cf. *Rokeby*, Canto II, st. 5 & note C.
150. Cf. ibid. Canto II, sts. 1–3; Canto V, st. 1.
151. Cf. ibid. II, sts. 1–3, note A.
152. Gala pp.267–8.
153. Ibid. pp.268–71. Cf. also *Letters* VIII, 259.
154. Canto V, st. XXXII & note LIV.
155. Cf. *Journal*, p.482; *Letters* I, 390; Lockhart V, 341.
156. Gala p.272, cf. *Letters* XII, 213, 255–6.
157. Gala p.272; *Journal*, p.452. *Letters* VIII, 13–14, 111–12.
158. Gala p.271.
159. Cf. *Letters* XI, 129. In this letter Scott mentioned 'Southey' instead of 'Humphry Davy' as his fellow-climber, together with Wordsworth, up Helvellyn. See *Letters of William and Dorothy Wordsworth: The Early Years 1787–1805*, ed E de Selincourt, revd C L Shaver (Oxford, 1967), p.621.
160. Gala pp.271–2.
161. *Letters* III, 274, 303, 315, 318.
162. Chs. XVII–XXII.
163. Chs. LIX–LX.
164. Gala pp.272–3; *Journal*, p.451; *Journal*, ed D Douglas (Edinburgh, 1891), p.612 & n.1.
165. Ch. LXIX; Gala p.273.
166. *Journal*, ed D Douglas (Edinburgh, 1891), p.612n.1.
167. Gala p.273.
168. Cf. *Letters* III, 318–19; XII, 173.
169. *Waverley*, Ch. LXIX, p.511.
170. *Letters* IV, 101.
171. Ibid.; Gala p.273.
172. Gala pp.273–4.
173. Ibid. p.275.
174. Cf. *Journal*, pp.43 & n.1, 368 & n.2, 374 & n.4, 376. Cf. also *Peveril of the Peak*, ch. XII, pp.137–8: '... In fine, there are few men who do not look back in secret to some period of their youth, at which a sincere and early affection was repulsed, or betrayed, or became abortive from opposing

circumstances. It is these little passages of secret history, which leave a tinge of romance in every bosom, scarce permitting us, even in the most advanced period of life, to listen with total indifference to a tale of true love ...'.

175. Cf. Johnson I, 108–24.
176. Cf. Lockhart IV, 55–6; Johnson I, 469–70.
177. Pp.275–6.
178. Ch. XXVII, p.366.
179. Chs. XXII–XXIII.
180. Gala pp.279–80.
181. Ch. XXIII, p.200.
182. Gala p.280; note to ballad of Lord Soulis in *Minstrelsy of the Scottish Border*,revd & ed T F Henderson (Edinburgh, 1932), IV, 257.
183. Ibid.
184. Gala p.281. Gala gave '26 September' as his and Scott's date of arrival at Abbotsford, whereas Scott wrote from Abbotsford on 25 September that 'I arrived here last night' (*Letters* I, 484).
185. Lockhart V, 89; Gala p.282.
186. Gala pp.282–3.
187. Lockhart V, 90.
188. *Letters* IV, 99–100.
189. Lockhart V, 94–5; *Letters* XII, 154. In point of fact, as has already been explained (see *ante* pp.93–4), Scott had not availed himself of Platoff's invitation to see the grand Russian review at Vertus beside him on 'a Ukraine charger', but John Buchan (*Sir Walter Scott*, 1932, p.147) seems to have concluded otherwise. Nor did Scott and Gala apparently ride on Cossack horses for the smaller Russian review before their departure from Paris (see *ante* p.106).
190. *Letters* IV, 114.
191. No. XXVIII, Jan. 1816, pp.283–333; *Letters* IV, 167, 168.
192. *Letters* IV, 169, 185.
193. *Misc. Pr.W.*, pp.10, 15, 32.
194. Cf. *Essay on the History of Civil Society* (Edinburgh, 1966), pp.80–81.

Bibliography

(*Place of publication is London unless otherwise stated.*)

Sir Walter Scott: Printed Works

The Letters of Sir Walter Scott, ed Sir H Grierson, 12 vols (centenary edn, 1932–7)
The Journal of Sir Walter Scott, ed W E K Anderson (Oxford, 1972)
The Poetical Works of Sir Walter Scott, ed J Logie Robertson (Oxford, 1951)
Minstrelsy of the Scottish Border, revd & ed T F Henderson, 4 vols (Edinburgh, 1932)
The Life of Napoleon Buonaparte, 9 vols (Edinburgh, 1827)
The Miscellaneous Prose Works of Sir Walter Scott, 3 vols (Edinburgh, 1841)
Paul's Letters to his Kinsfolk (Edinburgh, 1816)
The Tales of a Grandfather: Being the History of Scotland from the Earliest Period to 1746 (1925)
The Life and Works of John Dryden, 18 vols (1808)
The Life and Works of Jonathan Swift, 19 vols (1814)
The Lives and the Novelists (Oxford, World's Classics, 1906)
Contributions to *Edinburgh Annual Register* for 1809, 1814–15

Alexander, J H and Hewitt, D (eds), *Scott and his Influence: The Papers of the Aberdeen Scott Conference, 1982* (Aberdeen, 1983)
Alison, A *et al., Travels in France during the Years 1814–15* (published anonymously, 1815)
Alison, Sir A, *History of Europe from the Commencement of the French Revolution to the Restoration of the Bourbons,* 10 vols (Edinburgh & London, 1839–42)
——, *Some Account of my Life and Writings,* ed Lady Alison (Edinburgh & London, 1883)
Allentuck, Marcia, 'Scott and the Picturesque: Afforestation and History' in *Scott Bicentenary Essays,* ed A Bell (Edinburgh & London, 1973), pp.188–98
Anderson, J, *Sir Walter Scott and History* (Edinburgh, 1981)
Anonymous, *Caledonian Mercury* (Edinburgh, 1815)
——, *The Christian Observer,* vol.14 (Nov. 1815), pp.750–60 [For review of Scott's *The Field of Waterloo*]
——, *The Quarterly Review,* vols XIII–XIV (1815–16)

BIBLIOGRAPHY

Austen, Jane, *Letters*, ed R W Chapman (Oxford, 1959)

Barker, P, *Warwick Castle* (York, 1986)

Barrow, Sir J, *The Life and Correspondence of Admiral Sir Sidney Smith*, 2 vols (1848)

Bruce, R, *Journal of a Tour to the Continent in Autumn 1815 with Sir Walter Scott, John Scott of Gala, and Alexander Pringle of Whytbank* (MS 991, National Library of Scotland)

Bryan, M, *Dictionary of Painters and Engravers*, 5 vols (1901–2)

Bryant, Sir A, *The Age of Elegance 1812–22* (1950)

Burke, E, *Reflections on the Revolution in France*, ed A J Grieve (Everyman Library, 1964)

Byron, Lord G Gordon, *Poetical Works*, ed E H Coleridge (Oxford, 1964)

——, *Letters and Journals*, ed L Marchand, 12 vols (1973–81)

——, *Selected Letters and Journals*, ed L Marchand (1982)

Carhart, M S, *The Life and Work of Joanna Baillie* (New Haven, USA, 1923)

Cecil, Lord D, *Melbourne* (1955)

Cléry, J B, *Journal de la Captivité de Louis XVI à la Tour du Temple* (1798)

Cochrane, J B, *Catalogue of the Library at Abbotsford* (Edinburgh, 1838)

Corson, J C, *Bibliography of Sir Walter Scott* (Edinburgh, 1943)

——, *Notes and Index to Sir Herbert Grierson's Edition of 'The Letters of Sir Walter Scott'* (Oxford, 1979)

——, 'Scott Studies I–II', rpt from *University of Edinburgh Journal* (Autumn 1955)

Crabbe, G, *Selected Letters and Journals*, ed T Faulkner (Oxford, 1985)

Creevy, T, *The Creevy Papers*, ed J Gore (1963)

Croker, J W, *The Battles of Talavera, A Poem* (1811 edn)

Daiches, D, *Scott and his World* (1971)

——, *Edinburgh* (1980)

De Lancey, Lady, *A Week at Waterloo in June 1815* (1906)

Disraeli, B, *Sybil* (1845)

Douglas, D, ed, *The Journal of Sir Walter Scott 1825–32* (Edinburgh, 1891)

Elphinstone, M, *An Account of the Kingdom of Caubul* (1815)

Farington, J, *The Farington Diary*, ed J Greig, 8 vols (1923–8)

Ferguson, A, *Essay on the History of Civil Society* (1767)

Frazer, Sir A, *Letters*, ed General Sir Ed Sabine (1859)

Gell, Sir W, *Reminiscences of Sir Walter Scott's Residence in Italy, 1832*, ed J C Corson (Edinburgh, 1957)

Gordon, L P, *Personal Memoirs, or Reminiscences of Men and Manners at Home and Abroad* (1830)

Gordon, R C, 'Scott among the Partisans: A Significant Bias in his "Life of Napoleon Buonaparte"' in *Bicentenary Essays*, ed A Bell (Edinburgh & London, 1973), pp.115–33

Grierson, Sir H, *Sir Walter Scott, Bart.* (1938)

Haslip, Joan, *Lady Hester Stanhope* (1934)

Haydon, B, *Neglected Genius: The Diaries of Benjamin Haydon*, ed J Jolliffe (1990)

Jack, R D S, *The Italian Influence on Scottish Literature* (Edinburgh, 1972)

Johnson, E, *Sir Walter Scott: The Great Unknown*, 2 vols (1970)

Kaye, J W, *The Life and Correspondence of Major-General Sir John Malcolm*, 2 vols (1856)

Lachouque, H, *Waterloo* (1972)

Lewis, G, *Life in Revolutionary France* (1972)

Lockhart, J G, *Memoirs of the Life of Sir Walter Scott*, 10 vols (Edinburgh, 1856–8)

Longford, Elizabeth, *Wellington: The Years of the Sword* (1969)

——, *Wellington: Pillar of State* (1972)
Malcolm, Sir J, *History of Persia* (1815)
Mansel, P, *Louis XVIII* (1981)
Mathews, Mrs C, *Memoirs of Charles Mathews, Comedian*, 4 vols (1838)
Mitchell, J, *Scott, Chaucer, and Mediaeval Romance* (University of Kentucky Press, USA, 1988)
Moore, T, *The Poetical Works*, ed A D Godley (Oxford, 1910)
Nimmo, W P, ed, *Ballads: Scottish and English* (1878)
O'Leary, P, *Regency Editor: Life of John Scott* (Aberdeen, 1983)
Oman, Carola, *The Wizard of the North: The Life of Sir Walter Scott* (1973)
Partington, W M, *The Private Letter-Books of Sir Walter Scott* (1930)
——, *Sir Walter Scott's Post-Bag* (1932)
Pearson, H, *Walter Scott: His Life and Personality* (1954)
Ponsonby, A, *Henry Ponsonby Queen Victoria's Private Secretary* (1942)
Price, Sir U, *An Essay on the Picturesque as compared with the Sublime and the Beautiful* (1794)
Priestley, J B, *Prince of Pleasure and his Regency 1811–20* (1971)
Rogers, M, *The Waverley Dictionary* (Chicago, 1885)
Ryan, F W, *'The House of the Temple': A Study of Malta and its Knights in the French Revolution* (1930)
Scott, J, *A Visit to Paris in 1814* (1815)
——, *Paris Revisited in 1815* (1816)
Scott, J, of Gala, *Journal of a Tour to Waterloo and Paris, in company with Sir Walter Scott in 1815* (1842)
Scott, Maxwell, Mary Monica, *Catalogue of the Armour and Antiquities at Abbotsford* (Edinburgh, 1888, rpt 1900)
——, *The Personal Relics and Antiquarian Treasures of Sir Walter Scott* (1893)
Shankland, P, *Beware of Heroes: Admiral Sir Sidney Smith's War Against Napoleon* (1975)
Shelley, Lady F, *Diary*, ed R Edgcumbe, 2 vols (1912–13)
Simpson, J, *Paris after Waterloo, including a revised edition—the tenth—of 'A Visit to Flanders and the Field of Waterloo'* (Edinburgh & London, 1853)
Smiles, S, *A Publisher and his Friends: Memoir and Correspondence of John Murray*, 2 vols (1891)
Southey, R, *The Poet's Pilgrimage to Waterloo* (1816)
——, *Life and Correspondence*, ed C C Southey, 6 vols (1849–50)
——, *New Letters of Robert Southey*, ed K Curry, 2 vols (New York & London, 1965)
——, 'Life of Lord Wellington' in *Quarterly Review*, vol.XXIII, July 1815, pp.448–526
Stanhope, P H, 5th Earl, *Notes of Conversations with the Duke of Wellington 1831–51* (privately printed, 1886)
Sultana, D E, *The Journey of Sir Walter Scott to Malta* (Gloucester and New York, 1986)
——, 'Sir William Gell's Correspondence on Scott from Naples and his Reminiscences of Sir Walter Scott in Italy, 1832' in *Scott and his Influence*, ed J H Alexander and D Hewitt (Aberdeen, 1983)
——, *'The Siege of Malta' Rediscovered: An Account of Sir Walter Scott's Mediterranean Journey and his Last Novel* (Edinburgh, 1977)
Vere, de, A, *Ode to the Duchess of Angoulême* (1815)
Wedderburn-Webster, J, *Waterloo and Other Poems* (1816)

BIBLIOGRAPHY

Woodring, Carl, 'Three Poets on Waterloo' in *The Wordsworth Circle*, vol.XVIII, No.2, Spring 1987, pp.54–7

White, H A, *Sir Walter Scott's Novels on the Stage* (Yale University Press, rpt Hamden, Connecticut, 1973)

Wellington, Evelyn, *A Descriptive and Historical Atlas of the Collection of Pictures and Sculpture at Apsley House, London,* 2 vols (1901)

Young, A, *Travels in France during the Years, 1787, 1788, 1789,* ed M Betham-Edwards (1913)

Index

INDEX

Flanders *and* Netherlands, the, *and* Low Countries, the

Bell, Ch., *surgeon*, 14

Bell, G., *advocate*, 14

Belle Alliance, *see* La Belle Alliance

Belsches, Williamina, 140

Benedictines of Paris, 52 and n.70

Beresford, 143

Beresina, the, *river*, 73

Bergen-op-Zoom, 4–5, 8, 29, 33 n.1, 37, 45

Berkshire, 140

Berlin, 38

Bertram, Harry, *leading character in* Guy Mannering, 31

Bessborough, Earl of, 77

Bible, the, *see* Scripture

Bickerton, Mrs, *character in* The Heart of Midlothian, 135

Blenheim, battle of, 33

Blücher, Field Marshal G.L. von, 1, 16; his meeting with Wellington at victorious conclusion of battle of Waterloo, 25; 38–9, 47; is prevented by Wellington from destroying bridge of Jena, 55–6; 60; is first seen by S. at Wellington's ball in Paris, 71–2; 72; 82; his miraculous escape from death at battle of Ligny, 106; 121

Bohemia, 101

Boiardo, M.M., *It. poet*, 22

Boileau-Despréaux, N., *Fr. poet and critic*, 54

Bombay, 152

Bonaparte, J., *Napoleon's eldest brother*, 28

Bonaparte, N., *see* Napoleon I, Emperor of France

'Bonapartists', 100

Bonomi, J., *architect*, 65–7

Bordeaux, 109

Borghese, Prince C., 116–17

Borghese, Princess Pauline, *Napoleon's sister*, 102, 116, 118

Boswell, J., *biographer*, 133

Boucher, F., *Fr. painter*, 51

Bourbons, the, 40, 43, 46, 50; destruction of their property, tombs, and monuments in Fr. Revolution, 53, 103; 60; 97; Huguenots' distrust of, 99; 111

Bourbon, Duke of, 38, 40

Bourbon Restoration, ix; parallels and contrasts perceived by S. with Stuart Restoration, 3, 32, 56, 98; 99, *see also* Louis XVIII of France

Brantôme, P., *Fr. chronicler*, 36, 52

Branxholm Castle, 150

Brienne, 91

Brighton, 111, 124–5

Briquet, A.L., *Fr. watch-maker*, 119

Britain, 1, 2, 3, 10, 14, 15, 16, 28, 39, 42, 43, 49, 53, 65, 71, 97, 98, 104; *126–7*; 145

British army, 1, 16, 17; its celebrated 'squares' of infantry at Waterloo, 18; its numerical inferiority to Fr. army, 25; 26; 34; its discipline and restraint in contrast to Prussians' mercilessness, 35, 69; 38, 43, 55, 57; its strengths and weaknesses analysed by Gen. Müffling, 63; 77 n.221, 79, 110, 117, 120, 123, 131

British Embassy, Paris, *see* Paris: its buildings, etc

Brooke, Baron Henry Greville, *son and heir of 2nd Earl of Warwick*, 103 and n.129, 104, 135, 138

Brough, 146

Brougham Castle, 146–7

Bruce, Rob., *Scott's fellow-traveller*, 4, 69, 83, 84; parts from S. and Gala in Paris for Switzerland with Pringle, 93, 94 n.75, 111

Brunswick and Brunswickers, 2, 25

Brussels, 1, 2, 3, 4, 10, 11 and n.72; its buildings praised by S., 12, 65; also its citizens' kindness to wounded Br. troops, 13; their suspense over outcome of battle of Waterloo, 13–14, 22, 55; 15–23 *passim*, 28, 29; S.'s departure from, 33–4; 36, 42, 48, 51, 54, 55, 57, 59, 77, 78, 80, 86, 109, 111, 112; its royal palace's grounds laid out by Empress Josephine in 'the English fashion', 116; 122, 140

Bryant, Sir A., viii, 16 n.120, 20 n. 156

Buccleuch, 4th Duke of, 4; his former wartime service with S., 29; 38; is informed by S. of Gen. La Bédoyère's arrest and execution, 59–60, 61; 67

Buccleuch, Duchess of, 29, 59

Buchan, J., vii, viii, 151 n.189

Bunyan, J., 119

Buonaparte, N., *see* Napoleon I, Emperor of France

Burgundy, Duke of, *see* Charles the Bold

Burke, E., *statesman and orator*, 32, 98

Burnfoot, 59

Byron, Ada, *Lord Byron's daughter*, 132

Byron, G.G., 6th Baron, x, l; his first meeting with S., 2, 3, 15, 113; considers S. unrivalled in portrayal of Sc. 'manners', 10; his compliment to S. in Waterloo stanzas of *Childe Harold's Pilgrimage*, 15; 16, 20, 22 n.168; his verse lament over the dead at Waterloo, 26–7; 33; his perception of Napoleon's character at variance with S.'s, 47; 50, 57, 68, 78, 80, 90, 105, 113; dubs S. 'the Ariosto of the North', 117; his last meeting with S. in London on S.'s return from Paris, 125–33 and n.50; 132 n.57, 154

Byron, Lady A., (*née* Milbanke), 80, 128, 132

Cadiz, 73

Caledonian Mercury, 4 n.26, 74 n.206, 84 n.16, 90 n.51, 113 n.192

Calne, 147

Calvinists, 99–100

Cambrai, 29, 38, 39, 60

Cameron, Colonel J., 20

Campbell, Sir C., 19, 20, 22, 23, 25, 59, 71

Campbell, Captain Rob., 19, 22

Campbell, Th., *poet*, 45

Canaletto, A., *Venetian painter*, 135

Canova, A., *It. sculptor*, 49, 50, 51; his statue of Hebe at Malmaison impresses S., 116; is present at last assembly in Paris attended by S., 118

Cannes, 99

Canterbury Tales, The, 104

Carlisle, 105, 138, 146; its cathedral, as place of S.'s marriage in 1797, is revisited by him on return journey from Paris, 147–8; 149

Carnot, L.N., *Fr. general and military engineer*, 8

Caroline, *Queen Consort of George II*, 13 n.91, 68

Carpenter, Ch., *Mrs W. Scott's brother*, 2

Carpenter, Charlotte, *see* Scott, Mrs Walter

Castlereagh, Lady Amelia, 68; invites S. to an excursion to Montmorency, 81, 82; and to Versailles, 92; and to 'a great ball' for visiting Allied sovereigns, 100; and to an assembly for diplomatic corps before S.'s departure from Paris, 118

Castlereagh, Viscount F.W., *Foreign Secretary*, 10, 56; his and Lady Castlereagh's hospitality gratefully acknowledged by S., 68, 102; 71, 74; surprises S. by confessing to a belief in ghosts, 104 and n.133; 105; his diplomatic bag carries some of S.'s letters from Paris; 118

Castleton, 142

Cataline, L.S., *Roman conspirator*, 17

201

INDEX

INDEX

INDEX

207

208

INDEX